CONTENTS

S0-AEX-478

INTRODUCTION

The more we look at college texts, professional journals, and standardized exams, the more we realize one thing: the key to doing well academically and professionally is a strong working vocabulary of college-level words.

To have a good vocabulary, you don't need to memorize an entire dictionary; you need to work with a preselected, masterable group of words.

Barron's Basic Word List is your tool to help you master the working vocabulary you need efficiently and effectively. The 2,000-plus words of the *Basic Word List* are exactly that—basic. They are the foundations of a sophisticated vocabulary, the words you will encounter on the job, in the lecture hall, and on the SAT and GRE. In academic and professional circles, these words predominate.

Before you turn to the words themselves, take a moment to acquaint yourself with a few basic language-learning techniques. Some you have used in the past; others may be new to you. To discover which ones work best for you, try them all.

CREATE FLASH CARDS

Scan one of the word lists for unfamiliar terms; then make pocket-sized flash cards for those unmastered expressions. Be brief, but include all the information you need. On one side write the word. On the other side write *concise* definitions—two or three words at most— for each major meaning of the word you want to learn. Include an antonym, if you can; the synonym-antonym associations can help you remember both words. To fix the word in your mind, use it in a short phrase. Then write that phrase down.

Sample Flash Card

> ABSTRACT
>
> theoretical;
> nonrepresentational
>
> (ANT. concrete)
>
> "abstract notion"

You can pack an enormous
amount of information
onto a flash card in only
a few words. Use symbols
and simple sketches;
you may discover you
remember pictures
better than phrases.

Consider This Flash Card:

> virulent
>
>
>
> extremely poisonous
> bitterly hateful
>
> (ANT. benign)
>
> "virulent poison"

The skull-and-crossbones
symbol means poison
all around the world.

Consider This Card As Well:

Anyone can draw a dollar sign. What makes the dollar sign useful on this card is that it's something you added personally. You didn't just copy down definitions straight off the list—you translated the word insolvent into symbols with which you're comfortable.

Work up your own personal set of symbols and abbreviations. You can use simple plus and minus signs to clarify a word's connotations. The word thrifty, for example, has positive connotations; it's good to be a thrifty person, a person who has sense enough to save. Thrifty, + . The word parsimonious, however, has negative connotations. Though saving money is good, it's bad to carry thrift to an extreme; when old Scrooge wouldn't let his shivering clerk light a fire on the coldest day in winter, he showed just how stingy and parsimonious he was. Parsimonious, − .

dis joint ed

Visual cues can reinforce your sense of what a word means. Consider the word disjointed.

disconnected;
incoherent

(ANT. connected)

"disjointed phrases"

p
r
e
c
i
p
i
t
o
u
s

You can also write words at odd angles:

steep; headlong

(ANT. flat; gradual)

"a precipitous cliff"

prē - SIP - it - us

Or In Odd Shapes:

If you personalize your flash cards, you'll create something uniquely memorable, something that will stick in your mind because you thought it up yourself. That's the sort of flash card that will be most valuable to you.

circuitous

---

round about, winding

(ANT. direct)

"a circuitous route"

sur-KYOO-it-us

FLASH CARD POINTERS
Here are a few pointers to make you a flash card ace.

- Carry a few of your cards with you every day. Look them over whenever you have a spare moment or two. Work in short bursts. Try going through five flash cards at a time, shuffling through them rapidly to build up your rapid sight recognition of the words. You want these words to spring to your mind instantaneously.

- Test your memory; don't look at the back of the card unless you must. Go through your five cards several times a day. Then, when you have mastered two or three of the cards and have them down pat, set those cards aside and add a couple of new ones to your working pile. That way you will always be working with a limited group, but you won't be wasting time reviewing words you already recognize on sight.

- *Never* try to master a whole stack of flash cards in one long cram session. It won't work.

Dream Up Memory Tricks

As you can see, remembering words takes work. It also takes wit. You can spend hours memorizing dictionary definitions and get no place. You can also capitalize on your native intelligence to think up mnemonic devices—memory tricks—to help you remember new words.

Consider the word *hovel*. A hovel is a dirty, mean house. How can you remember that? *Hovel* rhymes with *shovel*. You need to shovel out the hovel to live in it. Rhymes can help you remember what words mean.

Now consider the word *hover*. To hover is to hang fluttering in the air or to wait around. Can rhyme help you here? *Hover* rhymes with *cover*. That doesn't seem to work. However, take another look at *hover*. Cut off the letter *h* and you are left with the word *over*. If a helicopter hovers over an accident, it hangs in the air. Hidden little words can help you remember bigger words.

Use Your Eyes: Visualize

Try creating mental pictures that remind you of the meanings of words; the more clearly you see the image, the better you will remember the words. The images can be silly or serious. Think of the word *rebuttal*. A rebuttal is a denial; someone comes up with evidence that contradicts what someone else has said. Picture the Three Stooges in an argument. Whenever one of them tries to make a point, another one kicks him in the *butt*.

What makes an image or mnemonic memorable? It has to grab you, has to be odd enough to stick in your mind. Weirdness works. If you want to remember *dogmatic* (stubborn about a claim; arbitrarily positive), think of a bulldog taking a stand on the welcome mat and refusing to budge. Then give the dog the face of the most opinionated teacher you ever had; you'll never forget the word.

Act It Out

Most techniques for mastering new vocabulary rely on visual or auditory learning, while many students find that they learn best kinesthetically (through physical movement). If you tend to excel at physical tasks such as dance, sports, or building things, you may be a kinesthetic learner. You can improve your retention of vocabulary by acting out the words, creating physical memories of their meanings. Studies have shown that this technique can significantly improve one's ability to recall what one has learned.

If you are learning the word *commodious*, meaning spacious and comfortable, you might act it out by opening your arms in a wide, expansive gesture. *Comprehensive*, meaning all inclusive, might be acted out by reaching out wide with your arms and then drawing them back to your body as if you were gathering up everything around you. *Nonchalance*, lack of concern or anxiety, could be depicted with a simple shrug. While you may not be able to come up with a gesture for every word on this list, the more words you learn in this manner, the more success you will have.

Adopt a Systematic Approach

To make any individual word your own, you need to use your imagination. To make more than 2,000 words your own, in addition to imagination you need a system.

If you intend to work your way through the entire Basic Word List, we recommend the following procedure:

1. Allot a specific time each day for the study of a list.

2. Devote at least one hour to each list.

3. First go through the list looking at the short, simple looking words (six letters at most). Mark those you don't know. In studying, pay particular attention to them.

4. Go through the list again looking at the longer words. Pay particular attention to words with more than one meaning and familiar looking words that have unusual definitions that come as a surprise to you. Standardized tests like the SAT and GRE often stump students with questions based on unfamiliar meanings of familiar looking words.

5. Note whether any of the words on the list contain familiar prefixes or roots. If you know the meaning of part of a word, you may find it easier to learn the word as a whole. (See our Word Parts Review).

6. List unusual words on index cards that you can shuffle and review from time to time. (Study no more than five cards at a time.)

7. Use the illustrative sentences in the list as models and make up new sentences of your own. Make them funny if you can.

8. Take the test following each list at least one day after studying the words. In this way, you will check your ability to remember what you have studied.

9. If you can answer correctly 18 of the 20 questions in the test, go on to the next list; if you cannot answer this number, restudy the list. Note any words you missed for later review.

10. Keep a record of your guesses and of your success as a guesser.

11. Try out your new words on your friends and acquaintances—but not all at once!

Learn by Reading

No matter what approach you take to learning individual words, one key to mastering an educated vocabulary remains: *read*.

The two elements of vocabulary study, memorization of individual words and reading, go hand in hand in helping you reach your goal of an expanded vocabulary. One reinforces and strengthens the other. If you have learned the word *capricious* by studying Word List 8 and then read a *Scientific American* article on weather patterns in which that word appears several times, you will strengthen your understanding of *capricious* by seeing it used in a larger context than the sample sentence the word list provides. On the flip side, you will get more out of the article because you know the exact definition of one of its key terms.

Read widely, read deeply, read daily. If you do, your vocabulary will grow. If you don't, it won't.

Challenge yourself to go beyond your usual fields of interest and sample current thinking in other fields. Reading widely, after all, involves more than merely reading every day. If you normally read only best-sellers and popular novels, try an issue or two of *Natural History* and *Scientific American* to rekindle your interest in science. If you're so caught up in business or school activities that you tend to ignore what is going on in the world, skim through *The New Yorker*, *Smithsonian*, *The Atlantic Monthly*, *Newsweek*, or *Time* for articles on literature, music, philosophy, history, world affairs, and the arts. It's not enough to be a habitual reader; be an adventurous one. Branch out. Open yourself to the full range of concepts and words you need to get the most out of your reading and your world.

The Word Lists

The 50 word lists are arranged in strict alphabetical order. For each word, the following is provided:

1. The word (printed in heavy type).

2. Its part of speech (abbreviated).

3. A brief definition.

4. A sentence illustrating the word's use.

There are tests after each word list and comprehensive tests after every ten word lists for practice.

Following the 50 word lists is a review of common prefixes and roots.

PRONUNCIATION SYMBOLS

ə	b**a**n**a**n**a**, c**o**llide, **a**but
ˈə, ˌə	h**u**mdr**u**m, ab**u**t
ə	immediately preceding \l\, \n\, \m\, \ŋ\, as in batt**le**, mitt**en**, eat**en**, and sometimes op**en** \ˈō-pᵊm\, lock **and** key \-ᵊŋ-\; immediately following \l\, \m\, \r\, as often in French tab**le**, pris**me**, tit**re**
ər	furth**er**, m**er**ger, b**ir**d
ˈər-, ˈə-r	as in two different pronunciations of h**urr**y \ˈhər-ē, ˈhə-rē\
a	m**a**t, m**a**p, m**a**d, g**a**g, sn**a**p, p**a**tch
ā	d**ay**, f**a**de, d**a**te, **a**orta, dr**a**pe, c**a**pe
ä	b**o**ther, c**o**t
är	c**ar**, h**ear**t, baz**aar**, biz**arre**
au̇	n**ow**, l**ou**d, **ou**t
b	**b**a**b**y, ri**b**
ch	**ch**in, natu**r**e \ˈnā-chər\
d	**d**i**d**, a**dd**er
e	b**e**t, b**e**d, p**e**ck
er	b**are**, f**air**, w**ear**, million**aire**
ˈē, ˌē	b**ea**t, nosebl**ee**d, **e**venly, **ea**sy
ē	eas**y**, meal**y**
f	**f**i**f**ty, cu**ff**
g	**g**o, bi**g**, **g**ift
h	**h**at, a**h**ead
hw	**wh**ale as pronounced by those who do not have the same pronunciation for both *whale* and *wail*

i   t**i**p, ban**i**sh, act**i**ve

ir   n**ear**, d**eer**, m**ere**, p**ier**

ī   s**i**te, s**i**de, b**uy**, tr**i**pe

j   **j**ob, **g**em, e**dge**, **j**oin, **j**u**dge**

k   **k**in, **c**ook, a**ch**e

k̲   German i**ch**, Bu**ch**; one pronunciation of lo**ch**

l   **l**i**l**y, poo**l**

m   **m**ur**m**ur, di**m**, ny**m**ph

n   **n**o, ow**n**

^{n} indicates that a preceding vowel or diphthong is pronounced with the nasal passages open, as in French *un bon vin blanc* \œ^n-bō^n-va^n-blä^n\

ŋ   si**ng** \'siŋ\, si**ng**er \'siŋ-ər\, fi**ng**er \'fiŋ-gər\, i**n**k \'iŋk\

ō   b**o**ne, kn**ow**, b**eau**

ȯ   s**aw**, **a**ll, gn**aw**, c**au**ght

œ   French b**oeu**f, f**eu**, German H**ö**lle, H**ö**hle

ȯi   c**oi**n, destr**oy**

ȯr   b**oar**, p**or**t, d**oor**, sh**or**e

p   **p**e**pp**er, li**p**

r   **r**ed, **r**a**r**ity

s   **s**our**c**e, le**ss**

sh   as in **sh**y, mi**ss**ion, ma**ch**ine, spe**ci**al (actually, this is a single sound, not two); with a hyphen between, two sounds as in *grasshopper* \'gras-ˌhä-pər\

t   **t**ie, a**tt**ack, la**t**e, la**t**er, la**tt**er

th   as in **th**in, e**th**er (actually, this is a single sound, not two; with a hyphen between, two sounds as in *knighthood* \'nīt-ˌhu̇d\

t̲h̲   **th**en, ei**th**er, **th**is (actually, this is a single sound, not two) ü **ru**le, y**ou**th, union \\'yün-yən\\, few \\'fyü\\

u̇ p**u**ll, w**oo**d, b**oo**k

ᴜᴇ German f**ü**llen, h**ü**bsch, f**üh**len, French r**u**e

u̇r b**oor**, t**our**, in**sure**

v **v**i**v**id, gi**ve**

w **w**e, a**w**ay

y **y**ard, **y**oung, cue \\'kyü\\, mute \\'myüt\\, union \\'yün-yən\\

ʸ indicates that during the articulation of the sound represented by the preceding character, the front of the tongue has substantially the position it has for the articulation of the first sound of *yard*, as in French *digne* \\dēnʸ\\

z **z**one, rai**s**e

zh as in vi**si**on, azure \\'a-zhər\\ (acutally, this is a single sound, not two); with hyphen between, two sounds as in *hogshead* \\'hȯgz-ˌhed, 'hägz-\\

\\ reversed virgule used in pairs to make the beginning and end of a transcription: \\'pen\\

' mark preceding a syllable with primary (strongest) stress: \\'pen-mən-ˌship\\

ˌ mark preceding a syllable with secondary (medium) stress: \\'pen-mən-ˌship\\

- mark of a syllable division

( ) indiate that what is symbolized between is present in some utterances but not in others: *factory* \\'fak-t(ə-)rē\\

÷ indicates that many regard as unacceptable the pronunciation variant immediately following: *nuclear* \\'nü-kēl-ər, 'nyü-, ÷-kyə-lər\\

BASIC
WORD
LIST

WORD LIST 1
abase–adroit

abase \ə-'bās\ v. LOWER; HUMILIATE. Defeated, Queen Zenobia was forced to *abase* herself before the conquering Romans, who made her march in chains before the Emperor in the procession celebrating his triumph. //abasement, n.

abash \ə-'bash\ v. EMBARRASS. He was not at all *abashed* by her open admiration.

abate \ə-'bāt\ v. SUBSIDE; DECREASE, LESSEN. Rather than leaving immediately, they waited for the storm to *abate*. //abatement, n.

abbreviate \ə-'brē-vē-,āt\ v. SHORTEN. Because we were running out of time, the lecturer had to *abbreviate* her speech.

abdicate \'ab-di-,kāt\ v. RENOUNCE; GIVE UP. When Edward VIII *abdicated* the British throne, he surprised the entire world.

aberrant \a-'ber-ənt; 'a-bə-rənt\ adj. ABNORMAL OR DEVIANT. Given the *aberrant* nature of the data, we doubted the validity of the entire experiment. //aberration, n.

abet \ə-'bet\ v. AID, USUALLY IN DOING SOMETHING WRONG; ENCOURAGE. She was unwilling to *abet* him in the swindle he had planned.

abeyance \ə-'bā-ən(t)s\ n. SUSPENDED ACTION. The deal was held in *abeyance* until her arrival.

abhor \əb-'hȯr, ab-\ v. DETEST; HATE. She *abhorred* all forms of bigotry. //abhorrence, n.

abnegation \,ab-ni-'gā-shən\ n. REPUDIATION; SELF-SACRIFICE. Though Rudolph and Duchess Flavia loved one another, their love was doomed, for she had to marry the king; their act of *abnegation* was necessary to preserve the kingdom.

abolish \ə-'bä-lish\ v. CANCEL; PUT AN END TO. The president of the college refused to *abolish* the physical education requirement. //abolition, n.

abominable \ə-'bäm-nə-bəl, -'bä-mə-\ adj. DETESTABLE; EXTREMELY UNPLEASANT; VERY BAD. Mary liked John until she learned that he was dating Susan; then she called him an *abominable* young man, with *abominable* taste in women.

aboriginal \ˌa-bə-'rij-nəl, -'ri-jə-nᵊl\ adj., n. BEING THE FIRST OF ITS KIND IN A REGION; PRIMITIVE; NATIVE. Her studies of the primitive art forms of the *aboriginal* Indians were widely reported in the scientific journals. //aborigines, n.

abortive \ə-'bȯr-tiv\ adj. UNSUCCESSFUL; FRUITLESS. Attacked by armed troops, the Chinese students had to abandon their *abortive* attempt to democratize Beijing peacefully.

abrade \ə-'brād\ v. WEAR AWAY BY FRICTION; ERODE. Because the sharp rocks had *abraded* the skin on her legs, she dabbed iodine on the scrapes and *abrasions*.

abridge \ə-'brij\ v. CONDENSE OR SHORTEN. Because the publishers felt the public wanted a shorter version of *War and Peace*, they proceeded to *abridge* the novel.

abscond \ab-'skänd, əb-\ v. DEPART SECRETLY AND HIDE. The teller who *absconded* with the bonds went uncaptured until someone recognized him from his photograph on *America's Most Wanted*.

absolve \əb-'zälv, -'sälv, -'zȯlv, -'sȯlv\ v. PARDON (AN OFFENSE). The father confessor *absolved* him of his sins. //absolution, n.

abstain \əb-'stān, ab-\ v. REFRAIN; HOLD ONESELF BACK VOLUNTARILY FROM AN ACTION OR PRACTICE. After considering the effect of alcohol on his athletic performance, he decided to *abstain* from drinking while he trained for the race. //abstinence, n.

abstemious \ab-'stē-mē-əs\ adj. SPARING IN EATING AND DRINKING; TEMPERATE. Concerned whether her vegetarian son's *abstemious* diet provided him with sufficient protein, the worried mother pressed food on him.

abstinence \'ab-stə-nən(t)s\ n. RESTRAINT FROM EATING OR DRINKING. The doctor recommended total *abstinence* from salted foods. //abstain, v., abstinent, adj.

abstract \ab-'strakt, 'ab-,\ adj. THEORETICAL; NOT CONCRETE; NONREPRESENTATIONAL. To him, hunger was an *abstract* concept; he had never missed a meal.

abstruse \əb-'strüs, ab-\ adj. OBSCURE; PROFOUND; DIFFICULT TO UNDERSTAND. Baffled by the *abstruse* philosophical texts assigned in class, Dave asked Lexy to explain Kant's *Critique of Pure Reason*.

abusive \ə-'byü-siv *also* -ziv\ adj. COARSELY INSULTING; PHYSICALLY HARMFUL. An *abusive* parent damages a child both mentally and physically.

abysmal \ə-'biz-məl, a-\ adj. IMMEASURABLY DEEP OR GREAT; BOTTOMLESS. His arrogance is exceeded only by his *abysmal* ignorance.

accede \ak-'sēd, ik-\ v. AGREE. If I *accede* to this demand for blackmail, I am afraid that I will be the victim of future demands.

accessible \ik-'se-sə-bəl, ak-, ek-\ adj. EASY TO APPROACH; OBTAINABLE. We asked our guide whether the ruins were *accessible* on foot.

accessory \ik-'se-sə-rē, ak-, ek-\ n. ADDITIONAL OBJECT; USEFUL BUT NOT ESSENTIAL THING. She bought an attractive handbag as an *accessory* for her dress. //also adj.

acclaim \ə-'klām\ v. APPLAUD; ANNOUNCE WITH GREAT APPROVAL. The NBC sportscasters *acclaimed* every American victory in the Olympics and decried every American defeat. //also n.

acclimate \'a-klə-,māt; ə-'klī-mət, -,māt\ v. ADJUST TO CLIMATE. One of the difficulties of our present air age is the need of travelers to *acclimate* themselves to their new and often strange environments.

accolade \'a-kə-,lād, -,läd\ n. AWARD OF MERIT. In Hollywood, an "Oscar" is the highest *accolade*.

accomplice \ə-'käm-pləs, -'kəm-\ n. PARTNER IN CRIME. Because he had provided the criminal with the lethal weapon, he was arrested as an *accomplice* in the murder.

accord \ə-'kord\ n. AGREEMENT. She was in complete *accord* with the verdict.

accost \ə-'kost, -'käst\ v. APPROACH AND SPEAK FIRST TO A PERSON. When the two young men *accosted* me, I was frightened because I thought they were going to attack me.

acerbity \ə-'sər-bə-tē\ n. BITTERNESS OF SPEECH AND TEMPER. The meeting of the United Nations Assembly was marked with such *acerbity* that reaching any useful settlement of the problem seemed unlikely. //acerbic, adj.

acknowledge \ik-'nä-lij, ak-\ v. RECOGNIZE; ADMIT. Although Iris *acknowledged* that the Beatles' tunes sounded pretty dated nowadays, she still preferred them to the hip-hop songs her brothers played.

acme \'ak-mē\ n. TOP; PINNACLE. Welles's success in *Citizen Kane* marked the *acme* of his career as an actor; never again did he achieve such popular acclaim.

acquiesce \ˌa-kwē-'es\ v. ASSENT; AGREE PASSIVELY. Although she appeared to *acquiesce* to her employer's suggestions, I could tell she had reservations about the changes he wanted made. //acquiescence, n.; acquiescent, adj.

acquittal \ə-'kwi-t³l\ n. DELIVERANCE FROM A CHARGE. His *acquittal* by the jury surprised those who had thought him guilty. //acquit, v.

acrid \'a-krəd\ adj. SHARP; BITTERLY PUNGENT. The *acrid* odor of burnt gunpowder filled the room after the pistol had been fired.

acrimonious \ˌa-krə-'mō-nē-əs\ adj. STINGING; CAUSTIC; BITTER IN WORDS OR MANNER. The candidate attacked his opponent in highly *acrimonious* terms.

acuity \ə-'kyü-ə-tē, a-\ n. SHARPNESS. In time his youthful *acuity* of vision failed him, and he needed glasses.

acumen \ə-'kyü-mən, 'a-kyə-mən\ n. MENTAL KEENNESS. His business *acumen* helped him to succeed where others had failed.

adage \'a-dij\ n. WISE SAYING; PROVERB. There is much truth in the old *adage* about fools and their money.

adamant \'a-də-mənt, -,mant\ adj. HARD; INFLEXIBLE. Bronson played the part of her revenge-driven man, *adamant* in his determination to punish the criminals who had destroyed his family. //adamancy, n.

adapt \ə-'dapt, a-\ v. ALTER; MODIFY. Some species of animals have become extinct because they could not *adapt* to a changing environment.

adept \'a-,dept, ə-'dept, a-'\ adj. EXPERT AT. She was *adept* at the fine art of irritating people. //also n.

adhere \ad-'hir, əd-\ v. STICK FAST. I will *adhere* to this opinion until proof that I am wrong is presented. //adhesion, n.

admonish \ad-'mä-nish\ v. WARN; REPROVE. When her courtiers questioned her religious beliefs, Mary Stuart *admonished* them, declaring that she would worship as she pleased. //admonition, n.

adorn \ə-'dorn\ v. DECORATE. Wall paintings and carved statues *adorned* the temple. //adornment, n.

adroit \ə-'droit\ adj. SOULFUL. His *adroit* handling of the delicate situation pleased his employers.

Synonym Test • Word List 1

Each of the questions below consists of a word in capital letters, followed by five words or phrases. Choose the word or phrase that is most similar in meaning to the word in capital letters and write the letter of your choice on your answer paper.

1. **ABASE** (A) incur (B) tax (C) descend (D) maltreat (E) humiliate

2. **ABERRATION** (A) deviation (B) abhorrence (C) dislike (D) absence (E) anecdote

3. **ABET** (A) conceive (B) wager (C) encourage (D) evade (E) protect

4. **ABEYANCE** (A) obedience (B) discussion (C) excitement (D) suspended action (E) editorial

5. **ABOLISH** (A) discuss (B) cancel (C) run off secretly (D) perjure (E) project

6. **ABOMINABLE** (A) explosive (B) temperate (C) obtainable (D) obscure (E) detestable

7. **ABNEGATION** (A) blackness (B) self-denial (C) selfishness (D) cause (E) effect

8. **ABORTIVE** (A) unsuccessful (B) consuming (C) financing (D) familiar (E) fruitful

9. **ABRIDGE** (A) stimulate (B) grasp (C) oppose (D) widen (E) shorten

10. **ABSOLUTION** (A) first design (B) rejection (C) finale (D) concept (E) pardon

11. **ABSTINENCE** (A) restrained eating or drinking (B) vulgar display (C) deportment (D) reluctance (E) population

12. **ABSTRUSE** (A) profound (B) irrespective (C) suspended (D) protesting (E) not thorough

13. **ABYSMAL** (A) bottomless (B) eternal (C) meteoric (D) diabolic (E) internal

14. **ACCEDE** (A) fail (B) compromise (C) correct (D) consent (E) mollify

15. **ACUMEN** (A) index (B) report (C) mental keenness (D) character (E) original idea

adulation \ˌa-jə-ˈlā-shən, -dyə, -də-\ n. FLATTERY; ADMIRATION. The rock star thrived on the *adulation* of his groupies and yes-men. //adulate, v.

adulterate \ə-ˈdəl-tə-ˌrāt\ v. MAKE IMPURE BY MIXING WITH BASER SUBSTANCES. It is a crime to *adulterate* foods without informing the buyer; when consumers learned that Beech-Nut had *adulterated* their apple juice by mixing it with water, they protested vigorously. //adulterated, adj.

adverse \ad-ˈvərs, ˈad-,\ adj. UNFAVORABLE; HOSTILE. The recession had a highly *adverse* effect on Father's investment portfolio: he lost so much money that he could no longer afford the butler and the upstairs maid.

adversity \ad-ˈvər-sə-tē\ n. POVERTY; MISFORTUNE. We must learn to meet *adversity* gracefully.

advocate \ˈad-və-kət, -ˌkāt\ v. URGE; PLEAD FOR. The abolitionists *advocated* freedom for the slaves. //also n.

aesthetic \es-ˈthe-tik\ adj. ARTISTIC; DEALING WITH OR CAPABLE OF APPRECIATION OF THE BEAUTIFUL. The beauty of Tiffany's stained-glass appealed to Esther's *aesthetic* sense. //aesthete, n.

affable \ˈa-fə-bəl\ adj. EASILY APPROACHABLE; WARMLY FRIENDLY. Accustomed to cold, aloof supervisors, Nicholas was amazed at how *affable* his new employer was.

affected \ə-ˈfek-təd, a-\ adj. ARTIFICIAL; PRETENDED; ASSUMED IN ORDER TO IMPRESS. His *affected* mannerisms—his "Harvard" accent, his air of boredom, his flaunting of obscure foreign words—irritated many of us who had known him before he had gone away to college. //affectation, n.

affidavit \ˌa-fə-ˈdā-vət\ n. WRITTEN STATEMENT MADE UNDER OATH. The court refused to accept his statement unless he presented it in the form of an *affidavit*.

affiliation \ ə-ˌfi-lē-ˈā-shən\ n. JOINING; ASSOCIATING WITH. His *affiliation* with the political party was brief for he soon disagreed with his colleagues.

affinity \ə-ˈfi-nə-tē\ n. KINSHIP. She felt an *affinity* with all who suffered; their pains were her pains.

affirmation \ˌa-fər-ˈmā-shən\ n. POSITIVE ASSERTION; CON-FIRMATION; SOLEMN PLEDGE BY ONE WHO REFUSES TO TAKE AN OATH. Despite Tom's *affirmations* of innocence, Aunt Polly still suspected he had eaten the pie.

affliction \ə-ˈflik-shən\ n. STATE OF DISTRESS; CAUSE OF SUFFERING. Even in the midst of her *affliction*, Elizabeth tried to keep up the spirits of those around her.

affluence \ˈa-flü-əns\ n. ABUNDANCE; WEALTH. Foreigners are amazed by the *affluence* and luxury of the American way of life. //affluent, adj.

agenda \ə-ˈjen-də\ n. ITEMS OF BUSINESS AT A MEETING; LIST OR PLAN OF THINGS TO BE DONE. We had so much diffi-culty agreeing upon an *agenda* that there was very lit-tle time for the meeting.

aggrandize \ə-ˈgran-ˌdīz *also* ˈa-grən-\ v. INCREASE OR INTENSIFY. The history of the past quarter century illustrates how a president may *aggrandize* his power to act aggressively in international affairs without con-sidering the wishes of Congress.

aggregate \ˈa-gri-ˌgāt\ v. GATHER; ACCUMULATE. Before the Wall Street scandals, dealers in so-called junk bonds managed to *aggregate* great wealth in short periods of time. //also n., adj.

aghast \ə-ˈgast\ adj. HORRIFIED; DUMBFOUNDED. Miss Manners was *aghast* at the crude behavior of the fra-ternity brothers at the annual toga party.

agility \ə-ˈji-lə-tē\ n. NIMBLENESS. The *agility* of the acro-bat amazed and thrilled the audience.

agitate \ˌa-jə-ˈtāt\ v. STIR UP; DISTURB. Her fiery remarks *agitated* the already angry mob.

agnostic \ag-ˈnäs-tik, əg-\ n. ONE WHO IS SKEPTICAL OF THE EXISTENCE OR KNOWABILITY OF A GOD OR ANY ULTIMATE REALITY. *Agnostics* say we can neither prove nor disprove the existence of God; we simply just can't know. //also adj.

agrarian \ə-ˈgrer-ē-ən\ adj. PERTAINING TO LAND OR ITS CULTIVATION. Because Korea's industrialization has transformed farmhands into factory workers, the country is gradually losing its *agrarian* traditions.

alacrity \ə-ˈla-krə-tē\ n. CHEERFUL PROMPTNESS. Eager to get away to the mountains, Phil and Dave packed up their ski gear and climbed into the van with *alacrity*.

alias \ˈā-lē-əs, ˈāl-yəs\ n. AN ASSUMED NAME. John Smith's *alias* was Bob Jones. //also adv.

alienate \ˈā-lē-ə-ˌnāt, ˈāl-yə-\ v. MAKE HOSTILE; SEPARATE. Her attempts to *alienate* the two friends failed because they had complete faith in each other.

alimony \ˈa-lə-ˌmō-nē\ n. PAYMENTS MADE TO AN EX-SPOUSE AFTER DIVORCE. Because Tony had supported Tina through medical school, on their divorce he asked the court to award him $500 a month in *alimony*.

allay \a-ˈlā, ə-\ v. CALM; PACIFY. The crew tried to *allay* the fears of the passengers by announcing that the fire had been controlled.

allege \ə-ˈlej\ v. STATE WITHOUT PROOF. Although the governor's critics *allege* that he has abused his office, they offer no proof of misconduct on his part. //allegation, n.

allegory \ˈa-lə-ˌgȯr-ē\ n. STORY IN WHICH CHARACTERS ARE USED AS SYMBOLS; FABLE. *Pilgrim's Progress* is an *allegory* of the temptations and triumphs of the human soul. //allegorical, adj.

alleviate \ə-lē-vē-ˈāt\ v. RELIEVE. This should *alleviate* the pain; if it does not, we shall have to use stronger drugs.

allocate \'a-lə-ˌkāt\ v. ASSIGN. Even though the Red Cross had *allocated* a large sum for the relief of the sufferers of the disaster, many people perished.

alloy \'a-ˌloi *also* ə-'loi\ n. A MIXTURE AS OF METALS. *Alloys* of gold are used more frequently than the pure metal.

allude \ə-'lüd\ v. REFER INDIRECTLY. Try not to mention divorce in Jack's presence because he will think you are *alluding* to his marital problems with Jill. //allusion, n.

allure \ə-'lur\ v. ENTICE; ATTRACT. *Allured* by the song of the sirens, the helmsman steered the ship toward the reef. //also n.

aloof \ə-'lüf\ adj. APART; RESERVED. Shy by nature, she remained *aloof* while all the rest conversed.

altercation \ˌol-tər-'kā-shən\ n. WORDY QUARREL. Throughout the entire *altercation*, not one sensible word was uttered.

altruistic \ˌal-trü-'is-tik\ adj. UNSELFISHLY GENEROUS; CONCERNED FOR OTHERS. In providing tutorial assistance and college scholarships for hundreds of economically disadvantaged youths, Eugene Lang performed a truly *altruistic* deed. //altruism, n.

amalgamate \ə-'mal-gə-ˌmāt\ v. COMBINE; UNITE IN ONE BODY. The unions will attempt to *amalgamate* their groups into one national body.

amass \ə-'mas\ v. COLLECT. The miser's aim is to *amass* and hoard as much gold as possible.

amazon \'a-mə-ˌzän, -zən\ n. FEMALE WARRIOR. Ever since the days of Greek mythology we refer to strong and aggressive women as *amazons*.

ambidextrous \ˌam-bi-'dek-strəs\ adj. CAPABLE OF USING EITHER HAND WITH EQUAL EASE. A switchhitter in baseball should be naturally *ambidextrous*.

ambience \'am-bē-ən(t)s\ n. ENVIRONMENT; ATMOSPHERE. She went to the restaurant not for the food but for the *ambience*.

ambiguous \am-'bi-gyə-wəs\ adj. UNCLEAR OR DOUBTFUL IN MEANING. His *ambiguous* instructions misled us; we did not know which road to take. //ambiguity, n.

ambivalence \am-'bi-və-lən(t)s\ n. THE STATE OF HAVING CONTRADICTORY OR CONFLICTING EMOTIONAL ATTITUDES. Torn between loving her parents one minute and hating them the next, she was confused by the *ambivalence* of her feelings. //ambivalent, adj.

ambulatory \'am-byə-lə-ˌtȯr-ē\ adj. ABLE TO WALK; NOT BEDRIDDEN. Juan was a highly *ambulatory* patient; not only did he refuse to be confined to bed, but he insisted on riding his skateboard up and down the halls.

ameliorate \ə-'mēl-yə-ˌrāt, -'mē-lē-ə-\ v. IMPROVE. Many social workers have attempted to *ameliorate* the conditions of people living in the slums.

amenable \ə-'mē-nə-bəl, -'me-\ adj. READILY MANAGED; WILLING TO BE LED. Although the ambassador was usually *amenable* to friendly suggestions, he balked when we hinted that he should waive his diplomatic immunity and pay his parking tickets.

amend \ə-'mend\ v. CORRECT; CHANGE, GENERALLY FOR THE BETTER. Hoping to *amend* his condition, he left Vietnam for the United States.

Synonym Test • Word List 2

Each of the questions below consists of a word in capital letters, followed by five words or phrases. Choose the word or phrase that is most similar in meaning to the word in capital letters and write the letter of your choice on your answer paper.

16. **ADULATION** (A) youth (B) purity (C) brightness (D) defense (E) flattery

17. **ADVOCATE** (A) define (B) urge (C) remove (D) inspect (E) discern

18. **AFFABLE** (A) courteous (B) ruddy (C) needy (D) useless (E) conscious

19. **AFFECTED** (A) weary (B) unfriendly (C) divine (D) pretended (E) slow

20. **AFFLUENCE** (A) plenty (B) fear (C) persuasion (D) consideration (E) neglect

21. **AGILITY** (A) nimbleness (B) solidity (C) temper (D) harmony (E) warmth

22. **ALACRITY** (A) promptness (B) plenty (C) filth (D) courtesy (E) despair

23. **ALLEVIATE** (A) endure (B) lessen (C) enlighten (D) maneuver (E) humiliate

24. **ALLURE** (A) hinder (B) tempt (C) ignore (D) leave (E) wallow

25. **ALOOF** (A) triangular (B) distant (C) comparable (D) honorable (E) savory

26. **AMALGAMATE** (A) equip (B) merge (C) generate (D) materialize (E) repress

27. **AMBIGUOUS** (A) salvageable (B) corresponding (C) responsible (D) obscure (E) auxiliary

28. **AMELIORATE** (A) make slow (B) improve (C) make young (D) make sure (E) make able

29. **AMBULATORY** (A) convalescent (B) impatient (C) mobile (D) chronic (E) congenital

30. **AMEND** (A) befriend (B) hasten (C) steal (D) correct (E) prattle

amenities \ə-'me-nə-tēs, -'mē-\ n. CONVENIENT FEATURES; COURTESIES. In addition to the customary *amenities* for the business traveler—fax machines, modems, a health club—the hotel offers the services of a concierge versed in the social *amenities*.

amiable \'ā-mē-ə-bəl\ adj. AGREEABLE; LOVABLE; WARMLY FRIENDLY. In *Little Women*, Beth is the *amiable* daughter whose loving disposition endears her to all who know her.

amicable \'a-mi-kə-bəl\ adj. POLITELY FRIENDLY; NOT QUARRELSOME. Beth's sister Jo is the hot-tempered tomboy who has a hard time maintaining *amicable* relations with those around her.

amiss \ə-'mis\ adj. WRONG; FAULTY. Seeing her frown, he wondered if anything were *amiss*. //also adv.

amity \'a-mə-tē\ n. FRIENDSHIP. Student exchange programs such as the Experiment in International Living were established to promote international *amity*.

amnesia \am-'nē-zhə\ n. LOSS OF MEMORY. Because she was suffering from *amnesia*, the police could not get the young girl to identify herself.

amoral \(ˌ)ā-'mȯr-əl, (ˌ)a-, -'mär-\ adj. NONMORAL. The *amoral* individual lacks a code of ethics; he cannot tell right from wrong. The immoral person can tell right from wrong; he chooses to do something he knows is wrong.

amorous \'a-mə-rəs, 'am-rəs\ adj. MOVED BY SEXUAL LOVE; LOVING. "Love them and leave them" was the motto of the *amorous* Don Juan.

amorphous \ə-'mȯr-fəs\ adj. FORMLESS; LACKING SHAPE OR DEFINITION. As soon as we have decided on our itinerary, we shall send you a copy; right now, our plans are still *amorphous*.

amphibian \am-'fi-bē-ən\ adj. ABLE TO LIVE BOTH ON LAND AND IN WATER. Frogs are classified as *amphibian.* //also n.

ample \'am-pəl\ adj. ABUNDANT. Bond had *ample* opportunity to escape. Why did he let us catch him?

amplify \'am-plə-,fī\ v. BROADEN OR CLARIFY BY EXPANDING; INTENSIFY; MAKE STRONGER. Charlie Brown tried to *amplify* his remarks, but he was drowned out by jeers from the audience. Lucy was smarter; she used a loudspeaker to *amplify* her voice.

anachronism \ə-'na-krə-,ni-zəm\ n. AN ERROR INVOLVING TIME IN A STORY. The reference to clocks in *Julius Caesar* is an *anachronism*; clocks did not exist in Caesar's time.

analogous \ə-'na-lə-gəs\ adj. COMPARABLE. She called our attention to the things that had been done in an *analogous* situation and recommended that we do the same. //analogy, n.

anarchist \'a-nər-kist, -,när-\ n. PERSON WHO SEEKS TO OVERTURN THE ESTABLISHED GOVERNMENT; ADVOCATE OF ABOLISHING AUTHORITY. Denying she was an *anarchist*, Katya maintained that she wished only to make changes in our government, not to destroy it entirely.

anarchy \'a-nər-kē, -,när-\ n. ABSENCE OF GOVERNING BODY; STATE OF DISORDER; LAWLESSNESS. The assassination of the leaders led to a period of *anarchy*.

anathema \ə-'na-thə-mə\ n. SOLEMN CURSE; SOMEONE OR SOMETHING REGARDED AS A CURSE. The Ayatollah Khomeini heaped *anathema* upon "the Great Satan," that is, the United States. //anathematize, v.

anchor \'aŋ-kər\ v. SECURE OR FASTEN FIRMLY; BE FIXED IN PLACE. We set the post in concrete to *anchor* it in place. //anchorage, n.

anesthetic \,a-nəs-'the-tik\ n. SUBSTANCE THAT REMOVES SENSATION WITH OR WITHOUT LOSS OF CONSCIOUSNESS. His monotonous voice acted like an *anesthetic*; his audience was soon asleep. //anesthesia, n.

animated \\'a-nə-ˌmā-təd\\ adj. LIVELY; SPIRITED. Jim Carrey's facial expressions are highly *animated*: when he played Ace Ventura, he looked practically rubber-faced. //animation, n.

animosity \\ˌa-nə-'mä-sə-tē\\ n. ACTIVE ENMITY. He incurred the *animosity* of the ruling class because he advocated limitations of their power.

annals \\'a-nəlz\\ n. RECORDS; HISTORY. "In this year our good King Richard died," wrote the chronicler in the kingdom's *annals*.

annihilate \\ə-'nī-ə-ˌlāt\\ v. DESTROY. During the Middle Ages, the Black Plague *annihilated* much of the population of Europe.

anomalous \\ə-'nä-mə-ləs\\ adj. ABNORMAL; IRREGULAR; OUT OF PLACE. A classical harpist in the middle of a heavy metal band is *anomalous*; she is also inaudible. //anomaly, n.

anonymity \\ˌa-nə-'ni-mə-tē\\ n. STATE OF BEING NAMELESS; ANONYMOUSNESS. The donor of the gift asked the college not to mention him by name; the dean readily agreed to respect his *anonymity*. //anonymous, adj.

antagonism \\an-'ta-gə-ˌni-zəm\\ n. HOSTILITY; ACTIVE RESISTANCE. Barry showed his *antagonism* toward his new stepmother by ignoring her whenever she tried talking to him. //antagonistic, adj.

antediluvian \\ˌan-ti-də-'lü-vē-ən, -(ˌ)dī-\\ adj. ANTIQUATED; ANCIENT. Looking at his great aunt's antique furniture, which must have been cluttering up her attic since the time of Noah's flood, the young heir exclaimed, "Heavens! How positively *antediluvian*!" //also n.

anthropoid \\'an(t)-thrə-ˌpȯid\\ adj. MANLIKE. The gorilla is the strongest of the *anthropoid* animals. //also n.

anthropologist \\ˌan(t)-thrə-'pä-lə-jist\\ n. A STUDENT OF THE HISTORY AND SCIENCE OF MANKIND. *Anthropologists* have discovered several relics of prehistoric man in this area.

anticlimax \,an-tī-'klī-,maks, ,an-tē-\ n. LETDOWN IN
THOUGHT OR EMOTION. After the fine performance in the
first act, the rest of the play was an *anticlimax*.
//anticlimactic, adj.

antidote \an-ti-,dōt\ n. MEDICINE TO COUNTERACT A POISON
OR DISEASE. When Margo's child accidentally swal-
lowed some cleaning fluid, the local poison control
hotline instructed Margo how to administer the
antidote.

antipathy \an-'ti-pə-thē\ n. AVERSION; DISLIKE. Tom's
extreme *antipathy* for disputes keeps him from getting into arguments with his temperamental wife.

antiseptic \,an-tə-'sep-tik\ n. SUBSTANCE THAT PREVENTS
INFECTION. It is advisable to apply an *antiseptic* to any
wound, no matter how slight or insignificant. //also
adj.

antithesis \an-'ti-thə-səs\ n. CONTRAST; DIRECT OPPOSITE OF
OR TO. This tyranny was the *antithesis* of all that he
had hoped for, and he fought it with all his strength.

apathy \'a-pə-thē\ n. LACK OF CARING; INDIFFERENCE. A
firm believer in democratic government, she could
not understand the *apathy* of people who never bothered to vote. //apathetic, adj.

apex \'ā-,peks\ n. TIP; SUMMIT; CLIMAX. At the *apex* of his
career, the star was deluged with offers of leading
roles; two years later, he was reduced to taking bit
parts in B-movies.

aphorism \'a-fə-,ri-zəm\ n. PITHY MAXIM. "The proper
study of mankind is man" is an *aphorism*. "There's no
smoke without a fire" is an adage. //aphoristic, adj.

aplomb \ə-'pläm, -'pləm\ n. POISE; ASSURANCE. Gwen's
aplomb in handling potentially embarrassing
moments was legendary around the office; when one
of her clients broke a piece of her best crystal, she
coolly picked up her own goblet and hurled it into the
fireplace.

apocalyptic \ə-ˌpä-kə-'lip-tik\ adj. PROPHETIC; PERTAINING TO REVELATIONS. The crowd jeered at the street preacher's *apocalyptic* predictions of doom.

apocryphal \ə-'pä-krə-fəl\ adj. UNTRUE; MADE UP; NOT GENUINE. To impress his friends, Tom invented *apocryphal* tales of his adventures in the big city.

apostate \ə-'päs-ˌtāt, -tət\ n. ONE WHO ABANDONS HIS RELIGIOUS FAITH OR POLITICAL BELIEFS. Because he switched from one party to another, his former friends shunned him as an *apostate*. //apostasy, n.

Synonym Test • Word List 3

Each of the questions below consists of a word in capital letters, followed by five words or phrases. Choose the word or phrase that is most similar in meaning to the word in capital letters and write the letter of your choice on your answer paper.

31. **AMICABLE**   (A) penetrating   (B) compensating   (C) friendly   (D) zig-zag   (E) inescapable

32. **AMORAL**   (A) unusual   (B) unfriendly   (C) without values   (D) suave   (E) firm

33. **AMORPHOUS**   (A) nauseous   (B) obscene   (C) providential   (D) indefinite   (E) happy

34. **AMPLIFY**   (A) distract   (B) infer   (C) publicize   (D) enlarge   (E) pioneer

35. **ANALOGOUS**   (A) similar   (B) not capable   (C) not culpable   (D) not corporeal   (E) not congenial

36. **ANATHEMATIZE**   (A) locate   (B) deceive   (C) regulate   (D) radiate   (E) curse

37. **ANIMATED**   (A) worthy   (B) humorous   (C) lively   (D) lengthy   (E) realistic

38. **ANIMOSITY**   (A) originality   (B) enmity   (C) mildness   (D) triviality   (E) understanding

39. **ANNIHILATE**   (A) advocate   (B) snub   (C) pardon   (D) grimace   (E) destroy

40. **ANOMALY**   (A) desperation   (B) requisition   (C) registry   (D) irregularity   (E) radiation

41. **ANONYMOUS**   (A) desperate   (B) nameless   (C) defined   (D) expert   (E) written

42. **ANTEDILUVIAN**   (A) transported   (B) subtle   (C) isolated   (D) celebrated   (E) ancient

43. **ANTIPATHY**   (A) profundity   (B) objection   (C) willingness   (D) abstention   (E) aversion

44. **ANTITHESIS**   (A) velocity   (B) maxim   (C) opposite   (D) acceleration   (E) reaction

45. **APLOMB**   (A) confidence   (B) necessity   (C) pain   (D) crack   (E) prayer

apotheosis \ə-ˌpä-thē-ˈō-səs, ˌa-pə-ˈthē-ə-səs\ n. DEIFICATION; GLORIFICATION; AN IDEAL EXAMPLE OF SOMETHING. The Roman empress Livia envied the late Emperor Augustus his *apotheosis*; she hoped that on her death she too would be exalted to the ranks of the gods.

appall \ə-ˈpȯl\ v. DISMAY; SHOCK. We were *appalled* by the horrifying conditions in the city's jails.

appease \ə-ˈpēz\ v. PACIFY; SOOTHE. Tom and Jody tried to *appease* the crying baby by offering him one toy after another.

apposite \ˈa-pə-zət\ adj. APPROPRIATE; FITTING. He was always able to find the *apposite* phrase, the correct expression for every occasion.

appraise \ə-ˈprāz\ v. ESTIMATE VALUE OF. It is difficult to *appraise* the value of old paintings; it is easier to call them priceless. //appraisal, n.

apprehension \ˌa-pri-ˈhen(t)-shən\ n. FEAR; ARREST; DISCERNMENT. The tourist refused to drive his rental car through downtown Miami because he felt some *apprehension* that he might be carjacked. //apprehensive, adj.; apprehend, v.

apprise \ə-ˈprīz\ v. INFORM. When NASA was *apprised* of the dangerous weather conditions, the head of the space agency decided to postpone the shuttle launch.

approbation \ˌa-prə-ˈbā-shən\ n. APPROVAL. She looked for some sign of *approbation* from her parents, hoping her good grades would please them.

appropriate \ə-ˈprō-prē-ˌāt\ v. ACQUIRE; TAKE POSSESSION OF FOR ONE'S OWN USE. The ranch owners *appropriated* the lands that had originally been set aside for the Indians' use.

aptitude \ˈap-tə-ˌtüd, -ˌtyüd\ n. FITNESS; TALENT. The American aviator Bessie Coleman grew up in Waxahatchie, Texas, where her mathematical *aptitude* freed her from working in the cotton fields with her 12 brothers and sisters.

arable \'a-rə-bəl, 'er-ə-\ adj. FIT FOR GROWING CROPS. The first settlers wrote home glowing reports of the New World, praising its vast acres of *arable* land ready for the plow.

arbiter \'är-bə-tər\ n. A PERSON WITH POWER TO DECIDE A DISPUTE; JUDGE. As an *arbiter* in labor disputes, she has won the confidence of the workers and the employers. //arbitrate, v.

arbitrary \'är-bə-,trer-ē, -,tre-rē\ adj. UNREASONABLE OR CAPRICIOUS. The coach claimed that the team lost because the umpire made some *arbitrary* calls.

arcane \är-'kān\ adj. SECRET; MYSTERIOUS; KNOWN ONLY TO THE INITIATED. Secret brotherhoods surround themselves with *arcane* rituals and trappings to mystify outsiders.

archaeology \,är-kē-'ä-lə-jē\ n. STUDY OF ARTIFACTS AND RELICS OF EARLY MANKIND. The professor of *archaeology* headed an expedition to the Gobi Desert in search of ancient ruins.

archaic \är-'kā-ik\ adj. ANTIQUATED. "Methinks," "thee," and "thou" are *archaic* words that are no longer part of our normal vocabulary.

archetype \'är-ki-,tīp\ n. PROTOTYPE; PRIMITIVE PATTERN. The Brooklyn Bridge was the *archetype* of the many spans that now connect Manhattan with Long Island and New Jersey.

archipelago \,är-kə-'pe-lə-,gō\ n. GROUP OF CLOSELY LOCATED ISLANDS. When he looked at the map and saw the *archipelagoes* in the South Seas, he longed to visit them.

archives \'är-,kīvz\ n. PUBLIC RECORDS; PLACE WHERE PUBLIC RECORDS ARE KEPT. These documents should be part of the *archives* so that historians may be able to evaluate them in the future.

ardor \\'är-dər\ n. HEAT; PASSION; ZEAL. Katya's *ardor* was contagious; soon all her fellow demonstrators were busily making posters and handing out flyers, inspired by her enthusiasm for the cause.

arduous \\'är-jə-wəs, -dyu̇-, -ju̇-əs\ adj. HARD; STRENUOUS. Even using a chainsaw, she found chopping down trees an *arduous*, time-consuming task.

aria \\'är-ē-ə\ n. OPERATIC SOLO. At her Metropolitan Opera audition, Marian Anderson sang an *aria* from *Norma*.

arid \\'a-rəd, 'er-əd\ adj. DRY; BARREN. The cactus has adapted to survive in an *arid* environment.

armada \är-'mä-də, -'mä-, *also* -'ma-\ n. FLEET OF WARSHIPS. Queen Elizabeth's navy defeated the mighty *armada* that threatened the English coast.

aromatic \ˌa-rə-'ma-tik, ˌer-ə-\ adj. FRAGRANT. Medieval sailing vessels brought *aromatic* herbs from China to Europe.

array \ə-'rā\ v. MARSHAL; DRAW UP IN ORDER. His actions were bound to *array* public sentiment against him. //also n.

array \ə-'rā\ v. CLOTHE; ADORN. She liked to watch her mother *array* herself in her finest clothes before going out for the evening. //also n.

arrogance \\'er-ə-gən(t)s, 'a-rə-\ n. PRIDE; HAUGHTINESS. Convinced that Emma thought she was better than anyone else in the class, Ed rebuked her for her *arrogance*.

articulate \är-'ti-kyə-lət\ adj. EFFECTIVE; DISTINCT. Her *articulate* presentation of the advertising campaign impressed her employers. //also v.

artifacts \\'är-ti-ˌfakts\ n. OBJECTS MADE BY HUMAN BEINGS, EITHER HAND-MADE OR MASS-PRODUCED. Archaeologists debated the significance of the *artifacts* discovered in the ruins of Asia Minor but came to no conclusion about the culture they represented.

artifice \\'är-tə-fəs\ n. DECEPTION; TRICKERY. The Trojan War proved to the Greeks that cunning and *artifice* were often more effective than military might.

artisan \\'är-tə-zən, -sən\ n. CRAFTSMAN, AS OPPOSED TO ARTIST. A noted *artisan*, Arturo was known for the fine craftsmanship of his inlaid cabinets.

ascendancy \ə-'sen-dən(t)-sē\ n. CONTROLLING INFLUENCE; DOMINATION. Leaders of religious cults maintain *ascendancy* over their followers by methods that can verge on brainwashing.

ascertain \\,a-sər-'tān\ v. FIND OUT FOR CERTAIN. Please *ascertain* her present address.

ascetic \ə-'se-tik, a-\ adj. PRACTICING SELF-DENIAL; AUSTERE. The wealthy, self-indulgent young man felt oddly drawn to the strict, *ascetic* life led by members of the monastic order. //also n.

ascribe \ə-'skrīb\ v. REFER; ATTRIBUTE; ASSIGN. I can *ascribe* no motive for her acts.

asperity \a-'sper-ə-tē, ə-, -'spe-rə-\ n. SHARPNESS (OF TEMPER). Exasperated by the boys' unruly behavior, she addressed them with considerable *asperity*.

aspire \ə-'spī(-ə)r\ v. SEEK TO ATTAIN; LONG FOR. Because he *aspired* to a career in professional sports, Philip enrolled in a graduate program in sports management.

assail \ə-'sāl\ v. ASSAULT. He was *assailed* with questions after his lecture.

assent \ə-'sent, a-\ v. AGREE; ACCEPT. It gives me great pleasure to *assent* to your request.

assessment \ə-'ses-mənt, a-\ n. ESTIMATION. I would like to have your *assessment* of the situation in South Africa.

assiduous \ə-'sij-wəs, -'si-jə-\ adj. DILIGENT. It took Rembrandt weeks of *assiduous* labor before he was satisfied with his portrait of his son. //assiduity, n.

assimilate \ə-'si-mə-ˌlāt\ v. ABSORB; CAUSE TO BECOME
HOMOGENEOUS. The manner in which the United States
was able to *assimilate* the hordes of immigrants during the nineteenth and the early part of the twentieth
centuries will always be a source of pride.

assuage \ə-'swāj *also* -'swäzh *or* -'swäzh\ v. EASE; LESSEN
(PAIN); SOOTHE. Jilted by Jane, Dick tried to *assuage*
his heartache by indulging in ice cream. //assuage-
ment, n.

asteroid \'as-tə-ˌroid\ n. SMALL PLANET. Most *asteroids*
are found in the region of space between Mars and
Jupiter, commonly known as the *asteroid* belt.

Each of the questions below consists of a word in capital letters, followed by five words or phrases. Choose the word or phrase that is most similar in meaning to the word in capital letters and write the letter of your choice on your answer paper.

46. **APPALL** (A) shock (B) distort (C) despise (D) cease (E) degrade

47. **APPEASE** (A) placate (B) qualify (C) display (D) predestine (E) interrupt

48. **APPREHEND** (A) obviate (B) capture (C) shiver (D) undermine (E) contrast

49. **APTITUDE** (A) sarcasm (B) inversion (C) adulation (D) talent (E) gluttony

50. **ARBITRARY** (A) watery (B) imperious (C) refined (D) antique (E) rodentlike

51. **ARCHAIC** (A) youthful (B) cautious (C) antiquated (D) placated (E) buttressed

52. **ARDOR** (A) zeal (B) paint (C) proof (D) group (E) excitement

53. **ARIA** (A) swindle (B) balance (C) operatic solo (D) dryness (E) musical theme

54. **ARMADA** (A) crevice (B) fleet (C) missile (D) food (E) fabric

55. **ARTIFICE** (A) spite (B) exception (C) anger (D) deception (E) loyalty

56. **ARTISAN** (A) educator (B) decider (C) sculptor (D) discourser (E) craftsman

57. **ASCERTAIN** (A) amplify (B) master (C) discover (D) retain (E) explode

58. **ASPERITY** (A) anguish (B) absence (C) innuendo (D) sharpness (E) snake

59. **ASSUAGE** (A) stuff (B) describe (C) wince (D) decrease (E) introduce

60. **ASTEROID** (A) Milky Way (B) radiance (C) small planet (D) rising moon (E) setting moon

WORD LIST 5

astronomical \ˌas-trə-ˈnä-mi-kəl\ adj. ENORMOUSLY LARGE OR EXTENSIVE. The government seems willing to spend *astronomical* sums on weapons development.

astute \ə-ˈstüt, a-, -ˈstyüt\ adj. WISE; SHREWD; KEEN. John Jacob Astor made *astute* investments in land, shrewdly purchasing valuable plots throughout New York City.

asylum \ə-ˈsī-ləm\ n. PLACE OF REFUGE OR SHELTER; PROTECTION. The refugees sought *asylum* from religious persecution in a new land.

atheist \ˈā-thē-ˌist\ n. ONE WHO DENIES THE EXISTENCE OF GOD. "An *atheist* is a person who has no invisible means of support."

atone \ə-ˈtōn\ v. MAKE AMENDS FOR; PAY FOR. He knew no way in which he could *atone* for his brutal crime.

atrocity \ə-ˈträ-sə-tē\ n. BRUTAL DEED. In time of war, many *atrocities* are committed by invading armies.

atrophy \ˈa-trə-fē\ v. WASTE AWAY. After three months in a cast, your calf muscles are bound to *atrophy*; you'll need physical therapy to get back in shape.

attest \ə-ˈtest\ v. TESTIFY, BEAR WITNESS. Having served as a member of the grand jury, I can *attest* that our system of indicting individuals is in need of improvement.

attribute \ˈa-trə-ˌbyüt\ n. ESSENTIAL QUALITY. His outstanding *attribute* was his kindness.

attribute \ə-ˈtri-ˌbyüt, -byət\ v. ASCRIBE; EXPLAIN. I *attribute* her success in science to the encouragement she received from her parents.

attrition \ə-ˈtri-shən, a-\ n. GRADUAL DECREASE IN NUMBERS; REDUCTION IN THE WORK FORCE WITHOUT FIRING EMPLOYEES; WEARING AWAY OF OPPOSITION BY MEANS OF HARASSMENT. In the 1960s urban churches suffered from *attrition* as members moved from the cities to the suburbs.

atypical \(ˌ)ā-'ti-pi-kəl\ adj. NOT NORMAL. The child psychiatrist reassured Mrs. Keaton that playing doctor was not *atypical* behavior for a child of young Alex's age. "Yes," she replied, "but not charging for house calls!"

audacity \ȯ-'da-sə-tē\ n. BOLDNESS. Luke could not believe his own *audacity* in addressing the princess. Where did he get the nerve?

audit \'ȯ-dət\ n. EXAMINATION OF ACCOUNTS. When the bank examiners arrived to hold their annual *audit*, they discovered the embezzlements of the chief cashier. //also v.

augment \ȯg-'ment\ v. INCREASE; ADD TO. Armies *augment* their forces by calling up reinforcements; teachers *augment* their salaries by taking after-school jobs.

august \ȯ-'gəst, 'ȯ-(ˌ)gəst\ adj. IMPRESSIVE; MAJESTIC. Visiting the palace at Versailles, she was impressed by the *august* surroundings in which she found herself.

auspicious \ȯ-'spi-shəs\ adj. FAVORING SUCCESS. With favorable weather conditions, it was an *auspicious* moment to set sail.

austerity \ȯ-'ster-ə-tē, -'ste-rə-\ n. STERNNESS; SEVERITY; LACK OF LUXURIES. The *austerity* and dignity of the court were maintained by the new justices, who were a strict and solemn group. //austere, adj.

authenticate \ə-'then-ti-ˌkāt, ȯ-\ v. CONFIRM AS GENUINE. After a thorough chemical analysis of the pigments and canvas, the experts were prepared to *authenticate* the painting as an original Rembrandt.

authoritarian \ȯ-ˌthär-ə-'ter-ē-ən, -ˌthȯr-\ adj. SUBORDINATING THE INDIVIDUAL TO THE STATE; COMPLETELY DOMINATING ANOTHER'S WILL. The leaders of the *authoritarian* regime ordered the suppression of the democratic protest movement. After years of submitting to the will of her *authoritarian* father, Elizabeth Barrett ran away from home with the poet Robert Browning. //also n.

authoritative \ə-'thär-ə-ˌtā-tiv, ȯ-, -'thȯr-\ adj. HAVING THE
WEIGHT OF AUTHORITY; DICTATORIAL. Impressed by the
young researcher's well-documented presentation,
we accepted her analysis of the experiment as
authoritative.

autocrat \'ȯ-tə-ˌkrat\ n. MONARCH WITH SUPREME POWER.
He ran his office like an *autocrat*, giving no one else
any authority. //autocracy, n; autocratic, adj.

autonomous \ȯ-'tä-nə-məs\ adj. SELF-GOVERNING.
Although the University of California at Berkeley is
just one part of the state university system, in many
ways, Cal Berkeley is *autonomous*, for it runs several
programs that are not subject to outside control.
//autonomy, n.

auxiliary \ȯg-'zil-yə-rē, -'zil-rē, -'zi-lə-\ adj. HELPER, ADDI-
TIONAL OR SUBSIDIARY. To prepare for the emergency,
they built an *auxiliary* power station. //also n.

avarice \'a-və-rəs, 'av-rəs\ n. GREEDINESS FOR WEALTH. It is
not poverty, but rather abundance, that breeds
avarice: the more shoes Imelda Marcos had, the more
she craved. //avaricious, adj.

averse \ə-'vərs\ adj. RELUCTANT. He was *averse* to reveal-
ing the sources of his information.

aversion \ə-'vər-zhən, -shən\ n. FIRM DISLIKE. Their
mutual *aversion* was so great that they refused to
speak to one another.

avert \ə-'vərt\ v. PREVENT; TURN AWAY. "Watch out!" she
cried, hoping to *avert* an accident.

aviary \'ā-vē-ˌer-ē\ n. ENCLOSURE FOR BIRDS. The *aviary* at
the zoo held nearly 300 birds.

avid \'a-vəd\ adj. GREEDY; EAGER FOR. *Avid* for pleasure,
Abner partied with great *avidity*. //avidity, n.

avocation \ˌa-və-'kā-shən\ n. SECONDARY OR MINOR OCCU-
PATION. His hobby proved to be so fascinating and

profitable that gradually he abandoned his regular occupation and concentrated on his *avocation*.

avow \ə-'vau̇\ v. DECLARE OPENLY. Lana *avowed* that she never meant to steal Debbie's boyfriend, but no one believed her *avowal* of innocence.

avuncular \ə-'vəŋ-kyə-lər\ adj. LIKE AN UNCLE. *Avuncular* pride did not prevent him from noticing his nephew's shortcomings.

awe \'ȯ\ n. SOLEMN WONDER. The tourists gazed with *awe* at the tremendous expanse of the Grand Canyon.

awry \ə-'rī\ adv. CROOKED; WRONG; AMISS. Noticing that the groom's tie was slightly *awry*, the bride reached over to set it straight. A careful organizer, she hated to have anything go *awry* with her plans. //also adj.

axiom \'ak-sē-əm\ n. SELF-EVIDENT TRUTH REQUIRING NO PROOF. The Declaration of Independence records certain self-evident truths or *axioms*, the first of which is "All men are created equal."

babble \'ba-bəl\ v. CHATTER IDLY. Now that Molly has a cell phone, she does nothing but *babble* on the phone all day. //also n.

badger \'ba-jər\ v. PESTER; ANNOY. She was forced to change her telephone number because she was *badgered* by obscene phone calls.

baffle \'ba-fəl\ v. FRUSTRATE; PERPLEX. The new code *baffled* the enemy agents.

bait \'bāt\ v. HARASS; TEASE. The school bully *baited* the smaller children, terrorizing them.

baleful \'bāl-fəl\ adj. HAVING A MALIGN INFLUENCE; OMINOUS. The fortune teller made *baleful* predictions of terrible things to come.

balk \'bȯk *sometimes* 'bȯlk\ v. FOIL; REFUSE TO PROCEED OR DO SOMETHING SPECIFIED. When the warden learned that several inmates were planning to escape, he took steps to *balk* their attempt.

ballast \'ba-ləst\ n. HEAVY SUBSTANCE USED TO ADD STABIL-ITY OR WEIGHT. The ship was listing badly to one side; it was necessary to shift the *ballast* in the hold to get her back on an even keel. //also v.

balm \'bä(l)m\ n. SOMETHING THAT RELIEVES PAIN. Friendship is the finest *balm* for the pangs of disappointed love.

balmy \'bä-mē, 'bäl-mē\ adj. MILD; FRAGRANT. A *balmy* breeze refreshed us after the sultry blast.

banal \bə-'nal, ba-, -'näl; bä-'nal; 'bä-nəl\ adj. HACKNEYED; COMMONPLACE; TRITE. The hack writer's worn-out clichés made his comic sketch seem *banal*. //banality, n.

bane \'bān\ n. CAUSE OF RUIN; POISON; CURSE. Lucy's little brother was the *bane* of her existence; he made her life a total misery. //baneful, adj.

banter \'ban-tər\ n. GOOD-NATURED RIDICULE. They made the mistake of taking his *banter* seriously. //also v; bantering, adj.

Each of the questions below consists of a word in capital letters, followed by five words or phrases. Choose the word or phrase that is most similar in meaning to the word in capital letters and write the letter of your choice on your answer paper.

61. **ASTUTE**   (A) sheer   (B) noisy   (C) astral
    (D) unusual   (E) clever

62. **ATROCITY**   (A) endurance   (B) fortitude   (C) session
    (D) heinous act   (E) hatred

63. **ATROPHY**   (A) capture   (B) waste away
    (C) govern   (D) award prize   (E) defeat

64. **ATTRIBUTE**   (A) appear   (B) be absent   (C) explain
    (D) testify   (E) soothe

65. **ATYPICAL**   (A) superfluous   (B) critical   (C) unusual
    (D) clashing   (E) lovely

66. **AUDACITY**   (A) boldness   (B) asperity   (C) strength
    (D) stature   (E) anchorage

67. **AUGMENT**   (A) make noble   (B) anoint   (C) increase
    (D) harvest   (E) reach

68. **AUXILIARY**   (A) righteous   (B) prospective
    (C) assistant   (D) archaic   (E) mandatory

69. **AVARICE**   (A) easiness   (B) greed   (C) statement
    (D) invoice   (E) power

70. **AVOCATION**   (A) promise   (B) hypnosis   (C) hobby
    (D) perfume   (E) disaster

71. **AWRY**   (A) recommended   (B) commiserating
    (C) startled   (D) crooked   (E) psychological

72. **BALEFUL**   (A) doubtful   (B) virtual   (C) deadly
    (D) conventional   (E) virtuous

73. **BALMY**   (A) venturesome   (B) dedicated   (C) mild
    (D) fanatic   (E) memorable

74. **BANAL**   (A) philosophical   (B) trite   (C) dramatic
    (D) heedless   (E) discussed

75. **BANEFUL**   (A) intellectual   (B) thankful   (C) decisive
    (D) poisonous   (E) remorseful

bard \'bärd\ n. POET. The ancient *bard* Homer sang of the fall of Troy.

baroque \bə-'rōk, ba-, -'räk, -'rȯk \ adj. HIGHLY ORNATE. Accustomed to the severe lines of contemporary buildings, the architecture students found the flamboyance of *baroque* architecture amusing. They simply didn't go for *baroque*.

bask \'bask\ v. LUXURIATE; TAKE PLEASURE IN WARMTH. *Basking* on the beach, she relaxed so completely that she fell asleep.

bastion \'bas-chən\ n. STRONGHOLD; SOMETHING SEEN AS A SOURCE OF PROTECTION. The villagers fortified the town hall, hoping this improvised *bastion* could protect them from the guerrilla raids.

bauble \'bȯ-bəl, 'bä-\ n. TRINKET; TRIFLE. The child was delighted with the *bauble* she had won in the grab bag.

beatific \ˌbē-ə-'ti-fik\ adj. SHOWING OR PRODUCING JOY; BLISSFUL. When Johnny first saw the new puppy, a *beatific* smile spread across his face.

befuddle \bi-'fə-dəl, bē-\ v. CONFUSE THOROUGHLY. His attempts to clarify the situation succeeded only in *befuddling* her further.

begrudge \bi-'grəj, bē-\ v. RESENT. I *begrudge* every minute I have to spend attending meetings; they're a complete waste of time.

beguile \bi-'gī(-ə)l, bē-\ v. AMUSE; DELUDE; CHEAT. He *beguiled* himself during the long hours by playing solitaire.

belated \bi-'lā-təd, bē-\ adj. DELAYED. He apologized for his *belated* note of condolence to the widow of his friend and explained that he had just learned of her husband's untimely death.

belie \bi-'lī, bē-\ v. CONTRADICT; GIVE A FALSE IMPRESSION. His coarse, hard-bitten exterior *belied* his inner sensitivity.

belittle \bi-'li-təl, bē-\ v. DISPARAGE; DEPRECIATE; PUT DOWN. Parents should not *belittle* their children's early attempts at drawing, but should encourage their efforts.

bellicose \'be-li-ˌkōs\ adj. WARLIKE; PUGNACIOUS. Someone who is spoiling for a fight is by definition *bellicose*.

belligerent \bə-'lij-rənt, -'li-jə-\ adj. QUARRELSOME. Whenever he had too much to drink, he became *belligerent* and tried to pick fights with strangers. //belligerence, n.

benediction \ˌbe-nə-'dik-shən\ n. BLESSING. The appearance of the sun after the many rainy days was like a *benediction*.

benefactor \'be-nə-ˌfak-tər\ n. GIFT GIVER; PATRON. Scrooge later became Tiny Tim's *benefactor* and gave him gifts.

beneficiary \ˌbe-nə-'fi-shē-ˌer-ē, -e-rē, -'fi-sh(ə-)rē\ n. PERSON ENTITLED TO BENEFITS OR PROCEEDS OF AN INSURANCE POLICY OR WILL. Scrooge's will named Tiny Tim as *beneficiary*; the one-time miser left his entire fortune to young Tim.

benevolent \bə-'nev-lənt, -'ne-və-\ adj. GENEROUS; CHARITABLE. Mr. Fezziwig was a *benevolent* employer who wished to make Christmas a merry time for Scrooge and his other employees. //benevolence, n.

benign \bi-'nīn\ adj. KINDLY; FAVORABLE; NOT MALIGNANT. Though her *benign* smile and gentle bearing made Miss Marple seem a sweet little old lady, in reality she was a tough-minded, shrewd observer of human nature. //benignity, n.

berate \bi-'rāt, bē-\ v. SCOLD STRONGLY. He feared she would *berate* him for his forgetfulness.

bereavement \bi-'rēv-mənt, bē-\ n. STATE OF BEING DEPRIVED OF SOMETHING VALUABLE OR BELOVED. His friends gathered to console him upon his sudden *bereavement*. //bereaved, adj.; bereft, adj.

berserk \bə(r)-'sərk, ˌbər-, -'zərk; 'bər-\ adv. FRENZIED. Angered, he went *berserk* and began to wreck the room.

beset \bi-'set, bē-\ v. HARASS; TROUBLE; HEM IN. Many vexing problems *beset* the American public school system. Sleeping Beauty's castle was *beset* on all sides by dense thickets that hid it from view.

besmirch \bi-'smərch, bē-\ v. SOIL, DEFILE. The scandalous remarks in the newspaper *besmirch* the reputations of every member of the society.

bestial \'bes-chəl, 'besh-, 'bēs-, 'bēsh-\ adj. BEASTLIKE; BRUTAL. According to legend, the werewolf was capable of retaining its human intelligence while assuming its *bestial* form.

bevy \'be-vē\ n. LARGE GROUP. The movie actor was surrounded by a *bevy* of starlets.

bicker \'bi-kər\ v. QUARREL. The children *bickered* morning, noon, and night, exasperating their parents.

biennial \(ˌ)bī-'e-nē-əl\ adj. EVERY TWO YEARS. Seeing no need to meet more frequently, the group held *biennial* meetings instead of annual ones.

bigotry \'bi-gə-trē\ n. STUBBORN INTOLERANCE. Brought up in a democratic atmosphere, the student was shocked by the *bigotry* and narrowness expressed by several of his classmates.

bilk \'bilk\ v. SWINDLE; CHEAT. The con man specialized in *bilking* insurance companies.

bizarre \bə-'zär\ adj. FANTASTIC; VIOLENTLY CONTRASTING. The plot of the novel was too *bizarre* to be believed.

blanch \'blanch\ v. BLEACH; WHITEN. Although age had *blanched* his hair, he was still vigorous and energetic.

bland \'bland\ adj. SOOTHING; MILD. She used a *bland* ointment for her sunburn. //blandness, n.

blandishment \'blan-dish-mənt\ n. FLATTERY. Despite the salesperson's *blandishments*, the customer did not buy the outfit.

blasé \blä-'zā\ adj. BORED WITH PLEASURE OR DISSIPATION. Although Beth was as thrilled by the idea of a trip to Paris as her classmates were, she tried to act super cool and *blasé*, as if she'd been abroad hundreds of times.

blasphemy \'blas-fə-mē\ n. IRREVERENCE; SACRILEGE; CURSING. In my father's house, the Dodgers were the holiest of holies; to cheer for another team was to utter words of *blasphemy*. //blasphemous, adj.

blatant \'blā-tənt\ adj. FLAGRANT; CONSPICUOUSLY OBVIOUS; LOUDLY OFFENSIVE. Caught in a *blatant* lie, the scoundrel had only one regret: he wished that he had lied more subtly. //blatancy, n.

bleak \'blēk\ adj. COLD; CHEERLESS. The frigid, inhospitable Aleutian Islands are *bleak* military outposts.

blighted \'blī-təd\ adj. SUFFERING FROM A DISEASE; DESTROYED. The extent of the *blighted* areas could be seen only when viewed from the air. //blight, n.

blithe \'blīth\ adj. CAREFREE AND UNCONCERNED (PERHAPS FOOLISHLY SO); CHEERFUL AND GAY. Marie Antoinette's famous remark "Let them eat cake!" epitomizes her *blithe* ignorance of the harsh realities endured by the common people.

bloat \'blōt\ v. EXPAND OR SWELL (WITH WATER OR AIR); PUFF UP WITH CONCEIT. Constant flattery from his hangers-on *bloated* the heavyweight champion's already sizable ego.

bludgeon \'blə-jən\ n. CLUB; HEAVY-HEADED WEAPON. Attacked by Dr. Moriarty, Holmes used his walking stick as a *bludgeon* to defend himself. //also v.

Each of the questions below consists of a word in capital letters, followed by five words or phrases. Choose the word or phrase that is most similar in meaning to the word in capital letters and write the letter of your choice on your answer paper.

76. **BAROQUE**   (A) polished   (B) constant   (C) transformed   (D) ornate   (E) aglow

77. **BEATIFIC**   (A) glorious   (B) blissful   (C) theatrical   (D) crooked   (E) handsome

78. **BELITTLE**   (A) disobey   (B) forget   (C) grandstand   (D) disparage   (E) envy

79. **BELLICOSE**   (A) warlike   (B) naval   (C) amusing   (D) piecemeal   (E) errant

80. **BENEFACTOR**   (A) dilettante   (B) bachelor   (C) wedding guest   (D) orgy   (E) patron

81. **BENIGN**   (A) harmless   (B) peaceful   (C) blessed   (D) wavering   (E) immortal

82. **BERATE**   (A) grant   (B) scold   (C) refer   (D) purchase   (E) deny

83. **BESTIAL**   (A) animated   (B) brutal   (C) zoological   (D) clear   (E) dusky

84. **BIGOTRY**   (A) arrogance   (B) approval   (C) mourning   (D) promptness   (E) intolerance

85. **BIZARRE**   (A) roomy   (B) veiled   (C) subdued   (D) triumphant   (E) fantastic

86. **BLANCH**   (A) soothe   (B) scatter   (C) whiten   (D) analyze   (E) subdivide

87. **BLAND**   (A) mild   (B) meager   (C) soft   (D) uncooked   (E) helpless

88. **BLASÉ**   (A) fiery   (B) clever   (C) intriguing   (D) slim   (E) bored

89. **BLEAK**   (A) pale   (B) sudden   (C) dry   (D) narrow   (E) cheerless

90. **BLITHE**   (A) spiritual   (B) profuse   (C) joyous   (D) hybrid   (E) comfortable

blunder \'blən-dər\ n. ERROR. The criminal's fatal *blunder* led to his capture. //also v.

bode \'bōd\ v. FORESHADOW; PORTEND. The gloomy skies and the sulphurous odors from the mineral springs seemed to *bode* evil to those who settled in the area.

bogus \'bō-gəs\ adj. COUNTERFEIT; NOT AUTHENTIC. The police quickly found the distributors of the *bogus* twenty-dollar bills.

boisterous \'boi-st(ə-)rəs\ adj. VIOLENT; ROUGH; NOISY. The unruly crowd became even more *boisterous* when he tried to quiet them.

bolster \'bōl-stər\ v. SUPPORT; PROP UP. The debaters amassed file boxes full of evidence to *bolster* their arguments. //also n.

bombastic \bäm-'bas-tik\ adj. POMPOUS; USING INFLATED LANGUAGE. The orator spoke in such a *bombastic* manner that we longed to deflate his pomposity. //bombast, n.

boorish \'bur-ish\ adj. INSENSITIVE. Though Mr. Collins constantly interrupted his wife, she ignored his *boorish* behavior, for she had lost hope of teaching him courtesy.

bountiful 'baun-ti-fəl\ adj. GENEROUS; ABUNDANT. Thanks to the good harvest, we had a *bountiful* supply of food, and we could be as *bountiful* as we liked in distributing food to the needy.

bourgeois \'burzh-,wä *also* 'buzh- *or* 'buzh- *or* burzh\ n. MIDDLE CLASS. The French Revolution was inspired by the *bourgeois*, who resented the aristocracy. //also adj.

brackish \'bra-kish\ adj. SOMEWHAT SALTY. Following the stream, we noticed that its fresh, springlike water grew increasingly *brackish* as we drew nearer to the bay.

braggart \'bra-gərt\ n. BOASTER. Modest by nature, she was no *braggart*, preferring to let her accomplishments speak for themselves.

brawn \'brȯn\ n. MUSCULAR STRENGTH; STURDINESS. It takes *brawn* to become a champion weight lifter. //brawny, adj.

brazen \'brā-zən\ adj. INSOLENT. Her *brazen* contempt for authority angered the officials.

breach \'brēch\ n. BREAKING OF CONTRACT OR DUTY; FISSURE; GAP. Jill sued Jack for *breach* of promise, claiming he had broken his promise to marry her. //also v.

breadth \'bretth, 'bredth, ÷'breth\ n. WIDTH; EXTENT. We were impressed by the *breadth* of her knowledge.

brevity \'bre-və-tē\ n. CONCISENESS. *Brevity* is essential when you send a telegram or cablegram; you are charged for every word.

brittle \'bri-təl\ adj. EASILY BROKEN; DIFFICULT. My employer's self-control was as *brittle* as an eggshell. Her *brittle* personality made it difficult for me to get along with her.

broach \'brōch\ v. INTRODUCE; OPEN UP. Jack did not even try to *broach* the subject of religion with his in-laws. If you *broach* a touchy subject, it may cause a breach.

brochure \brō-'shu̇r\ n. PAMPHLET. This *brochure* on farming was issued by the Department of Agriculture.

brusque \'brəsk\ adj. BLUNT; ABRUPT. Was Bruce too *brusque* when he brushed off Bob's question with an abrupt "Not now!"?

buffoonery \(,)bə-'fü-nə-rē, -'fün-rē\ n. CLOWNING. Despite Cesar's *buffoonery* and fooling around in class, he had a serious side to his personality.

bulwark \'bu̇l-(,)wərk, -,wȯrk; 'bəl-(,)wərk\ n. EARTHWORK OR OTHER STRONG DEFENSE; PERSON WHO DEFENDS. The navy is our principal *bulwark* against invasion.

bungle \'bəŋ-gəl\ v. MISMANAGE; BLUNDER. Don't botch this assignment, Bumstead; if you *bungle* the job, you're fired!

bureaucracy \byu̇-'rä-krə-sē, byə-, byər-'ä-\ n. OVER-REGULATED ADMINISTRATIVE SYSTEM MARKED BY RED TAPE. The Internal Revenue Service is the ultimate *bureaucracy*: taxpayers wasted so much paper filling out IRS forms that the IRS *bureaucrats* printed up a new set of rules requiring taxpayers to comply with the Paperwork Reduction Act. //bureaucrat, n.

burgeon \'bər-jən\ v. GROW FORTH; SEND OUT BUDS. In the spring, the plants that *burgeon* are a promise of the beauty that is to come.

burlesque \(,)bər-'lesk\ v. GIVE AN IMITATION THAT RIDICULES. In *Spaceballs*, Rick Moranis *burlesques* Darth Vader of *Star Wars*, outrageously parodying Vader's stiff walk and hollow voice. //also n.

burnish \'bər-nish\ v. MAKE SHINY BY RUBBING; POLISH. The maid *burnished* the brass fixtures until they reflected the lamplight.

buttress \'bə-trəs\ v. SUPPORT; PROP UP. The attorney came up with several far-fetched arguments in a vain attempt to *buttress* his weak case.

cache \'kash\ n. HIDING PLACE. The detectives followed the suspect until he led them to the *cache* where he had stored his loot. //also v.

cacophony \ka-'kä-fə-nē, -'kȯ- *also* -'ka-\ n. HARSH OR DISCORDANT SOUND; DISSONANCE. Does anyone enjoy the *cacophony* of an orchestra that is tuning up? What a racket! //cacophonous, adj.

cajole \kə-'jōl\ v. COAX; WHEEDLE. Diane tried to *cajole* her father into letting her drive the family car.

calamity \kə-'la-mə-tē\ n. DISASTER; MISERY. As news of the *calamity* spread, offers of relief poured in to the stricken community.

caliber \'ka-lə-bər\ n. ABILITY; CAPACITY. The scholarship committee searched for students of high *caliber*, ones with the intelligence and ability to be a credit to the school.

callous \'ka-ləs\ adj. HARDENED; UNFEELING. He had worked in the hospital for so many years that he was *callous* to the suffering in the wards. //callousness, n.

callow \'ka-(,)lō\ adj. YOUTHFUL; IMMATURE. As a freshman, Frank was sure he and his classmates were men of the world; as a sophomore, he made fun of freshmen as inexperienced, *callow* youths.

calumny \'ka-ləm-nē *also* 'kal-yəm-\ n. MALICIOUS MISREPRESENTATION; SLANDER. He could endure his financial failure, but he could not bear the *calumny* that his foes heaped upon him.

camaraderie \,käm-'rä-d(ə-)rē, ,kam-, ,kä-mə-, ,ka-, -'ra-\ n. GOOD FELLOWSHIP. What he loved best about his job was the sense of *camaraderie* he and his coworkers shared.

candor \'kan-dər, -,dȯr\ n. FRANKNESS. Jack can carry *candor* too far: when he told Jill his honest opinion of her, she felt like slapping his face. //candid, adj.

canine \'kā-,nīn\ adj. RELATED TO DOGS; DOG-LIKE. Some days the *canine* population of Berkeley seems almost to outnumber the human population.

canny \'ka-nē\ adj. SHREWD; THRIFTY. The *canny* Scotsman was more than a match for the swindlers.

cantankerous \kan-'taŋ-k(ə-)rəs, kən-\ adj. ILL HUMORED; IRRITABLE. Constantly complaining about his treatment and refusing to cooperate with the hospital staff, he was a *cantankerous* patient.

Each of the questions below consists of a word in capital letters, followed by five words or phrases. Choose the word or phrase that is most similar in meaning to the word in capital letters and write the letter of your choice on your answer paper.

91. **BOISTEROUS**   (A) conflicting   (B) noisy
     (C) testimonial   (D)   grateful   (E) adolescent

92. **BOMBASTIC**   (A) sensitive   (B) pompous   (C) rapid
     (D) sufficient   (E) expensive

93. **BOORISH**   (A) brave   (B) oafish   (C) romantic
     (D) speedy   (E) dry

94. **BOUNTIFUL**   (A) insightful   (B) respectable
     (C) golden   (D) abundant   (E) cautious

95. **BRACKISH**   (A) careful   (B) salty   (C) chosen
     (D) tough   (E) wet

96. **BRAGGART**   (A) weaponry   (B) boaster   (C) skirmish
     (D) enchanter   (E) traitor

97. **BRAZEN**   (A) shameless   (B) quick   (C) modest
     (D) pleasant   (E) melodramatic

98. **BRITTLE**   (A) shiny   (B) pathetic   (C) hasty
     (D) easily broken   (E) mild tasting

99. **BROCHURE**   (A) opening   (B) pamphlet   (C) censor
     (D) bureau   (E) pin

100. **BRUSQUE**   (A) diseased   (B) repulsive   (C) abrupt
      (D) twinkling   (E) cold

101. **BUNGLING**   (A) voluminous   (B) incisive
      (C) convincing   (D) incompetent   (E) bookish

102. **CACHE**   (A) lock   (B) hiding place   (C) tide
      (D) automobile   (E) grappling hook

103. **CACOPHONY**   (A) discord   (B) dance   (C) applause
      (D) type of telephone   (E) rooster

104. **CALLOW**   (A) youthful   (B) holy   (C) mild
      (D) colored   (E) seated

105. **CANDID**   (A) vague   (B) outspoken   (C) experienced
      (D) anxious   (E) sallow

canvass \'kan-vəs\ v. DETERMINE VOTES, ETC. After *canvassing* the sentiments of his constituents, the congressman was confident that he represented the majority opinion of his district. //also n.

capacious \kə-'pā-shəs\ adj. SPACIOUS. In the *capacious* rotunda of the railroad terminal, thousands of travelers lingered while waiting for their train.

capitulate \kə-'pi-chə-ˌlāt\ v. SURRENDER. The enemy was warned to *capitulate* or face annihilation.

capricious \kə-'pri-shəs, -'prē-\ adj. UNPREDICTABLE; FICKLE. The storm was *capricious*: it changed course constantly. Jill was *capricious*, too; she changed boyfriends almost as often as she changed clothes. //caprice, n.

caption \'kap-shən\ n. TITLE; CHAPTER HEADING; TEXT UNDER ILLUSTRATION. The *captions* that accompany *The Far Side* cartoons are almost as funny as the pictures. //also v.

cardinal \'kärd-nəl, 'kär-də-\ adj. CHIEF. If you want to increase your word power, the *cardinal* rule of vocabulary building is to read.

caricature \'ker-i-kə-ˌchu̇r, -ˌchər, -ˌtyu̇r, -ˌtu̇r, -'ka-ri-\ n. DISTORTION; BURLESQUE. The cartoonist's *caricature* of President Bush grossly exaggerated the size of the president's ears. //also v.

carnage \'kär-nij\ n. DESTRUCTION OF LIFE. The film *The Killing Fields* vividly depicts the *carnage* wreaked by Pol Pot's followers in Cambodia.

carnal \'kär-nəl\ adj. OF THE FLESH. Is the public more interested in *carnal* pleasures than in spiritual matters? Compare the number of people who read *Playboy* daily to the number of those who read the Bible or Koran every day.

carnivorous \kär-'ni-v(ə-)rəs\ adj. MEAT EATING. The lion's a *carnivorous* beast. A hunk of meat makes up his feast. A cow is not a *carnivore*. She likes the taste of grain, not gore. //carnivore, n.

carping \'kär-piŋ\ adj. FINDING FAULT. A *carping* critic is a nit-picker: he loves to point out flaws. If you don't like this definition, feel free to *carp*. //carp, v.

cartographer \kär-'tä-grə-fər\ n. MAP MAKER. Though not a professional *cartographer*, Tolkien was able to construct a map of his fictional world.

caste \'kast *also* 'käst\ n. ONE OF THE HEREDITARY CLASSES IN HINDU SOCIETY; SOCIAL STRATIFICATION. The differences created by *caste* in India must be wiped out if true democracy is to prevail in that country.

castigate \'kas-tə-,gāt\ v. SEVERELY CRITICIZE; PUNISH. Ben Jonson was a highly moral playwright: in his plays, his purpose was to *castigate* vice and hypocrisy by exposing them publicly.

casualty \'ka-zhəl-tē, 'kazh-wəl-, 'ka-zhə-wəl-\ n. SERIOUS OR FATAL ACCIDENT. The number of automotive *casualties* on this holiday weekend was high.

cataclysm \'ka-tə-,kli-zəm\ n. VIOLENT UPHEAVAL; DELUGE. The Russian Revolution was a political and social *cataclysm* that overturned czarist society. //cataclysmic, adj.

catalyst \'ka-tə-ləst\ n. SOMETHING THAT PRECIPITATES A CHANGE OR BRINGS ABOUT AN EVENT; AGENT BRINGING ABOUT A CHEMICAL CHANGE, WHILE IT REMAINS UNAFFECTED. The IRA faction known as the Provos argued that terrorism was a necessary *catalyst* for unification: only violence could bring about the united Ireland they desired.

catapult \'ka-tə-,pəlt, -,pült\ n. SLINGSHOT; A HURLING MACHINE. Airplanes are sometimes launched from battleships by *catapults*. //also v.

catastrophe \kə-'tas-trə-(ˌ)fē\ n. CALAMITY; DISASTER. The 1906 San Francisco earthquake was a *catastrophe* that destroyed most of the city.

catharsis \kə-'thär-səs\ n. RELEASE OF PENT-UP FEELINGS; EMOTIONAL CLEANSING. To some behavioral scientists, sports are a form of *catharsis*, for they provide a channel for the safe release of the aggression that forms part of every person's makeup.

catholic \'kath-lik, 'ka-thə-\ adj. BROADLY SYMPATHETIC; LIBERAL; UNIVERSAL. He was extremely *catholic* in his taste and read everything he could find in the library. (secondary meaning)

caucus \'kȯ-kəs\ n. PRIVATE MEETING OF MEMBERS OF A PARTY TO SELECT OFFICERS OR DETERMINE POLICY. At the opening of Congress, the members of the Democratic Party held a *caucus* to elect the Majority Leader of the House and the Party Whip.

caustic \'kȯs-tik\ adj. BURNING; SARCASTICALLY BITING. The Anglo-Welsh author Caradoc Evans bitterly criticized the Welsh religious and educational systems in *caustic* satires undiluted with sympathy.

cavalcade \ˌka-vəl-'kād, 'ka-vəl-ˌ\ n. PROCESSION; PARADE. As described by Chaucer the *cavalcade* of Canterbury pilgrims was a motley group.

cede \'sēd\ v. YIELD (TITLE, TERRITORY) TO; SURRENDER FORMALLY. Eventually the descendants of England's Henry II were forced to *cede* their French territories to the King of France.

celerity \sə-'ler-ə-tē, -'le-rə-\ n. SPEED; RAPIDITY. Hamlet resented his mother's *celerity* in remarrying within a month after his father's death.

celestial \sə-'les-chəl, -'lesh-, -'les-tē-əl\ adj. HEAVENLY. Pointing his primitive telescope at the heavens, Galileo explored the *celestial* mysteries.

celibate \'se-lə-bət\ adj. ABSTAINING FROM SEXUAL INTERCOURSE; UNMARRIED. Though the late Havelock Ellis wrote extensively about sexual customs and was considered an expert in such matters, recent studies maintain he was *celibate* throughout his life. //celibacy, n.

censor \'sen(t)-sər\ n. OVERSEER OF MORALS; PERSON WHO READS TO ELIMINATE INAPPROPRIATE REMARKS. Soldiers dislike having their mail read by a *censor* but understand the need for this precaution. //also v.

censorious \sen-'sȯr-ē-əs\ adj. CRITICAL. *Censorious* people delight in casting blame.

censure \'sen(t)-shər\ v. BLAME; CRITICIZE. The senator was *censured* for behavior inappropriate to a member of Congress. //also n.

centrifugal \sen-'tri-fyə-gəl, -'tri-fi-\ adj. RADIATING; DEPARTING FROM THE CENTER. Many automatic drying machines remove excess moisture from clothing by *centrifugal* force.

centripetal \sen-'tri-pə-təl\ adj. TENDING TOWARD THE CENTER. Does *centripetal* force or the force of gravity bring orbiting bodies to the earth's surface?

cerebral \sə-'rē-brəl, 'ser-ə-, 'se-rə-\ adj. PERTAINING TO THE BRAIN OR INTELLECT. The heroes of *Dumb and Dumber* were poorly equipped for *cerebral* pursuits.

ceremonious \ˌser-ə-'mō-nē-əs, ˌse-rə-\ adj. MARKED BY FORMALITY. Ordinary dress would be inappropriate at so *ceremonious* an affair.

cessation \se-'sā-shən\ n. STOPPAGE. Greenpeace activists campaigned for the *cessation* of the dumping of toxic chemicals at sea. //cease, v.

chafe \'chāf\ v. WARM BY RUBBING; MAKE SORE BY RUBBING. The collar *chafed* his neck. //also n.

chaff \'chaf\ n. WORTHLESS PRODUCTS OF AN ENDEAVOR. When you separate the wheat from the *chaff*, be sure you throw out the *chaff*.

chagrin \shə-'grin\ n. VEXATION; DISAPPOINTMENT; HUMILIA-
TION. Embarrassed by his parents' shabby, working-
class appearance, Richard felt their visit to his school
would bring him nothing but *chagrin*.

chameleon \kə-'mēl-yən\ n. LIZARD THAT CHANGES COLOR
IN DIFFERENT SITUATIONS. Like the *chameleon*, he
assumed the political thinking of every group he met.

Synonym Test • Word List 8

Each of the questions below consists of a word in capital letters, followed by five words or phrases. Choose the word or phrase that is most similar in meaning to the word in capital letters and write the letter of your choice on your answer paper.

106. **CAPACIOUS** (A) warlike (B) cordial (C) curious (D) roomy (E) not capable

107. **CAPRICIOUS** (A) satisfied (B) insured (C) photographic (D) scattered (E) changeable

108. **CARDINAL** (A) chief (B) capable (C) unholy (D) winning (E) recollected

109. **CARNAL** (A) impressive (B) minute (C) sensual (D) actual (E) private

110. **CARNIVOROUS** (A) gloomy (B) tangential (C) productive (D) weak (E) meat eating

111. **CARPING** (A) criticizing (B) mean (C) limited (D) farming (E) racing

112. **CATASTROPHE** (A) awakening (B) disaster (C) acceleration (D) direction (E) production

113. **CATHOLIC** (A) religious (B) pacific (C) universal (D) weighty (E) funny

114. **CAUSTIC** (A) capitalistic (B) lengthy (C) important (D) burning (E) current

115. **CELERITY** (A) assurance (B) state (C) acerbity (D) rapidity (E) infamy

116. **CENSORIOUS** (A) investing (B) critical (C) witty (D) commodious (E) dubious

117. **CENSURE** (A) process (B) enclose (C) interest (D) blame (E) penetrate

118. **CENTRIFUGAL** (A) radiating (B) ephemeral (C) lasting (D) barometric (E) algebraic

119. **CESSATION** (A) premium (B) gravity (C) ending (D) composition (E) apathy

120. **CHAGRIN** (A) achievement (B) disappointment (C) silence (D) serious endeavor (E) expensive taste

champion \\'cham-pē-ən\ v. SUPPORT MILITANTLY. Martin Luther King, Jr., won the Nobel Peace Prize because he *championed* the oppressed in their struggle for equality.

chaotic \kā-'ä-tik\ adj. IN UTTER DISORDER. He tried to bring order to the *chaotic* state of affairs. //chaos, n.

charisma \kə-'riz-mə\ n. GREAT POPULAR CHARM OR APPEAL OF A POLITICAL LEADER. Political commentators have deplored the importance of a candidate's *charisma* in these days of television campaigning. //charismatic, adj.

charlatan \\'shär-lə-tən\ n. QUACK; FAKER; FRAUD; PRETENDER TO KNOWLEDGE. When they realized that the Wizard didn't know how to get them back to Kansas, Dorothy and her companions were indignant that they'd been duped by a *charlatan*.

chary \\'cher-ē\ adj. CAUTIOUSLY WATCHFUL; SPARING OR RESTRAINED ABOUT GIVING. A prudent, thrifty New Englander, DeWitt was as *chary* of investing money in junk bonds as he was *chary* of paying people unnecessary compliments.

chasm \\'ka-zəm\ n. ABYSS. Looking down from the Cliffs of Doom, Frodo and his companions could not see the bottom of the *chasm*.

chaste \\'chāst\ adj. PURE; VIRGINAL; MODEST. To ensure that his bride would stay *chaste* while he was off to the wars, the crusader had her fitted out with a chastity belt. //chastity, n.

chasten \\'chā-sən\ v. DISCIPLINE; PUNISH IN ORDER TO CORRECT. Whom God loves, God *chastens*.

chastise \(,)chas-'tīz\ v. PUNISH. "Spare the rod and spoil the child" was Miss Watson's motto: she relished whipping Huck with a birch rod to *chastise* him.

chauvinist \'shō -və-nist\ n. BLINDLY DEVOTED PATRIOT. A *chauvinist* cannot recognize any faults in his country, no matter how flagrant they may be. Likewise, a male *chauvinist* cannot recognize his bias in favor of his own sex, no matter how flagrant that may be. //chauvinistic, adj.

chicanery \shi-'kān-rē, -'kā-nə-, chi-\ n. TRICKERY; DECEPTION. Those sneaky lawyers misrepresented what occurred, made up all sorts of implausible alternative scenarios to confuse the jurors, and in general depended on *chicanery* to win the case.

chide \'chīd\ v. SCOLD. Grandma began to *chide* Steven for his lying.

chimerical \kī-'mer-i-kəl, kə-, -'mir-\ adj. FANTASTICALLY IMPROBABLE; HIGHLY UNREALISTIC; IMAGINATIVE. As everyone expected, Ted's *chimerical* scheme to make a fortune by raising ermines in his backyard proved a dismal failure. //chimera, n.

choleric \'kä-lə-rik, kə-'ler-ik\ adj. HOT-TEMPERED. His flushed, angry face indicated a *choleric* nature.

choreography \,kȯr-ē-'ä-grə-fē\ n. ART OF REPRESENTING DANCES IN WRITTEN SYMBOLS; ARRANGEMENT OF DANCES. Merce Cunningham uses a computer in designing *choreography*: a software program allows him to compose sequences of possible moves and immediately view them on screen.

chronic \'krä-nik\ adj. CONSTANT; HABITUAL; LONG ESTABLISHED. The doctors were finally able to attribute his *chronic* headaches and nausea to traces of formaldehyde gas in his apartment.

churlish \'chər-lish\ adj. BOORISH, RUDE. Dismayed by his *churlish* manners at the party, the girls vowed never to invite him again.

circuitous \(,)sər-'kyü-ə-təs\ adj. ROUNDABOUT. To avoid the traffic congestion on the main highways, she took a *circuitous* route. //circuit, n.

circumlocution \ˌsər-kəm-lō-'kyü-shən\ n. INDIRECT OR ROUNDABOUT EXPRESSION. He was afraid to call a spade a spade and resorted to *circumlocutions* to avoid direct reference to his subject.

circumscribe \'sər-kəm-ˌskrīb\ v. LIMIT; CONFINE. School regulations *circumscribed* Elle's social life: she hated having to follow rules that limited her activities.

circumspect \'sər-kəm-ˌspekt\ adj. PRUDENT; CAUTIOUS. Investigating before acting, she tried always to be *circumspect*.

circumvent \'sər-kəm-ˌvent\ v. BYPASS; OUTWIT; BAFFLE. In order to *circumvent* the enemy, we will make two preliminary attacks in other sections before starting our major campaign.

citadel \'si-tə-dəl, -ˌdel\ n. FORTRESS. The *citadel* overlooked the city like a protecting angel.

cite \'sīt\ v. QUOTE. She could *cite* passages in the Bible from memory. //citation, n.

clairvoyant \kler-'vȯi-ənt\ adj., n. HAVING FORESIGHT; FORTUNETELLER. Cassandra's *clairvoyant* warning was not heeded by the Trojans. //clairvoyance, n.

clamor \'kla-mər\ n. NOISE. The *clamor* of the children at play outside made it impossible for her to take a nap. //also v.

clandestine \klan-'des-tən *also* -ˌtīn *or* -ˌtēn *or* 'klan-dəs-\ adj. SECRET. After avoiding their chaperon, the lovers had a *clandestine* meeting.

claustrophobia \ˌklȯs-trə-'fō-bē-ə\ n. FEAR OF BEING IN ENCLOSED OR NARROW PLACES. Because patients undergoing magnetic resonance imaging (MRI) must lie quietly inside a narrow tube, the procedure may raise anxiety levels in the patients, especially if they suffer from *claustrophobia*.

cleave \'klēv\ v. SPLIT; DIVIDE WITH A BLOW; SEVER. With her heavy *cleaver*, Julia Child could *cleave* a whole roast duck in two. //cleavage, n.

cleave \\'klēv\\ v. STICK TO; CLING TO. Note how the tenacious ivy still *cleaves* to the fallen tree.

cleft \\'kleft\\ n. SPLIT. Trying for a fresh handhold, the mountaineer grasped the edge of a *cleft* in the sheer rock face. //also adj.

clemency \\'kle-mən(t)-sē\\ n. DISPOSITION TO BE LENIENT; MILDNESS, AS OF THE WEATHER. The lawyer was pleased when the case was sent to Judge Smith's chambers because Smith was noted for her *clemency* toward first offenders.

cliché \\klē-'shā, 'klē-,, kli-'\\ n. PHRASE DULLED IN MEANING BY REPETITION. High school compositions are often marred by such *clichés* as "strong as an ox."

clientele \\,klī-ən-'tel, ,klē-ən- *also* ,klē-,än-\\ n. BODY OF CUSTOMERS. The rock club attracted a young, stylish *clientele*.

climactic \\klī-'mak-tik, klə-\\ adj. RELATING TO THE HIGHEST POINT. When he reached the *climactic* portions of the book, he could not stop reading. //climax, n.

clime \\'klīm\\ n. REGION; CLIMATE. His doctor advised him to move to a milder *clime*.

clique \\'klēk, 'klik\\ n. SMALL EXCLUSIVE GROUP. Scott Fitzgerald wished that he belonged to the *clique* of popular athletes and big men on campus who seemed to run Princeton's social life.

cloister \\'klöi-stər\\ n. MONASTERY OR CONVENT. The nuns lived in the *cloister*.

coalesce \\,kō-ə-'les\\ v. COMBINE; FUSE. When minor political parties *coalesce*, their *coalescence* may create a major coalition. //coalescence, n.

coddle \\'kä-dəl\\ v. TO TREAT GENTLY. Don't *coddle* the children so much; they need a taste of discipline.

codicil \\'kä-də-səl, -,sil\\ n. SUPPLEMENT TO THE BODY OF A WILL. Miss Havisham kept her lawyers busy drawing up *codicils* to add to her already complicated will.

coercion \kō-ˈər-zhən, -shən\ n. USE OF FORCE TO GET SOMEONE TO OBEY. The inquisitors used both physical and psychological *coercion* to force Joan of Arc to deny that her visions were sent by God. //coerce, v.

cogent \ˈkō-jənt\ adj. CONVINCING. Katya mustered such *cogent* arguments in presenting her case that the jury had to decide in favor of her clients.

cognizance \ˈkäg-nə-zən(t)s\ n. KNOWLEDGE. During the election campaign, the two candidates were kept in full *cognizance* of the international situation. //cognizant, adj.

cohesion \kō-ˈhē-zhən\ n. FORCE THAT KEEPS PARTS TOGETHER. A firm believer in the maxim "Divide and conquer," the evil emperor, by means of lies and trickery, sought to disrupt the *cohesion* of the federation of free nations. //cohere, v.; coherent, adj.

Each of the questions below consists of a word in capital letters, followed by five words or phrases. Choose the word or phrase that is most similar in meaning to the word in capital letters and write the letter of your choice on your answer paper.

121. **CHASTE**   (A) loyal   (B) timid   (C) curt   (D) pure
    (E) outspoken

122. **CHIDE**   (A) unite   (B) fear   (C) record   (D) skid
    (E) scold

123. **CHIMERICAL**   (A) developing   (B) brief   (C) distant
    (D) economical   (E) fantastic

124. **CHOLERIC**   (A) musical   (B) episodic   (C) hotheaded
    (D) global   (E) seasonal

125. **CHURLISH**   (A) marine   (B) economical
    (C) impolite   (D) compact   (E) young

126. **CIRCUITOUS**   (A) tortured   (B) complete
    (C) obvious   (D) aware   (E) indirect

127. **CIRCUMSCRIBE**   (A) limit   (B) collect   (C) restore
    (D) collaborate   (E) manage

128. **CITE**   (A) galvanize   (B) visualize   (C) locate
    (D) quote   (E) signal

129. **CLANDESTINE**   (A) abortive   (B) secret
    (C) tangible   (D) doomed   (E) approved

130. **CLAUSTROPHOBIA**   (A) lack of confidence
    (B) fear of spiders   (C) love of books
    (D) fear of grammar   (E) fear of closed places

131. **CLEFT**   (A) split   (B) waterfall   (C) assembly
    (D) parfait   (E) surplus

132. **CLICHÉ**   (A) increase   (B) vehicle   (C) morale
    (D) platitude   (E) pique

133. **COERCE**   (A) recover   (B) total   (C) force
    (D) license   (E) ignore

134. **COGNIZANCE**   (A) policy   (B) knowledge
    (C) advance   (D) omission   (E) examination

135. **COHESION**   (A) attachment   (B) dimness
    (C) suspicion   (D) jealousy   (E) sincerity

collaborate \kə-'la-bə-,rāt\ v. WORK TOGETHER. Two writers *collaborated* in preparing this book.

collage \kə-'läzh, kȯ-, kō-\ n. WORK OF ART PUT TOGETHER FROM FRAGMENTS. Scraps of cloth, paper doilies, and old photographs all went into her *collage*.

colloquial \kə-'lō-kwē-əl\ adj. PERTAINING TO CONVERSATIONAL OR COMMON SPEECH. Some of the new, less formal reading passages on the SAT have a *colloquial* tone that is intended to make them more appealing to students.

collusion \kə-'lü-zhən\ n. CONSPIRING IN A FRAUDULENT SCHEME. The swindlers were found guilty of *collusion*.

colossal \kə-'lä-səl\ adj. HUGE. People living on fixed incomes have been complaining about the *colossal* increase in the cost of living.

comatose \'kō-mə-,tōs, 'kä-\ adj. IN A COMA; EXTREMELY SLEEPY. The long-winded orator soon had his audience in a *comatose* state.

combustible \kəm-'bəs-tə-bəl\ adj. EASILY BURNED. After the recent outbreak of fires in private homes, the fire commissioner ordered that all *combustible* materials be kept in safe containers. //also n.

comely \'kəm-lē *also* 'kōm- *or* 'käm-\ adj. ATTRACTIVE; AGREEABLE. I would rather have a poor and *comely* wife than a rich and homely one.

commiserate \kə-'mi-zə-,rāt\ v. FEEL OR EXPRESS PITY OR SYMPATHY FOR. Her friends *commiserated* with the widow.

commodious \kə-'mō-dē-əs\ adj. SPACIOUS AND COMFORTABLE. After sleeping in small roadside cabins, they found their hotel suite *commodious*.

communal \kə-'myü-nəl, 'käm-yə-nəl\ adj. HELD IN COMMON; OF A GROUP OF PEOPLE. When they were divorced, they had trouble dividing their *communal* property.

compact \kəm-'pakt, käm-', 'käm-,\ n. AGREEMENT; CON-
TRACT. The signers of the Mayflower *Compact* were
establishing a form of government.

compact \kəm-'pakt, käm-', 'käm-,\ adj. TIGHTLY PACKED;
FIRM; BRIEF. His short, *compact* body was better suited
to wrestling than to basketball.

compatible \kəm-'pa-tə-bəl\ adj. HARMONIOUS; IN HARMONY
WITH. They were *compatible* neighbors, never quarrel-
ing over unimportant matters. //compatibility, n.

compendium \kəm-'pen-dē-əm\ n. BRIEF COMPREHENSIVE
SUMMARY. This text can serve as a *compendium* of the
tremendous amount of new material being developed
in this field.

compensatory \kəm-'pen(t)-sə-,tȯr-ē\ adj. MAKING UP FOR;
REPAYING. Can a *compensatory* education program
make up for the inadequate schooling he received in
earlier years?

compile \kəm-'pī(-ə)l\ v. ASSEMBLE; GATHER; ACCUMULATE.
We plan to *compile* a list of the words most frequently used on SAT examinations. //compilation, n.

complacent \kəm-'plā-sənt\ adj. SELF-SATISFIED; SMUG.
Complacent about his latest victories, he looked
smugly at the row of trophies on his mantelpiece.
//complacency, n.

complement \'käm-plə-mənt\ v. COMPLETE; CONSUMMATE;
MAKE PERFECT. The waiter recommended a glass of
port to *complement* the cheese.

compliance \kəm-'plī-ən(t)s\ n. READINESS TO YIELD; CONFOR-
MITY IN FULFILLING REQUIREMENTS. Stubborn to the point
of bullheadedness, Bill was not noted for easy *compliance* with the demands of others. //compliant, adj.

complicity \kəm-'pli-s(ə-)tē\ n. INVOLVEMENT IN A CRIME; PAR-
TICIPATION. Queen Mary's marriage to Lord Darnley, her
suspected *complicity* in his murder, and her hasty marriage to the Earl of Bothwell stirred the Protestant
lords to revolt.

component \kəm-'pō-nənt, 'käm-,, käm-'\ n. ELEMENT; INGREDIENT. I wish all the *components* of my stereo system were working at the same time.

composure \kəm-'pō-zhər\ n. MENTAL CALMNESS. Even the latest work crisis failed to shake her *composure*.

comprehensive \,käm-pri-'hen(t)-siv\ adj. THOROUGH; INCLUSIVE. This book provides a *comprehensive* review of the vocabulary you will need in preparing for the SAT or ACT.

compress \kəm-'pres\ v. SQUEEZE OR PRESS TOGETHER; MAKE MORE COMPACT. Miss Watson *compressed* her lips in disapproval as she noted the bedraggled state of Huck's clothes. On farms, roller-packers are used in dry seasons to *compress* and pack down the soil after plowing. //compression, n.

compromise \'käm-prə-,mīz\ v. ADJUST OR SETTLE BY MAKING MUTUAL CONCESSIONS; ENDANGER THE INTERESTS OR REPUTATION. Sometimes the presence of a neutral third party can help adversaries *compromise* their differences. Unfortunately, you are not neutral; therefore, your presence here *compromises* our chances of reaching an agreement. //also n.

compunction \kəm-'pəŋ(k)-shən\ n. REMORSE. The judge was especially severe in his sentencing because he felt that the criminal had shown no *compunction* for his heinous crime.

concave \kän-'kāv, 'kän-,\ adj. HOLLOW. The back-packers found partial shelter from the storm by huddling against the *concave* wall of the cliff.

concede \kən-'sēd\ v. ADMIT; YIELD. Despite all the evidence Monica had assembled, Mark refused to *concede* that she was right.

concession \kən-'se-shən\ n. AN ACT OF YIELDING. Before they could reach an agreement, both sides had to make certain *concessions*.

conciliatory \kən-'sil-yə-ˌtȯr-ē, -'si-lē-ə-\ adj. RECONCIL-ING; SOOTHING. She was still angry despite his *conciliatory* words. //conciliate, v.

concise \kən-'sīs\ adj. BRIEF AND COMPACT. When you define a new word, be *concise*: the shorter the definition, the easier it is to remember. //concision, concise-ness, n.

conclusive \kən-'klü-siv, -ziv\ adj. DECISIVE; ENDING ALL DEBATE. When the stolen books turned up in John's locker, we finally had *conclusive* evidence of the identity of the mysterious thief.

concoct \kən-'käkt, kän-\ v. PREPARE BY COMBINING; DEVISE. How did the inventive chef ever *concoct* such a strange dish? //concoction, n.

concur \kən-'kər, kän-\ v. AGREE. Did you *concur* with the decision of the court or did you find it unfair?

concurrent \kən-'kər-ənt, -'kə-rənt\ adj. HAPPENING AT THE SAME TIME. In America, the colonists were resisting the demands of the mother country; at the *concurrent* moment in France, the middle class was sowing the seeds of rebellion.

condescend \ˌkän-di-'send\ v. ACT CONSCIOUS OF DESCEND-ING TO A LOWER LEVEL; PATRONIZE. Though Jill had been a star softball player in college, when she played a pickup game at the park she never *condescended* to her less experienced teammates. //condescension, n.

condole \kən-'dōl\ v. EXPRESS SYMPATHETIC SORROW. His friends gathered to *condole* with him over his loss. //condolence, n.

condone \kən-'dōn\ v. OVERLOOK; FORGIVE. Unlike Widow Douglass, who *condoned* Huck's minor offenses, Miss Watson did nothing but scold.

conducive \kən-'dü-siv, -'dyü-\ adj. CONTRIBUTIVE; TEND-ING TO. Rest and proper diet are *conducive* to good health.

confidant \\'kän-fə-,dänt *also* -,dant, -dənt\\ n. TRUSTED FRIEND. He had no *confidants* with whom he could discuss his problems at home. //confide, v.

confiscate \\'kän-fə-,skāt\\ v. SEIZE; COMMANDEER. The army *confiscated* all available supplies of uranium.

conflagration \\,kän-flə-'grā-shən\\ n. GREAT FIRE. In the *conflagration* that followed the 1906 earthquake, much of San Francisco was destroyed.

confluence \\'kän-,flü-ən(t)s, kən-'\\ n. FLOWING TOGETHER; CROWD. They built the city at the *confluence* of two rivers.

conformity \\kən-'for-mə-tē\\ n. HARMONY; AGREEMENT. In *conformity* with our rules and regulations, I am calling a meeting of our organization.

confound \\kən-'faund, kän-\\ v. CONFUSE; PUZZLE. No mystery could *confound* Sherlock Holmes for long.

congeal \\kən-'jēl\\ v. FREEZE; COAGULATE. His blood *congealed* in his veins as he saw the dread monster rush toward him.

congenial \\kən-'jē-nē-əl, -'jēn-yəl\\ adj. PLEASANT; FRIENDLY. My father loved to go out for a meal with *congenial* companions.

congenital \\kən-'je-nə-təl, kän-\\ adj. EXISTING AT BIRTH, INNATE. Doctors are able to cure some *congenital* problems such as cleft palates by performing operations on infants.

Each of the questions below consists of a word in capital letters, followed by five words or phrases. Choose the word or phrase that is most similar in meaning to the word in capital letters and write the letter of your choice on your answer paper.

136. **COLLAGE**   (A) furor   (B) lack of emphasis   (C) distance   (D) spree   (E) work of art

137. **COLLOQUIAL**   (A) burnt   (B) informal   (C) political   (D) gifted   (E) problematic

138. **COLLUSION**   (A) dialect   (B) diversion   (C) announcement   (D) conspiracy   (E) expansion

139. **COMATOSE**   (A) coy   (B) restrained   (C) unconscious   (D) dumb   (E) grim

140. **COMBUSTIBLE**   (A) flammable   (B) industrious   (C) waterproof   (D) specific   (E) plastic

141. **COMELY**   (A) vigorous   (B) attractive   (C) liquid   (D) soothing   (E) circumvented

142. **COMMISERATE**   (A) communicate   (B) expand   (C) repay   (D) diminish   (E) sympathize

143. **COMMODIOUS**   (A) numerous   (B) yielding   (C) leisurely   (D) spacious   (E) expensive

144. **COMPLIANT**   (A) numerous   (B) veracious   (C) soft   (D) yielding   (E) livid

145. **CONCILIATE**   (A) defend   (B) activate   (C) integrate   (D) soothe   (E) react

146. **CONCOCT**   (A) thrive   (B) wonder   (C) intrude   (D) drink   (E) invent

147. **CONDONE**   (A) build   (B) evaluate   (C) pierce   (D) infuriate   (E) overlook

148. **CONFISCATE**   (A) discuss   (B) discover   (C) seize   (D) exist   (E) convey

149. **CONFORMITY**   (A) agreement   (B) ambition   (C) confinement   (D) pride   (E) restraint

150. **CONGENITAL**   (A) slight   (B) obscure   (C) thorough   (D) existing at birth   (E) classified

Comprehensive Test • Word Lists 1–10

Each of the questions below consists of a sentence from which one word is missing. Choose the most appropriate replacement from among the five choices.

1. Though I had requested a _____ critique of my work, I was not prepared for the harsh criticism that I received.
   (A) candid (B) commodious (C) benign
   (D) compensatory (E) baleful

2. The community's _____ efforts to build a new library led many to conclude that there was little local support for civic projects.
   (A) ambiguous (B) cardinal (C) abortive
   (D) combustible (E) benevolent

3. The _____ equipment in many public schools undermines our efforts to prepare students to meet the demands of modern business.
   (A) animated (B) antediluvian (C) capacious
   (D) callow (E) brackish

4. King Lear was startled that when he _____ his power to rule he lost the respect that had come with his throne.
   (A) absolved (B) censored (C) chided
   (D) abdicated (E) augmented

5. The clock striking in *Julius Caesar* is a good example of an _____, as there were no clocks in Caesar's Rome.
   (A) amphibian (B) apocalypse (C) apprehension
   (D) anachronism (E) apotheosis

6. Despite her _____ for calculus, she had trouble with basic arithmetic.
   (A) claustrophobia (B) circumlocution (C) aptitude
   (D) chicanery (E) abeyance

7. The _____ of his admirers caused him to grow complacent.
   (A) adulation (B) acumen (C) apex
   (D) animosity (E) assimilation

8. The tragedy of Othello's murder of Desdemona is intensified by the _____ of their love for each other.
   (A) cacophony (B) artifice (C) ardor
   (D) anonymity (E) adversity

9. The office was designed with practical, rather than
   _____, concerns in mind.
   (A) aesthetic   (B) amorphous   (C) appropriate
       (D) canny   (E) catholic

10. It seemed that nothing, not even the heckling of the
    drunks in the audience, could ruffle the _____ of the
    stand-up comedian.
    (A) conflagration   (B) collusion   (C) amenities
        (D) composure   (E) accord

11. Because its members feared an adverse public reaction,
    the city council's vote on its pay raise was held in
    _____ until after the general election.
    (A) abeyance   (B) affirmation   (C) bevy
        (D) brevity   (E) concession

12. After her promotion to management our new director
    would no longer _____ to eat lunch with us in the
    employee lounge.
    (A) bolster   (B) condescend   (C) banter
        (D) apprise   (E) cajole

13. Accepting illegal campaign contributions is a serious, and
    all too common, _____ of ethics among candidates
    for public office.
    (A) breach   (B) calamity   (C) confluence
        (D) autocrat   (E) atrophy

14. Despite strong _____ from public safety officials, most
    Californians are inadequately prepared for a moderate to
    large earthquake.
    (A) artisans   (B) archives   (C) admonitions
        (D) caches   (E) concessions

15. Drinking a cup of coffee before bed is not _____ to
    getting an adequate night's sleep.
    (A) concave   (B) atypical   (C) ascetic
        (D) antagonistic   (E) conducive

conglomeration \kən-glä-mə-'rā-shən,'kän-\ n. MASS OF MATERIAL STICKING TOGETHER; AGGREGATE. Our public schools grew out of a disorganized *conglomeration* of reading and writing schools, dame schools, private academies, Latin grammar schools, and colleges into a coordinated system.

congruent \kən-'grü-ənt, \'käŋ-grü-ənt\ adj. IN AGREEMENT; CORRESPONDING. In formulating a hypothesis, we must keep it *congruent* with what we know of the real world; it cannot disagree with our experience.

conjecture \kən-'jek-chər\ v. SURMISE; GUESS. Although there was no official count, the organizers *conjectured* that more than 10,000 marchers took part in the March for Peace. //also n.

conjure \'kän-jər *also* 'kən-\ v. SUMMON A DEVIL; PRACTICE MAGIC; IMAGINE; INVENT. Sorcerers *conjure* devils to appear. Magicians *conjure* white rabbits out of hats. Political candidates *conjure* up images of reformed cities and the world at peace.

connivance \kə-'nī-vən(t)s\ n. PURPOSEFUL REFUSAL TO NOTICE SOMETHING WRONG; SECRET COOPERATION OR ASSISTANCE. In 1930 charges were made against the Liberian government that slave trading had gone on with the government's *connivance*. //connive, v.

connoisseur \,kä-nə-'sər *also* -'sür\ n. PERSON COMPETENT TO ACT AS A JUDGE OF ART, ETC.; A LOVER OF AN ART. Bernard Berenson, the American art critic and *connoisseur* of Italian art, was hired by wealthy art lovers to select paintings for their collections.

connotation \,kä-nə-'tā-shən\ n. SUGGESTED OR IMPLIED MEANING OF AN EXPRESSION. Foreigners frequently are unaware of the *connotations* of the words they use.

conscientious \,kän(t)-shē-'en(t)-shəs\ adj. SCRUPULOUS; CAREFUL. A *conscientious* editor, she checked every definition for its accuracy.

consecrate \'kän(t)-sə-,krāt\ v. DEDICATE; SANCTIFY. In 1804, Napoleon forced Pope Pius VII to come to Paris to *consecrate* him as emperor, only to humiliate Pius at the last minute by taking the crown from the pope's hands and crowning himself.

consensus \kən-'sen(t)-səs\ n. GENERAL AGREEMENT. Every time the garden club members had nearly reached a *consensus* about what to plant, Mistress Mary, quite contrary, disagreed.

consequential \,kän(t)-sə-'kwen(t)-shəl\ adj. FOLLOWING AS AN EFFECT; IMPORTANT; SELF-IMPORTANT. Convinced of his own importance, the actor strutted about the dressing room with a *consequential* air. //consequence, n.; consequent, adj.

consonance \'kän(t)-s(ə-)nən(t)s\ n. HARMONY; AGREEMENT. Her agitation seemed out of *consonance* with her usual calm.

conspicuous \kən-'spi-kyə-wəs, -kyü-əs\ adj. EASILY SEEN; NOTICEABLE; STRIKING. Janet was *conspicuous* both for her red hair and for her height.

conspiracy \kən-'spir-ə-sē\ n. TREACHEROUS PLOT. Brutus and Cassius joined in the *conspiracy* to kill Julius Caesar.

constituent \kən-'stich-wənt, -'sti-chə-, -'sti-chü-ənt\ n. SUPPORTER. The congressman received hundreds of letters from angry *constituents* after the Equal Rights Amendment failed to pass.

constraint \kən-'strānt\ n. LIMITATION OR RESTRICTION; REPRESSION OF FEELINGS. There was a feeling of *constraint* in the room because no one dared to criticize the speaker. //constrain, v.

construe \kən-'strü\ v. EXPLAIN; INTERPRET. If I *construe* your remarks correctly, you disagree with the theory already advanced.

consummate \'kän(t)-sə-mət, kən-'sə-mət\ adj. WHOLLY WITHOUT FLAW; SUPREMELY SKILLED; COMPLETE AND UTTER.

Da Vinci depicted in his drawings, with scientific precision and _consummate_ artistry, subjects ranging from flying machines to intricate anatomical studies of people, animals, and plants. //also v.

contagion \kən-'tā-jən\ n. INFECTION; RAPID SPREADING OF AN INFLUENCE (AS A DOCTRINE OR EMOTIONAL STATE). Fearing _contagion_, they took great steps to prevent the spread of the disease //contagious, adj.

contaminate \kən-'ta-mə-ˌnāt\ v. POLLUTE. Leaks from the city's sewage system _contaminated_ the water so badly that swimming was forbidden.

contempt \kən-'tem(p)t\ n. SCORN; DISDAIN. The heavyweight boxer looked on ordinary people with _contempt_, scorning them as weaklings who couldn't punch their way out of a paper bag. //contemptuous, contemptible, adj.

contend \kən-'tend\ v. STRUGGLE; COMPETE; ASSERT EARNESTLY. Sociologist Harry Edwards _contends_ that young black athletes are exploited by some college recruiters.

contentious \kən-'ten(t)-shəs\ adj. QUARRELSOME. Disagreeing violently with the referee's ruling, the coach became so _contentious_ that the referees threw him out of the game.

contest \kən-'test, 'kän-ˌ\ v. DISPUTE. The defeated candidate attempted to _contest_ the election results.

context \'kän-ˌtekst\ n. WRITINGS PRECEDING AND FOLLOWING THE PASSAGE QUOTED. Because these lines are taken out of _context_, they do not convey the message the author intended.

contiguous \kən-'ti-gyə-wəs, -gyü-əs\ adj. ADJACENT TO; TOUCHING UPON. The two countries are _contiguous_ for a few miles; then they are separated by the gulf.

continence \'kän-tə-nən(t)s\ n. SELF-RESTRAINT; SEXUAL CHASTITY. At the convent, Connie vowed to lead a life of _continence_. The question was, could Connie be content with always being _continent_? //continent, adj.

contingent \kən-'tin-jənt\ adj. CONDITIONAL; DEPENDENT ON. Karen's father informed her that any raise in her allowance was *contingent* on the quality of her final grades. //contingency, n.

contortions \kən-'tȯr-shəns\ n. TWISTINGS; DISTORTIONS. At Cirque du Soleil, the acrobats perform extraordinary *contortions*, twisting their bodies into seemingly impossible positions. //contort, v.

contrite \'kän-ˌtrīt, kən-'\ adj. PENITENT; REMORSEFUL; REPENTANT. Although Heather wept copious tears and pretended to regret her malicious acts, we knew she was not truly *contrite*. //contrition, n.

contusion \kən-'tü-zhən, -'tyü-\ n. BRUISE. Black and blue after her fall, Sue was treated for *contusions* and abrasions.

convene \kən-'vēn\ v. ASSEMBLE. Because much needed legislation had to be enacted, the governor ordered the legislature to *convene* in special session by January 15.

conventional \kən-'vench-nəl, -'ven(t)-shə-nəl\ adj. ORDINARY; TYPICAL. His *conventional* upbringing left him wholly unprepared for his wife's eccentric family.

converge \kən-'vərj\ v. COME TOGETHER. African American men from all over the United States *converged* on Washington to take part in the historic Million Man March.

conviction \kən-'vik-shən\ n. STRONGLY HELD BELIEF. Nothing could shake his *conviction* that she was innocent. (secondary meaning)

convivial \kən-'viv-yəl, -'vi-vē-əl\ adj. FESTIVE; GAY; CHARACTERIZED BY JOVIALITY. The class reunion was a highly *convivial* gathering, for the returning alumni were delighted to see their old friends.

convoluted \'kän-və-ˌlü-təd\ adj. COILED AROUND; INVOLVED; INTRICATE. The new tax regulations are so *convoluted* that even my accountant has trouble following their twists and turns.

copious \'kō-pē-əs\ adj. PLENTIFUL; LARGE IN NUMBER. During the meeting, she took *copious* notes that she later summarized when she typed up the minutes.

cordial \'kȯr-jəl\ adj. GRACIOUS; HEARTFELT. Our hosts greeted us at the airport with a *cordial* welcome and a hearty hug.

corollary \'kȯr-ə-ˌler-ē, 'kär-, -le-rē\ n. CONSEQUENCE; ACCOMPANIMENT. Brotherly love is a complex emotion, with sibling rivalry its natural *corollary*.

corporeal \kȯr-'pȯr-ē-əl\ adj. BODILY; MATERIAL. During the Crimean war, Florence Nightingale was appalled by the extreme *corporeal* suffering of the wounded soldiers.

corpulent \'kȯr-pyə-lənt\ adj. VERY FAT. The *corpulent* man resolved to reduce his weight. //corpulence, n.

correlation \ˌkȯr-ə-'lā-shən, ˌkär-\ n. MUTUAL RELATIONSHIP. He sought to determine the *correlation* that existed between ability in algebra and ability to interpret reading exercises. //correlate, v., n.

corroborate \kə-'rä-bə-ˌrāt\ v. CONFIRM. Though Huck was quite willing to *corroborate* Tom's story, Aunt Polly knew better than to believe either of them.

corrosive \kə-'rō-siv, -ziv\ adj. EATING AWAY BY CHEMICALS OR DISEASE. Stainless steel is able to withstand the effects of *corrosive* chemicals. //corrode, v.

cosmic \'käz-mik\ adj. PERTAINING TO THE UNIVERSE; VAST. *Cosmic* rays derive their name from the fact that they bombard the earth's atmosphere from outer space. //cosmos, n.

countenance \'kaȯn-tᵊn-ən(t)s, 'kaȯnt-nən(t)s\ v. APPROVE; TOLERATE. Miss Manners refused to *countenance* such rude behavior on their part.

countenance \'kaȯn-tᵊn-ən(t)s, 'kaȯnt-nən(t)s\ n. FACE; FACIAL EXPRESSION. When José saw his newborn daughter, a proud smile spread across his *countenance*.

countermand \'kaȯn-tər-ˌmand, ˌkaȯn-tər-'\ v. CANCEL; REVOKE. The general *countermanded* the orders issued in his absence.

Each of the questions below consists of a word in capital letters, followed by five words or phrases. Choose the word or phrase that is most similar in meaning to the word in capital letters and write the letter of your choice on your answer paper.

151. **CONJECTURE** (A) magic (B) guess (C) position (D) form (E) place

152. **CONNOISSEUR** (A) gourmand (B) lover of art (C) humidor (D) delinquent (E) interpreter

153. **CONNOTATION** (A) implied meaning (B) friendship (C) bloodletting (D) relief (E) understanding

154. **CONSENSUS** (A) general agreement (B) project (C) insignificance (D) sheaf (E) crevice

155. **CONSTRUE** (A) explain (B) promote (C) reserve (D) erect (E) block

156. **CONTAMINATE** (A) arrest (B) prepare (C) pollute (D) beam (E) inform

157. **CONTENTIOUS** (A) squealing (B) surprising (C) quarrelsome (D) smug (E) creative

158. **CONTINENCE** (A) humanity (B) research (C) embryology (D) bodies of land (E) self-restraint

159. **CONTINGENCY** (A) strong purpose (B) sensation (C) rascality (D) difficulty (E) conditional state

160. **CONTORT** (A) turn over (B) twist (C) mind (D) explain (E) swing

161. **CONTRITE** (A) smart (B) penitent (C) restful (D) recognized (E) perspiring

162. **CONVENE** (A) propose (B) restore (C) question (D) gather (E) motivate

163. **CONVENTIONAL** (A) nonconformist (B) speaking (C) incorporated (D) familiar (E) pedantic

164. **COPIOUS** (A) plentiful (B) cheating (C) dishonorable (D) adventurous (E) inspired

165. **CORPULENT** (A) regenerate (B) obese (C) different (D) hungry (E) bloody

counterpart \ 'kaún-tər-ˌpärt\ n. CORRESPONDING PERSON OR THING; A PERSON OR THING THAT CLOSELY RESEMBLES ANOTHER; COMPLEMENT. The mischievous Norse god Loki is a trickster who has his *counterpart* in the Navajo god Coyote.

coup \'kü\ n. HIGHLY SUCCESSFUL ACTION OR SUDDEN ATTACK. As the news of his *coup* spread throughout Wall Street, his fellow brokers dropped by to congratulate him.

couple \'kə-pəl\ v. JOIN; UNITE. The Flying Karamazovs *couple* expert juggling and amateur joking in their nightclub act.

courier \'kúr-ē-ər, 'kər-ē-, 'kə-rē-\ n. MESSENGER. The publisher sent a special *courier* to pick up the manuscript.

covenant \'kəv-nənt, 'kə-və-\ n. AGREEMENT, USUALLY FORMAL; TREATY; PACT. We must comply with the terms of the *covenant*.

covetous \'kə-və-təs\ adj. AVARICIOUS; EAGERLY DESIROUS OF. The poor man wants many things; the *covetous* man wants everything. //covet, v.

cower \'kaú(-ə)r\ v. SHRINK QUIVERING, AS FROM FEAR. The frightened child *cowered* in the corner of the room.

coy \'koi\ adj. SHY; MODEST; COQUETTISH. Reluctant to commit herself so early in the game, Kay was *coy* in her answers to Ken's offer.

crabbed \'kra-bəd\ adj. SOUR; PEEVISH. He was a *crabbed* old man, always scolding the children when they made any noise and complaining whenever his meals weren't served on time.

crass \'kras\ adj. VERY UNREFINED; GROSSLY INSENSIBLE. Film critics deplore the *crass* commercialism of moviemakers who abandon artistic standards in order to make a quick buck.

credence \'krē-dən(t)s\ n. BELIEF. Do not place any *credence* in his promises; he is an incorrigible liar.

credulity \kri-'dü-lə-tē, -'dyü-\ n. BELIEF ON SLIGHT EVIDENCE; GULLIBILITY. Con artists take advantage of the *credulity* of inexperienced investors to swindle them out of their savings. //credulous, adj.

creed \'krēd\ n. SYSTEM OF RELIGIOUS OR ETHICAL BELIEF. I have a dream that one day this nation will rise up and live out the true meaning of its *creed*: "We hold these truths to be self-evident that all men are created equal." (Martin Luther King, Jr.)

crescendo \krə-'shen-(,)dō\ n. INCREASE IN VOLUME OR INTENSITY, AS IN A MUSICAL PASSAGE; CLIMAX. The overture suddenly changed from a quiet pastoral theme to a *crescendo* featuring blaring trumpets and clashing cymbals.

cringe \'krinj\ v. SHRINK BACK, AS IF IN FEAR. The dog *cringed*, expecting a blow.

criterion \krī-'tir-ē-ən *also* krə-\ n. STANDARD USED IN JUDGING. What *criterion* did you use when you selected this essay as the prizewinner? //criteria, pl.

crux \'krəks, 'krùks\ n. CRUCIAL POINT. The *crux* of our problems today is the increasing disparity in wealth between the haves and the have-nots.

cryptic \'krip-tik\ adj. MYSTERIOUS; PUZZLING; AMBIGUOUS; SECRET. Thoroughly baffled by Holmes's *cryptic* remarks, Watson wondered whether Holmes was intentionally concealing his thoughts about the crime.

culinary \'kə-lə-,ner-ē, 'kyü-, 'kü-\ adj. RELATING TO COOKING. Many chefs attribute their *culinary* skill to the wise use of spices.

culmination \'kəl-mə-,nā-shən\ n. ATTAINMENT OF HIGHEST POINT. His inauguration as President of the United States marked the *culmination* of his political career. //culminate, v.

culpable \\'kəl-pə-bəl\ adj. DESERVING BLAME. Corrupt building inspectors who take bribes to overlook flaws in construction are as *culpable* as the contractors who perform the substandard work.

cupidity \kyü-'pi-də-tē\ n. GREED. The defeated people could not satisfy the *cupidity* of the conquerors, who demanded excessive tribute.

curator \\'kyur-ˌā-tər, kyü-'rā-, 'kyur-ə-\ n. SUPERINTENDENT; MANAGER. The members of the board of trustees of the museum expected the new *curator* to plan events and exhibitions that would make the museum more popular.

curmudgeon \(ˌ)kər-'mə-jən\ n. CHURLISH, MISERLY INDIVID-UAL. ; ILL-TEMPERED GROUCH. Lighten up, pal, and quit being such a sourpuss, or you'll wind up turning into an old *curmudgeon*.

cursive \\'kər-siv\ adj. FLOWING, RUNNING. In normal writing we run our letters together in *cursive* form; in printing, we separate the letters.

cursory \\'kərs-rē, 'kər-sə-\ adj. CASUAL; HASTILY DONE. Because a *cursory* examination of the ruins indicates the possibility of arson, we believe that the insurance agency should undertake a more extensive investigation of the fire's cause.

curtail \(ˌ)kər-'tāl\ v. SHORTEN; REDUCE. Barbie declined Ken's invitation to go to the movies, saying her father had ordered her to *curtail* her social life.

cynical \\'si-ni-kəl\ adj. SKEPTICAL OR DISTRUSTFUL OF HUMAN MOTIVES. *Cynical* from birth, Sidney was suspicious whenever anyone offered to give him a gift "with no strings attached." //cynic, n.

dank \\'daŋk\ adj. DAMP. The walls of the dungeon were *dank* and slimy.

daub \\'dȯb, 'däb\ v. SMEAR (AS WITH PAINT). From the way he *daubed* his paint on the canvas, I could tell he knew nothing of oils. //also n.

daunt \'dȯnt, 'dänt\ v. INTIMIDATE; FRIGHTEN; DISHEARTEN. Although we thought the amount of work left to do might *daunt* her, she refused to become discouraged and resolutely settled down to the job.

dauntless \'dȯnt-ləs, 'dänt-\ adj. BOLD. Despite the dangerous nature of the undertaking, the *dauntless* soldier volunteered for the assignment.

dawdle \'dȯ-dᵊl\ v. LOITER; WASTE TIME. We have to meet a deadline, so don't *dawdle*; just get down to work.

deadlock \'ded-ˌläk\ n. STANDSTILL; STALEMATE. Because negotiations had reached a *deadlock*, some of the delegates had begun to mutter about breaking off the talks. //also v.

deadpan \'ded-ˌpan\ adj. WOODEN; IMPERSONAL; EXPRESSIONLESS. Serious and wooden faced, the comedian Buster Keaton was a master of *deadpan* humor.

dearth \'dərth\ n. SCARCITY. The *dearth* of skilled labor compelled the employers to open trade schools.

debacle \dē-'bä-kəl, di-, -'ba-; ÷'de-bə-kəl\ n. SUDDEN DOWNFALL; COMPLETE DISASTER. In the *Airplane* movies, every flight turns into a *debacle*, with passengers and crewmembers collapsing, engines falling apart, and carry-on baggage popping out of the overhead bins.

debase \di-'bās, dē-\ v. REDUCE IN QUALITY OR VALUE; LOWER IN ESTEEM; DEGRADE. In *The King and I*, Anna refuses to kneel down and prostrate herself before the king, for she feels that to do so would *debase* her position. //debasement, n.

debauch \di-'bȯch, -'bäch, dē-\ v. CORRUPT; SEDUCE FROM VIRTUE. Did Socrates' teachings lead the young men of Athens to be virtuous citizens, or did they *debauch* the young men, causing them to question the customs of their fathers? //debauchery, n.

debilitate \di-'bi-lə-ˌtāt, dē-\ v. WEAKEN; ENFEEBLE. Michael's severe bout of the flu *debilitated* him so much that he was too tired to go to work for a week.

debris \də-'brē, dā-', 'dā-,\ n. RUBBLE. A full year after the earthquake in Mexico City, they were still carting away the *debris*.

decadence \'de-kə-dən(t)s *also* di-'kā-\ n. DECAY; DECLINE, ESPECIALLY MORAL; SELF-INDULGENCE. We named our best-selling ice cream flavor "chocolate *decadence*" because only truly self-indulgent people would treat themselves to something so calorific and cholesterol laden.

decapitate \di-'ka-pə-,tāt, dē-\ v. BEHEAD. "Off with her head!" cried the Duchess, eager to *decapitate* poor Alice.

decelerate \(,)dē-'se-lə-,rāt\ v. SLOW DOWN. Seeing the emergency blinkers in the road ahead, he *decelerated* quickly.

Each of the questions below consists of a word in capital letters, followed by five words or phrases. Choose the word or phrase that is most similar in meaning to the word in capital letters and write the letter of your choice on your answer paper.

166. **COWER**   (A) amuse   (B) quiver   (C) prate
(D) shackle   (E) vilify

167. **COY**   (A) weak   (B) airy   (C) shy
(D) old   (E) tiresome

168. **CRASS**   (A) desirous   (B) direct   (C) crude
(D) minute   (E) controlled

169. **CRUX**   (A) affliction   (B) spark   (C) events
(D) crucial point   (E) belief

170. **CRYPTIC**   (A) tomblike   (B) futile   (C) famous
(D) mysterious   (E) indifferent

171. **CUPIDITY**   (A) anxiety   (B) tragedy   (C) greed
(D) entertainment   (E) love

172. **CURTAIL**   (A) mutter   (B) cut short   (C) express
(D) burden   (E) shore up

173. **CYNICAL**   (A) distrustful   (B) effortless
(C) conclusive   (D) gallant   (E) vertical

174. **DANK**   (A) clammy   (B) guiltless   (C) warm
(D) babbling   (E) reserved

175. **DAUNT**   (A) reveal   (B) intimidate   (C) coax
(D) warm   (E) punish

176. **DAUNTLESS**   (A) stolid   (B) courageous
(C) irrelevant   (D) peculiar   (E) particular

177. **DEARTH**   (A) life   (B) shortage   (C) brightness
(D) terror   (E) width

178. **DEBACLE**   (A) downfall   (B) refusal   (C) masque
(D) cowardice   (E) traffic

179. **DEBILITATE**   (A) bedevil   (B) repress   (C) weaken
(D) animate   (E) deaden

180. **DECELERATION**   (A) slowing   (B) destination
(C) application   (D) praise   (E) strength

WORD LIST 13
decimate–derivative

decimate \\'de-sə-ˌmāt\ v. KILL, USUALLY ONE OUT OF TEN. We do more to *decimate* our population in automobile accidents than we do in war.

decipher \dē-'sī-fər\ v. DECODE; MAKE OUT THE MEANING OF. The pharmacist could not *decipher* the doctor's almost illegible handwriting.

decomposition \(ˌ)dē-ˌkäm-pə-'zi-shən\ n. DECAY. Despite the body's advanced state of *decomposition*, the police were able to identify the murdered man. //decompose, v.

decorous \'de-kər-əs\ adj. PROPER; ORDERLY. Even the best mannered students have trouble behaving in a *decorous* fashion on the last day of school. //decorum, n.

decoy \'dē-ˌkȯi, di-'\ n. LURE OR BAIT. The wild ducks were not fooled by the *decoy*. //also v.

decrepit \di-'kre-pət\ adj. WORN OUT BY AGE. The *decrepit* car blocked traffic on the highway. //decrepitude, n.

decry \di-'krī, dē-\ v. EXPRESS STRONG DISAPPROVAL OF; DISPARAGE. The founder of the Children's Defense Fund, Marion Wright Edelman, strongly *decries* the lack of financial and moral support for children in America today.

deducible \di-'d(y)ü-sə-bəl\, dē-\ adj. DERIVED BY REASONING. If we accept your premise, your conclusions are easily *deducible*. //deduce, v.

defamation \ˌde-fə-'mā-shən\ n. HARMING A PERSON'S REPUTATION. If you try to harm my good name, my lawyers will sue you for *defamation* of character. //defame, v.

default \di-'fȯlt, dē-; 'dē-ˌfȯlt\ n. FAILURE TO DO. When the visiting team failed to show up for the big game, they lost the game by *default*. //also v.

defeatist \di-'fē-tist, dē-\ adj. ATTITUDE OF ONE WHO IS READY TO ACCEPT DEFEAT AS A NATURAL OUTCOME. If you maintain your *defeatist* attitude, you will never succeed. //also n.

defection \di-'fek-shən\ n. DESERTION. The children, who had made him an idol, were hurt most by his *defection* from our cause.

deference \'de-fə-rən(t)s, 'def-rən(t)s\ n. COURTEOUS REGARD FOR ANOTHER'S WISH. In *deference* to the minister's request, please do not take photographs during the wedding service. //defer, v.

defile \di-'fī(-ə)l, dē-\ v. POLLUTE; PROFANE. The hoodlums *defiled* the church with their obscene writing.

definitive \di-'fi-nə-tiv\ adj. AUTHORITATIVE AND APPARENTLY EXHAUSTIVE; FINAL; COMPLETE. Carl Sandburg's *Abraham Lincoln* may be regarded as the *definitive* work on the life of the Great Emancipator.

deflect \di-'flekt, dē-\ v. TURN ASIDE. His life was saved when his cigarette case *deflected* the bullet.

deft \'deft\ adj. NEAT; SKILLFUL. The *deft* waiter uncorked the champagne without spilling a drop.

defunct \di-'fəŋkt, dē-\ adj. DEAD; NO LONGER IN USE OR EXISTENCE. The lawyers sought to examine the books of the *defunct* corporation.

degradation \,de-grə-'dā-shən\ n. HUMILIATION; DEBASEMENT; DEGENERATION. Some secretaries object to fetching the boss a cup of coffee because they resent the *degradation* of being made to do such lowly tasks.

deify \'dē-ə-,fī, 'dā-\ v. TURN INTO A GOD; IDOLIZE. Admire the rock star all you want; just don't *deify* him.

delectable \di-'lek-tə-bəl\ adj. DELIGHTFUL; DELICIOUS. We thanked our host for a most *delectable* meal.

delete \di-'lēt, dē-\ v. ERASE; STRIKE OUT. Less is more: if you *delete* this paragraph, your whole essay will have greater appeal.

deleterious \,de-lə-'tir-ē-əs\ adj. HARMFUL. If you believe that smoking is *deleterious* to your health (and the Surgeon General certainly does), then quit!

deliberate \di-'li-bə-ˌrāt\ v. CONSIDER; PONDER. Offered the new job, she asked for time to *deliberate* before she told them her decision.

delineate \di-'li-nē-ˌāt, dē-\ n. PORTRAY. Using only a few descriptive phrases, Jane Austen *delineates* the character of Mr. Collins so well that we can predict his every move. //delineation, n.

delude \di-'lüd, dē-\ v. DECEIVE. The mistress *deluded* herself into believing that her lover would leave his wife and marry her. //delusion, n. delusive, adj.

deluge \'del-ˌyüj, -,yüzh; ÷də-'lüj, 'dā-ˌlüj\ n. FLOOD; RUSH. When we advertised the position, we received a *deluge* of applications.

demagogue \'de-mə-ˌgäg\ n. PERSON WHO APPEALS TO PEOPLE'S PREJUDICE; FALSE LEADER OF PEOPLE. A consummate *demagogue*, Huey Long played upon the voters' economic fears, fiercely attacking the utilities industry and corporate privileges in order to sway poor rural Louisianans into voting him into office.

demean \di-'mēn\ v. DEGRADE; HUMILIATE. If you truly believed in the dignity of labor, you would not think that it would *demean* you to work as a janitor.

demeanor \di-'mē-nər\ n. BEHAVIOR; BEARING. His sober *demeanor* quieted the noisy revelers.

demise \di-'mīz\ n. DEATH. Upon the *demise* of the dictator, a bitter dispute about succession to power developed.

demolition \ˌde-mə-'li-shən, ˌdē-mə-\ n. DESTRUCTION. In the course of a typical *demolition* derby, 10 or more drivers deliberately ram their vehicles into one another until every car but one has been *demolished*. //demolish, v.

demure \di-'myur\ adj. GRAVE; SERIOUS; COY. She was *demure* and reserved, a nice modest girl whom any young man would be proud to take home to his mother.

denigrate \'de-ni-,grāt\ v. BLACKEN. All attempts to *denigrate* the character of our late president have failed; the people still love him and cherish his memory.

denizen \'de-nə-zən\ n. INHABITANT OF. In *The Untouchables*, Eliot Ness fights Al Capone and the other *denizens* of Chicago's underworld.

denotation \,dē-nō-'tā-shən\ n. MEANING; DISTINGUISHING BY NAME. A dictionary will always give us the *denotation* of a word; frequently, it will also give us its connotation.

denouement \,dā-,nü-'mä\u207f, dā-,nü-'\ n. OUTCOME; FINAL DEVELOPMENT OF THE PLOT OF A PLAY. The play was childishly written; the *denouement* was obvious to sophisticated theatergoers as early as the middle of the first act.

denounce \di-'nau\u0307n(t)s, dē-\ v. CONDEMN; CRITICIZE. The reform candidate *denounced* the corrupt city officers for having betrayed the public's trust. //denunciation, n.

depict \di-'pikt, dē-\ v. PORTRAY. In this sensational exposé, the author *depicts* Beatle John Lennon as a drug-crazed neurotic. Do you question the accuracy of this *depiction* of Lennon? //depiction, n.

deplete \di-'plēt\ v. REDUCE; EXHAUST. We must wait until we *deplete* our present inventory before we order replacements.

deplore \di-'plȯr\ v. REGRET; DISAPPROVE OF. Although Ann Landers *deplored* the disintegration of the modern family, she recognized that not every marriage could be saved.

depose \di-'pōz, dē-\ v. DETHRONE; REMOVE FROM OFFICE. The army attempted to *depose* the king and set up a military government.

deposition \,de-pə-'zi-shən, ,dē-pə-\ n. TESTIMONY UNDER OATH. He made his *deposition* in the judge's chamber.

depravity \di-'pra-və-tē *also* -'prā-\ n. CORRUPTION; WICKEDNESS. The *depravity* of Caligula's behavior

came to sicken even those who had willingly partici-
pated in his earlier, comparatively innocent orgies.
//deprave, v.

deprecate \'de-pri-ˌkāt\ v. EXPRESS DISAPPROVAL OF; PROTEST
AGAINST; BELITTLE. A firm believer in old-fashioned
courtesy, Miss Post *deprecated* the modern tendency
to address new acquaintances by their first names.
//deprecatory, adj.

depreciate \di-'prē-shē-ˌāt\ v. LESSEN IN VALUE. If you
neglect this property, it will *depreciate*.

deranged \di-'rānjd\ adj. INSANE. Hamlet's cruel rejection left poor Ophelia *deranged*; in her madness, she
drowned herself.

derelict \'der-ə-ˌlikt, 'de-rə-\ adj. ABANDONED; NEGLECTFUL
OF DUTY. Whoever abandoned the *derelict* craft in the
middle of the harbor was *derelict* in living up to his
responsibilities as a boat owner. //also n.

derision \di-'ri-zhən\ n. RIDICULE. The critics greeted
the new play with *derision*, ridiculing its pretentious
dialogue and refusing to take it seriously. //derisive,
adj.; deride v.

derivative \di-'ri-və-tiv\ adj. UNORIGINAL; DERIVED FROM
ANOTHER SOURCE. Although her early poetry was clearly
derivative in nature, the critics thought she had
promise and eventually would find her own voice.

Each of the questions below consists of a word in capital letters, followed by five words or phrases. Choose the word or phrase that is most similar in meaning to the word in capital letters and write the letter of your choice on your answer paper.

181. **DECIMATE** (A) kill (B) disgrace (C) search (D) collide (E) deride

182. **DECIPHER** (A) trap (B) reduce (C) quarter (D) split (E) decode

183. **DECOROUS** (A) flavored (B) artistic (C) flowery (D) proper (E) sweet

184. **DECREPIT** (A) momentary (B) emotional (C) suppressed (D) worn out (E) unexpected

185. **DEFAMATION** (A) slander (B) disease (C) coolness (D) melee (E) crowd

186. **DEFEATIST** (A) pessimist (B) eloper (C) observer (D) conqueror (E) investor

187. **DEFECTION** (A) determination (B) desertion (C) invitation (D) affection (E) reservation

188. **DEFILE** (A) manicure (B) ride (C) pollute (D) assemble (E) order

189. **DEGRADATION** (A) assessment (B) humiliation (C) expulsion (D) desertion (E) resolution

190. **DELETERIOUS** (A) delaying (B) experimental (C) harmful (D) graduating (E) glorious

191. **DELUGE** (A) confusion (B) deception (C) flood (D) mountain (E) weapon

192. **DENIGRATE** (A) refuse (B) blacken (C) terrify (D) admit (E) review

193. **DENOUEMENT** (A) action (B) scenery (C) resort (D) character (E) solution

194. **DEPRAVITY** (A) wickedness (B) sadness (C) heaviness (D) tidiness (E) seriousness

195. **DERANGED** (A) insane (B) announced (C) neighborly (D) alphabetical (E) surrounded

derogatory \di-'rä-gə-ˌtȯr-ē\ adj. EXPRESSING A LOW OPINION. Because the word *Eskimo* has come under strong attack in recent years for its supposedly *derogatory* connotations, many Americans today either avoid the term or feel uneasy using it.

desecrate \'de-si-ˌkrāt\ v. PROFANE; VIOLATE THE SANCTITY OF. Shattering the altar and trampling the holy objects underfoot, the invaders *desecrated* the sanctuary.

desiccate \'de-si-ˌkāt\ v. DRY UP. A tour of this smoke-house will give you an idea of how the pioneers used to *desiccate* food in order to preserve it.

desolate \'de-sə-ˌlāt\ v. ROB OF JOY; LAY WASTE TO; FORSAKE. The bandits *desolated* the countryside, burning farms and carrying off the harvest.

despicable \di-'spi-kə-bəl, 'des-(ˌ)pi-\ adj. CONTEMPTIBLE. Mr. Bond, I despise spies; I look down on them as mean, *despicable*, honorless men. //despise, v.

despondent \di-'spän-dənt\ adj. DEPRESSED; GLOOMY. To the dismay of his parents, William became seriously *despondent* after he broke up with Jan. //despondency, n.

despot \'des-pət\ n. TYRANT; HARSH, AUTHORITARIAN RULER. How could a benevolent king turn overnight into a *despot*?

destitute \'des-tə-ˌtüt, -ˌt(y)üt\ adj. EXTREMELY POOR. Because the family had no health insurance, the father's costly illness left them *destitute*.

desultory \'de-səl-ˌtȯr-ē *also* -zəl-\ adj. HAPHAZARD; DIGRESSING AT RANDOM. In prison Malcolm X set himself the task of reading straight through the dictionary; to him, reading was purposeful, not *desultory*.

detached \di-'tacht, dē-\ adj. EMOTIONALLY REMOVED; CALM AND OBJECTIVE; INDIFFERENT; PHYSICALLY UNCONNECTED. A psychoanalyst must maintain a *detached* point of view and stay uninvolved with her patients' personal lives. //detachment, n. (secondary meaning)

deterrent \di-'tər-ənt, dē-\ n. SOMETHING THAT DISCOURAGES; HINDRANCE. The threat of capital punishment may serve as a *deterrent* to potential killers. //deter, v.

detraction \di-'trak-shən, dē-\ n. DAMAGING COMMENT; DISPARAGEMENT; SLANDER. Because Susan B. Anthony and Elizabeth Cady Stanton dared to fight for women's rights, their motives, manners, dress, personal appearance, and character were held up to ridicule and *detraction*.

detrimental \ˌde-trə-'men-təl\ adj. HARMFUL; DAMAGING. Senator Obama's relationship with his controversial minister proved not to be *detrimental* to his chances of being elected president? //detriment, n.

deviate \'dē-vē-ˌāt\ v. TURN AWAY FROM; DIVERGE. Richard never *deviated* from his daily routine: every day, he set off for work at eight o'clock, had his sack lunch at noon, and headed home at the stroke of five.

devious \'dē-vē-əs, -vyəs\ adj. ROUNDABOUT; ERRATIC; NOT STRAIGHTFORWARD. The Joker's plan was so *devious* that it was only with great difficulty we could follow its shifts and dodges.

devoid \di-'void\ adj. LACKING. You may think Sherry's mind is a total void, but she's actually not *devoid* of intelligence. She just sounds like an airhead.

devotee \ˌde-ˌvō-'tē, ˌdē-, ˌdā-, də-, -'tā\ n. ENTHUSIASTIC FOLLOWER. A *devotee* of the opera, he bought season tickets every year.

devout \di-'vaut\ adj. PIOUS. The *devout* man prayed daily.

dexterous \'dek-st(ə-)rəs\ adj. SKILLFUL. The magician was so *dexterous* that we could not follow him as he performed his tricks.

diabolical \ˌdī-ə-'bä-li-kəl\ adj. DEVILISH. "What a fiend I am, to devise such a *diabolical* scheme to destroy Gotham City," chortled the Joker.

dialectical \ˌdī-ə-'lek-ti-kəl\ adj. RELATING TO THE ART OF DEBATE; MUTUAL OR RECIPROCAL. The debate coach's students grew to develop great forensic and *dialectical* skill.

diaphanous \dī-'a-fə-nəs\ adj. SHEER; TRANSPARENT. Sexy nightgowns are *diaphanous*; Uncle Donald's woolen long johns, fortunately, are not.

diatribe \'dī-ə-'trīb\ n. BITTER SCOLDING; INVECTIVE. ; HARANGUE; RANT. Infuriated by what he considered unfair attacks in the press, the candidate delivered a lengthy *diatribe* against biased reporting.

dichotomy \dī-'kä-tə-mē *also* də-\ n. SPLIT; BRANCHING INTO TWO PARTS (ESPECIALLY CONTRADICTORY ONES). According to Carl Jung, the distinction between mind and body is an artificial *dichotomy*, a division that is not necessarily inherent in the nature of things.

dictum \'dik-təm\ n. AUTHORITATIVE AND WEIGHTY STATEMENT; SAYING; MAXIM. University administrators still follow the old *dictum* of "Publish or perish."

didactic \dī-'dak-tik, də-\adj. TEACHING; INSTRUCTIONAL. Pope's lengthy poem *An Essay on Man* is too *didactic* for my taste: I dislike it when poets turn preachy and moralize.

diffidence \'di-fə-dən(t)s, -fə-ˌden(t)s\ n. SHYNESS; MODESTY. Doubting her ability to write English correctly, the young Japanese student felt some *diffidence* about replying to the first letter she received from her American pen pal. //diffident, adj.

diffuse \di-'fyüs\ adj. WORDY; RAMBLING; SPREAD OUT (LIKE A GAS). If you pay authors by the word, you tempt them to produce *diffuse* manuscripts rather than brief ones. //diffusion, n.

digression \dī-'gre-shən, də-\ n. WANDERING AWAY FROM THE SUBJECT. Nobody minded when Professor Renoir's lectures wandered away from their official theme; his *digressions* were always more fascinating than the topic of the day. //digress, v.

dilapidated \də-'la-pə-ˌdā-tid, -təd\ adj. RUINED BECAUSE OF NEGLECT. The *dilapidated* old building needed far more work than just a new coat of paint. //dilapidation, n.

dilate \'dī-lāt, dī-'\ v. EXPAND. In the dark, the pupils of your eyes *dilate*.

dilatory \'di-lə-ˌtȯr-ē\ adj. DELAYING. If you are *dilatory* in paying bills, your credit rating may suffer.

dilemma \də-'le-mə *also* dī-\ n. PROBLEM; CHOICE OF TWO UNSATISFACTORY ALTERNATIVES. In this *dilemma*, he knew no one to whom he could turn for advice.

dilettante \'di-lə-ˌtänt, -ˌtant; ˌdi-lə-'\ n. AIMLESS FOLLOWER OF THE ARTS; AMATEUR; DABBLER. According to Turgenev, without painstaking work, any writer or artist is doomed to remain a *dilettante*.

diligence \'di-lə-jən(t)s\ n. STEADINESS OF EFFORT; PERSISTENT HARD WORK. Her employers were greatly impressed by her *diligence* and offered her a partnership in the firm. //diligent, adj.

dilute \dī-'lüt, də-\ v. MAKE LESS CONCENTRATED; REDUCE IN STRENGTH. She preferred her coffee *diluted* with milk.

diminution \ˌdi-mə-'nü-shən *also* -'nyü-\ n. LESSENING; REDUCTION IN SIZE. Old Jack was as sharp at 80 as he had been at 50; increasing age led to no *diminution* of his mental acuity.

dire \'dī(-ə)r\ adj. DISASTROUS; URGENT; DESPERATE. People ignored her *dire* predictions of an approaching depression.

dirge \'dərj\ n. LAMENT WITH MUSIC. Walt Whitman's *Drum-Taps*, published in 1865, included a moving *dirge* commemorating the death of the martyred Abraham Lincoln.

disapprobation \(ˌ)dis-ˌa-prə-'bā-shən\ n. DISAPPROVAL; CONDEMNATION. The conservative father viewed his daughter's radical boyfriend with *disapprobation*.

disarray \\,dis-ə-'rā\ n. A DISORDERLY OR UNTIDY STATE.
After the New Year's party, the once orderly house
was in total *disarray*.

disavowal \\,dis-ə-'vaủ (-ə)l\ n. DENIAL; DISCLAIMING.
The novelist Andre Gide was controversial both for
his early support of communism and for his later
disavowal of it after a visit to the Soviet Union.
//disavow, v.

disband \dis-'band\ v. DISSOLVE; DISPERSE. The chess club
disbanded after its disastrous initial season.

disburse \dis-'bərs\ v. PAY OUT. When you *disburse*
money on the company's behalf, be sure to get a
receipt.

discerning \di-'sər-niŋ, -'zər-\ adj. MENTALLY QUICK AND
OBSERVANT; HAVING INSIGHT. Though she was no genius,
the star was sufficiently *discerning* to tell her true
friends from the countless phonies who flattered her.
//discern, v., discernment, n.

disclaimer \dis-'klā-mər\ n. DENIAL OF A LEGAL CLAIM OR
RIGHT; DISAVOWAL. Although reporter Joe Klein issued a
disclaimer stating that he was not Anonymous, the
author of *Primary Colors*, eventually he admitted
that he had written the controversial novel.
//disclaim, v.

disclose \dis-'klōz\ v. REVEAL. Although competitors
offered him bribes, he refused to *disclose* any information about his company's forthcoming product.
//disclosure, n.

disconcert \\,dis-kən-'sərt\ v. CONFUSE; UPSET; EMBARRASS.
The lawyer was *disconcerted* by the evidence produced
by her adversary.

disconsolate \dis-'kän(t)-sə-lət\ adj. SAD. The death of
his wife left him *disconsolate*.

discordant \dis-'kȯr-dᵊnt\ adj. INHARMONIOUS; CONFLICTING.
Nothing is quite as *discordant* as the sound of a
junior high school orchestra tuning up. //discord, n.

discount \'dis-ˌkau̇nt, dis-'\ v. DISREGARD. Be prepared to *discount* what he has to say about his ex-wife. (secondary meaning)

discredit \(ˌ)dis-'kre-dət\ v. DEFAME; DESTROY CONFIDENCE IN; DISBELIEVE. The campaign was highly negative in tone; each candidate tried to *discredit* the other

discrepancy \dis-'kre-pən-sē\ n. LACK OF CONSISTENCY; DIFFERENCE; CONTRADICTION. "Observe, Watson, the significant *discrepancies* between Sir Percy's original description of the crime and his most recent testimony. What do these contradictions suggest?"

Each of the questions below consists of a word in capital letters, followed by five words or phrases. Choose the word or phrase that is most similar in meaning to the word in capital letters and write the letter of your choice on your answer paper.

196. **DEROGATORY**   (A) roguish   (B) immediate   (C) opinionated   (D) insulting   (E) conferred

197. **DESECRATE**   (A) desist   (B) integrate   (C) confuse   (D) intensify   (E) profane

198. **DESPICABLE**   (A) steering   (B) contemptible   (C) inevitable   (D) featureless   (E) incapable

199. **DESTITUTE**   (A) impoverished   (B) dazzling   (C) stationary   (D) characteristic   (E) explanatory

200. **DEVOID**   (A) latent   (B) eschewed   (C) lacking   (D) suspecting   (E) evident

201. **DEVOUT**   (A) quiet   (B) dual   (C) pious   (D) straightforward   (E) wrong

202. **DIABOLICAL**   (A) mechanical   (B) lavish   (C) devilish   (D) azure   (E) red

203. **DIATRIBE**   (A) mass   (B) range   (C) scolding   (D) elegy   (E) starvation

204. **DIFFIDENCE**   (A) sharpness   (B) bashfulness   (C) malcontent   (D) dialogue   (E) catalog

205. **DILATE**   (A) procrastinate   (B) expand   (C) conclude   (D) participate   (E) divert

206. **DILATORY**   (A) narrowing   (B) delaying   (C) enlarging   (D) portentous   (E) sour

207. **DIMINUTION**   (A) expectation   (B) context   (C) validity   (D) shrinking   (E) difficulty

208. **DISAPPROBATION**   (A) realism   (B) cost   (C) disapproval   (D) sincerity   (E) delay

209. **DISCLOSE**   (A) violate   (B) control   (C) recover   (D) renege   (E) reveal

210. **DISCONSOLATE**   (A) examining   (B) thankful   (C) theatrical   (D) cheerless   (E) prominent

discrete \dis-'krēt, 'dis-,\ adj. SEPARATE; UNCONNECTED. Because human populations have been migrating and intermingling for hundreds of centuries, it is hard to classify humans into *discrete* racial groups. (Do not confuse *discrete* with *discreet*, or tactful.)

discretion \dis-'kre-shən\ n. PRUDENCE; ABILITY TO ADJUST ACTIONS TO CIRCUMSTANCES. Because we trusted our architect's judgment, we left many decisions about the house renovation to his *discretion*. //discreet, adj.

discriminating \dis-'kri-mə-,nā-tiŋ\ adj. ABLE TO SEE DIFFERENCES. Renowned as an expert on Picasso, she was sufficiently *discriminating* to judge the most complex works of modern art. //discrimination, n.; discriminate, v.

discursive \dis-'kər-siv\ adj. DIGRESSING; RAMBLING. As the lecturer wandered from topic to topic, we wondered what if any point there was to his *discursive* remarks.

disdain \dis-'dān\ v. TREAT WITH SCORN OR CONTEMPT. In the film *Funny Face*, the bookish heroine *disdains* fashion models for their lack of intellectual interests. //also n.

disfigure \dis-'fi-gyər\ v. MAR IN BEAUTY; SPOIL. An ugly frown *disfigured* his normally pleasant face.

disgruntle \dis-'grən-təl\ v. MAKE DISCONTENTED. The passengers were *disgruntled* by the numerous delays.

disheartened \(,)dis-'här-t°nd\ adj. LACKING COURAGE AND HOPE. His failure to pass the bar exam *disheartened* him.

disinclination \(,)dis-,in-klə-'nā-shən, -,siŋ-\ n. UNWILLINGNESS. Some mornings I feel a great *disinclination* to get out of bed.

disingenuous \,dis-in-'jen-yə-wəs, -yü-əs-\ adj. LACKING GENUINE CANDOR; INSINCERE. Now that we know that the mayor and his wife are engaged in a bitter divorce fight, we find their earlier remarks regretting their lack of time together remarkably *disingenuous*.

disinterested \(ˌ)dis-ˈin-trəs-təd; -ˈin-tə-ˌres-təd\ adj. UNPREJUDICED. Given the judge's political ambitions and the lawyers' financial interest in the case, the only *disinterested* person in the courtroom may have been the court reporter.

disjointed \(ˌ)dis-ˈjȯin-təd\ adj. DISCONNECTED. Unable to think of anything coherent to say about the assigned topic, the unprepared student scribbled a few *disjointed* sentences on his answer sheet.

dismantle \(ˌ)dis-ˈman-təl\ v. TAKE APART. When the show closed, they *dismantled* the scenery before storing it.

dismiss \dis-ˈmis\ v. PUT AWAY FROM CONSIDERATION; REJECT. Believing in John's love for her, she *dismissed* the notion that he might be unfaithful. (secondary meaning)

disparage \di-ˈsper-ij, -ˈspa-rij\ v. BELITTLE. A doting mother, Emma was far more likely to praise her son's crude attempts at art than to *disparage* them. //disparaging, adj.

disparity \di-ˈsper-ə-tē, -ˈspa-rə-\ n. DIFFERENCE; CONDITION OF INEQUALITY. Their *disparity* in rank made no difference at all to the Prince and Cinderella. //disparate, adj.

dispassionate \(ˌ)dis-ˈpa-sh(ə-)nət\ adj. CALM; IMPARTIAL. Known in the company for his cool judgment, Bill could impartially examine the causes of a problem, give a *dispassionate* analysis of what had gone wrong, and go on to suggest how to correct the mess.

dispel \di-ˈspel\ v. SCATTER; DRIVE AWAY; CAUSE TO VANISH. The bright sunlight eventually *dispelled* the morning mist.

disperse \di-ˈspərs\ v. SCATTER. The police fired tear gas into the crowd to *disperse* the protesters. //dispersion, n.

dispirited \(ˌ)dis-ˈpir-ə-təd, -ˈpi-rə-\ adj. LACKING IN SPIRIT. The coach used all the tricks at his command to buoy up the enthusiasm of his team, which had become *dispirited* at the loss of the star player.

disputatious \ˌdis-pyə-ˈtā-shəs\ adj. ARGUMENTATIVE; FOND OF ARGUMENT. Convinced he knew more than his lawyers, Tony was a *disputatious* client, ready to argue about the best way to conduct the case.

dissection \dī-ˈsek-shən *also* di-, ˈdī-ˌ\ n. ANALYSIS; CUTTING APART IN ORDER TO EXAMINE. The *dissection* of frogs in the laboratory is particularly unpleasant to some students.

dissemble \di-ˈsem-bəl\ v. DISGUISE; PRETEND. Bond realized that the only way he could fool his captors was to *dissemble*, to pretend that he was still unconscious.

disseminate \di-ˈse-mə-ˌnāt\ v. DISTRIBUTE; SPREAD; SCATTER (LIKE SEEDS). By their use of the Internet, propagandists have been able to *disseminate* their pet doctrines to new audiences around the globe.

dissent \di-ˈsent\ v. DISAGREE. In a recent Supreme Court decision, Justice Ginsburg *dissented* from the majority opinion. //also n.

dissimulate \(ˌ)di-ˈsim-yə-ˌlāt\ v. PRETEND; CONCEAL BY FEIGNING. Although the governor tried to *dissimulate* his feelings about the opposing candidate, we all knew that he despised his rival.

dissipate \ˈdi-sə-ˌpāt\ v. SQUANDER. Although Jon had the potential to become a fine actor, he seemed content to *dissipate* his talents appearing in burlesque shows and soap operas.

dissonance \ˈdi-sə-nən(t)s\ n. INHARMONIOUS OR HARSH SOUND; DISCORD. Composer Charles Ives often used *dissonance*—clashing or unresolved chords—for special effects in his musical works. //dissonant, adj.

dissuade \di-ˈswād\ v. PERSUADE NOT TO DO; DISCOURAGE. Since Tom could not *dissuade* Huck from running away from home, he decided to accompany his friend. //dissuasion, n.

distant \'dis-tənt\ adj. RESERVED OR ALOOF; COLD IN MANNER. His *distant* greeting made me feel unwelcome from the start. (secondary meaning)

distend \di-'stend\ v. EXPAND; SWELL. I can tell when he is under stress by the way the veins *distend* on his forehead.

distort \di-'stȯrt\ v. TWIST OUT OF SHAPE. In the fun house, Betty refused to look at the wall of mirrors because she hated the way the mirrors *distorted* her reflection. //distortion, n.

distraught \di-'strȯt\ adj. UPSET; DISTRACTED BY ANXIETY. The *distraught* parents frantically searched the ravine for their lost child.

diva \'dē-və\ n. OPERATIC SINGER; PRIMA DONNA. Although world famous as a *diva*, she did not indulge in fits of temperament.

divergent \də-'vər-jənt, dī-\ adj. DIFFERING; DEVIATING. Since graduating from medical school, the two doctors have taken *divergent* paths, one going on to become a nationally prominent surgeon, the other dedicating himself to a small family practice in his hometown. //divergence, n.; diverge, n.

diverse \dī-'vərs, də-', 'dī-,\ adj. MANY AND DIFFERENT; DISTINCTLY UNLIKE. San Francisco offers tourists *diverse* pleasures, some as simple as a ride on a cable car, others as sophisticated as a night at the Opera. //diversity, n.

diversion \də-'vər-zhən, dī-, -shən\ n. ACT OF TURNING ASIDE; PASTIME. After studying for several hours, he needed a *diversion* from work. //divert, v.

divest \dī-'vest, də-\ v. STRIP; DEPRIVE. He was *divested* of his power to act and could no longer govern. //divestiture, n.

divulge \də-'vəlj, dī-\ v. REVEAL. No lover of gossip, Charlotte would never *divulge* anything that a friend told her in confidence.

docile \'dä-səl *also* -ˌsī(-ə)l\ adj. OBEDIENT; EASILY MANAGED. As *docile* as he seems today, that old lion was once a ferocious, snarling beast. //docility, n.

document \'dä-kyə-ˌment\ v. PROVIDE WRITTEN EVIDENCE. She kept all the receipts from her business trip in order to *document* her expenses for the firm. //also n.

doggerel \'dȯ-g(ə-)rəl, 'dä-\ n. POOR VERSE. Although we find occasional snatches of genuine poetry in her work, most of her writing is mere *doggerel*.

dogmatic \dȯg-'ma-tik, däg-\ adj. OPINIONATED; ARBITRARY; DOCTRINAL. We tried to discourage Doug from being so *dogmatic*, but we never could convince him that his opinions might be wrong.

domicile \'dä-mə-ˌsī(-ə)l, 'dō-; 'dä-mə-sil\ n. HOME. Although his legal *domicile* was in New York City, his work kept him away from his residence for many years. //also v.

domineer \ˌdä-mə-'nir\ v. RULE OVER TYRANNICALLY. Students prefer teachers who guide, not ones who *domineer*.

dormant \'dȯr-mənt\ adj. SLEEPING; LETHARGIC; TORPID; LATENT. At 50 her long-*dormant* ambition to write flared up once more; within a year she had completed the first of her great historical novels. //dormancy, n.

dour \'dùr, 'daù(-ə)r\ adj. SULLEN; STUBBORN. Although New Englanders are by reputation *dour* and humorless, Captain Don was a jovial, outgoing soul.

douse \'daùs *also* 'daùz\ v. PLUNGE INTO WATER; DRENCH; EXTINGUISH. They *doused* each other with hoses and water balloons.

drone \'drōn\ n. IDLE PERSON; MALE BEE. Content to let his wife support him, the would-be writer was in reality nothing but a *drone*.

drone \'drōn\ v. TALK DULLY; BUZZ OR MURMUR LIKE A BEE. On a gorgeous day, who wants to be stuck in a classroom listening to the teacher *drone*.

dross \'dräs, 'dròs\ n. WASTE MATTER; WORTHLESS IMPURITIES. At the smelter, the workers skimmed the *dross* from the surface of the molten metal, discarding the hot scum with great care.

dubious \'dü-bē-əs *also* dyü-\ adj. DOUBTFUL; QUESTIONABLE; FILLED WITH DOUBT. Many critics of the SAT contend that the test is of *dubious* worth. Jack claimed he could get a perfect 2400 on the SAT, but Ellen was *dubious*: she knew he hadn't cracked a book in three years.

duplicity \dü-'pli-sə-tē *also* dyü-\ n. DOUBLE-DEALING; HYPOCRISY. When Tanya learned that Mark had been two-timing her, she was furious at him for his *duplicity*.

Each of the questions below consists of a word in capital letters, followed by five words or phrases. Choose the word or phrase that is most similar in meaning to the word in capital letters and write the letter of your choice on your answer paper.

211. **DISINGENUOUS** (A) uncomfortable (B) eventual (C) insincere (D) complex (E) enthusiastic

212. **DISINTERESTED** (A) unbiased (B) horrendous (C) affected (D) arbitrary (E) bored

213. **DISJOINTED** (A) satisfied (B) carved (C) understood (D) disconnected (E) evicted

214. **DISPARITY** (A) resonance (B) elocution (C) relief (D) difference (E) symbolism

215. **DISPASSIONATE** (A) sensual (B) immoral (C) inhibited (D) impartial (E) scientific

216. **DISPIRITED** (A) current (B) dented (C) drooping (D) removed (E) dallying

217. **DISSIPATE** (A) waste (B) clean (C) accept (D) anticipate (E) withdraw

218. **DISSUADE** (A) advise against (B) adjust (C) exist (D) materialize (E) finish with

219. **DIVERGENT** (A) clever (B) industrial (C) differing (D) narrow (E) crooked

220. **DIVULGE** (A) look (B) refuse (C) deride (D) reveal (E) harm

221. **DOCUMENT** (A) withdraw (B) provide evidence (C) remain active (D) control (E) start

222. **DOGMATIC** (A) benign (B) canine (C) impatient (D) petulant (E) arbitrary

223. **DORMANT** (A) latent (B) silent (C) sensitive (D) aloof (E) obedient

224. **DOUR** (A) sullen (B) ornamental (C) grizzled (D) lacking speech (E) international

225. **DUBIOUS** (A) rotund (B) doubtful (C) fearsome (D) tiny (E) strange

dwindle \'dwin-dəl\ v. SHRINK; REDUCE. The food in the lifeboat gradually *dwindled* away to nothing; in the end, they ate the ship's cook.

dynamic \dī-'na-mik\ adj. ENERGETIC; ACTIVE. The *dynamic* aerobics instructor kept her students on the run; she was a little dynamo.

earthy \'ər-thē\ adj. UNREFINED; COARSE. His *earthy* remarks often embarrassed the women in his audience.

ebb \'eb\ v. RECEDE; LESSEN. Sitting on the beach, Mrs. Dalloway watched the waters recede as the tide slowly *ebbed*. //also n.

ebullient \i-'búl-yənt, -'bəl-\ adj. SHOWING EXCITEMENT; OVERFLOWING WITH ENTHUSIASM. Amy's *ebullient* nature could not be repressed; she was always bubbling over with excitement. //ebullience, n.

eccentric \ik-'sen-trik, ek-\ adj. ODD; WHIMSICAL; IRREGULAR. The comet veered dangerously close to the earth in its *eccentric* orbit. //eccentricity, n.

eclectic \e-'klek-tik, i-\ adj. COMPOSED OF ELEMENTS DRAWN FROM DISPARATE SOURCES. Dale's taste in interior decoration was *eclectic*: he would select bits and pieces of furnishings from widely divergent periods and strikingly juxtapose them to create a unique decor.

eclipse \i-'klips\ v. DARKEN; EXTINGUISH; SURPASS. The new stock market high *eclipsed* the previous record set in 1985.

ecologist \i-'kä-lə-jist, e-\ n. A PERSON CONCERNED WITH THE INTERRELATIONSHIP BETWEEN LIVING ORGANISMS AND THEIR ENVIRONMENT. The *ecologist* was concerned that the new dam would upset the natural balance of the creatures living in Glen Canyon.

ecstasy \'ek-stə-sē\ n. RAPTURE; JOY; ANY OVERPOWERING EMOTION. When Allison received her long-hoped-for letter of acceptance from Yale, she was in *ecstasy*. //ecstatic, adj.

edify \'e-də-ˌfī\ v. INSTRUCT; CORRECT MORALLY. Although his purpose was to *edify* and not to entertain his audience, many of his listeners were amused and not enlightened.

eerie \'ir-ē\ adj. WEIRD. In that *eerie* setting, it was easy to believe in ghosts and other supernatural beings.

efface \i-'fās, e-\ v. RUB OUT. The coin had been handled so many times that its date had been *effaced*.

effectual \i-'fek-chə(-wə)l, -chü(-ə)l; -'feksh-wəl\ adj. ABLE TO PRODUCE THE DESIRED EFFECT; VALID. Medical researchers are concerned because of the development of drug-resistant strains of bacteria; many once useful antibiotics are no longer *effectual* in curing bacterial infections.

effeminate \ə-'fe-mə-nət\ adj. HAVING WOMANLY TRAITS. "*Effeminate* men intrigue me more than anything in the world. I see them as my alter egos. I feel very drawn to them. I think like a guy, but I'm feminine. So I relate to feminine men." (Madonna)

effervescence \ˌe-fər-'ve-sən(t)s\ n. INNER EXCITEMENT; EXUBERANCE. Nothing depressed her for long; her natural *effervescence* soon reasserted itself. //effervescent, adj.; effervesce, v.

efficacy \'e-fi-kə-sē\ n. POWER TO PRODUCE DESIRED EFFECT. I'm not convinced of the *efficacy* of this decongestant; although I've been taking it regularly for three weeks, my sinuses are still blocked. //efficacious, adj.

effrontery \i-'frən-tə-rē, e-\ n. SHAMELESS BOLDNESS. When his boss told Frank that she was firing him for laziness and insubordination, he had the *effrontery* to ask her for a letter of recommendation.

effusive \i-'fyü-siv, e-, -ziv\ adj. POURING FORTH; GUSHING. Unmoved by Martha's many compliments on his performance, George dismissed her *effusive* words of praise as the outpourings of an overemotional fool. //effusion, n.

egoism \\'ē-gə-ˌwi-zəm, -gō-ˌi- *also* 'e-\\ n. EXCESSIVE INTEREST IN ONE'S SELF; BELIEF THAT ONE SHOULD BE INTERESTED IN ONE'S SELF RATHER THAN IN OTHERS. His *egoism* prevented him from seeing the needs of his colleagues.

egotistical \\ˌē-gə-'tis-ti-kəl\\ adj. EXCESSIVELY SELF-CENTERED; SELF-IMPORTANT; CONCEITED. Typical *egotistical* remark: "But enough of this chit-chat about you and your little problems. Let's talk about what's really important: me!"

egregious \\i-'grē-jəs\\ adj. NOTORIOUS; CONSPICUOUSLY BAD OR SHOCKING. She was an *egregious* liar; we all knew better than to believe a word she said.

egress \\'ē-ˌgres\\ n. EXIT. If you were at the circus and saw a sign "This Way to the *Egress*," would you think you were going to see a wild animal or would you realize that you had found the way out?

elaboration \\i-ˌla-bə-'rā-shən\\ n. ADDITION OF DETAILS; INTRICACY. Tell what happened simply, without any *elaboration*. //elaborate, v.

elated \\i-'lā-təd\\ adj. OVERJOYED; IN HIGH SPIRITS. Grinning from ear to ear, Janet Evans was clearly *elated* by her Olympic victory. //elation, n.

elegy \\'e-lə-ˌjē \\ n. MOURNFUL POEM; LAMENT FOR THE DEAD. Moved by the death of his college friend Edward King, John Milton wrote his famous *elegy* "Lycidas." //elegiacal, adj.

elicit \\i-'li-sət\\ v. DRAW OUT (BY DISCUSSION); CALL FORTH. The camp counselor's humorous remarks finally *elicited* a smile from the shy new camper.

eloquence \\'e-lə-kwən(t)s\\ n. EXPRESSIVENESS; PERSUASIVE SPEECH. The crowds were stirred by Martin Luther King, Jr.'s *eloquence*.

elucidate \i-'lü-sə-ˌdāt\ v. EXPLAIN; ENLIGHTEN. He was called upon to *elucidate* the disputed points in his article.

elusive \ē-'lü-siv, -'lü-ziv\ adj. EVASIVE; BAFFLING; HARD TO GRASP. No matter how hard Tom tried to lure the trout into taking the bait, the fish was too *elusive* for him to catch. //elude, v.

emaciated \i-'mā-shē-ˌā- təd\ adj. THIN AND WASTED. Many severe illnesses leave the victims so *emaciated* that they must gain back their lost weight before they can fully recover.

emanate \'e-mə-ˌnāt\ v. ISSUE FORTH. A strong odor of sulphur *emanated* from the spring.

emancipate \i-'man(t)-sə-ˌpāt\ v. SET FREE. At first, the attempts of the Abolitionists to *emancipate* the slaves were unpopular in New England as well as in the South.

embark \im-'bärk\ v. COMMENCE; GO ON BOARD A BOAT OR AIRPLANE; BEGIN A JOURNEY. In devoting herself to the study of gorillas, Dian Fossey *embarked* on a course of action that was to cost her her life.

embed \im-'bed\ v. ENCLOSE; PLACE IN SOMETHING. Tales of actual historical figures like King Alfred have become *embedded* in legends.

embellish \im-'be-lish\ v. ADORN. The costume designer *embellished* the leading lady's ball gown with yards and yards of ribbon and lace.

embezzlement \im-'be-zəl- mənt, em-\ n. STEALING. The bank teller confessed his *embezzlement* of the funds. //embezzle, v.; embezzler n.

embroil \im-'brȯi(-ə)l\ v. THROW INTO CONFUSION; INVOLVE IN STRIFE; ENTANGLE. He became *embroiled* in the heated discussion when he tried to arbitrate the dispute.

embryonic \ˌem-brē-'ä-nik\ adj. UNDEVELOPED; RUDIMEN-TARY. The CEO reminisced about the good old days when the computer industry was still in its *embryonic* stage and a startup company could be founded in the family garage.

emend \ē-'mend\ v. CORRECT (USUALLY A TEXT). In editing *Beowulf* for his new scholarly edition, Professor Oliver freely *emended* the manuscript's text whenever it seemed to make no sense. //emendation, n.

eminent \'e-mə-nənt\ adj. HIGH; LOFTY; FAMOUS; CELEBRATED. After his appointment to this *eminent* position, he seldom had time for his former friends.

emissary \'e-mə-,ser-ē, -,se-rē\ n. AGENT; MESSENGER. The secretary of state was sent as the president's special *emissary* to the conference on disarmament.

emollient \i-'mäl-yənt\ n. SOOTHING OR SOFTENING REMEDY. *Emollients* such as lanolin or almond oil are used to soften the skin by slowing the evaporation of water. //also adj.

empirical \im-'pir-i-kəl, em-\ adj. BASED ON EXPERIENCE; VERIFIABLE BY EXPERIMENT OR OBSERVATION; PRAGMATIC. He distrusted hunches and intuitive flashes; he placed his reliance entirely on *empirical* data.

emulate \'em-yə-,lāt, -yü-\ v. RIVAL; IMITATE. In a brief essay, describe a person you admire, someone whose virtues you would like to *emulate*.

encompass \in-'kəm-pəs, en- *also* -'käm-\ v. SURROUND OR ENCIRCLE; ENCLOSE; INCLUDE. A moat, or deep water-filled trench, *encompassed* the castle, protecting it from attack.

encroachment \in-'krōch- mənt, en-\ n. GRADUAL INTRUSION. The *encroachment* of the factories upon the neighborhood lowered the value of the real estate. //encroach, v.

Each of the questions below consists of a word in capital letters, followed by five words or phrases. Choose the word or phrase that is most similar in meaning to the word in capital letters and write the letter of your choice on your answer paper.

226. **DWINDLE** (A) blow (B) inhabit (C) spin (D) lessen (E) combine

227. **ECSTASY** (A) joy (B) speed (C) treasure (D) warmth (E) lack

228. **EDIFY** (A) mystify (B) suffice (C) improve (D) erect (E) entertain

229. **EFFACE** (A) countenance (B) encourage (C) recognize (D) blackball (E) rub out

230. **EFFERVESCENCE** (A) requisition (B) warmth (C) charge (D) accord (E) exuberance

231. **EGREGIOUS** (A) pious (B) shocking (C) anxious (D) sociable (E) gloomy

232. **EGRESS** (A) entrance (B) bird (C) exit (D) double (E) progress

233. **ELATED** (A) debased (B) respectful (C) drooping (D) gay (E) charitable

234. **ELUSIVE** (A) deadly (B) eloping (C) evasive (D) simple (E) petrified

235. **EMACIATED** (A) garrulous (B) primeval (C) vigorous (D) disparate (E) thin

236. **EMANCIPATE** (A) set free (B) take back (C) make worse (D) embolden (E) run away

237. **EMBELLISH** (A) doff (B) don (C) balance (D) adorn (E) equalize

238. **EMBEZZLEMENT** (A) stealing (B) interpretation (C) exhumation (D) inquiry (E) fault

239. **EMEND** (A) cherish (B) repose (C) correct (D) assure (E) worry

240. **EMINENT** (A) purposeful (B) high (C) delectable (D) curious (E) urgent

encumber \in-'kəm-bər\ v. BURDEN. Some people *encumber* themselves with too much luggage when they take short trips.

endemic \en-'de-mik, in-\ adj. PREVAILING AMONG A SPECIFIC GROUP OF PEOPLE OR IN A SPECIFIC AREA OR COUNTRY. This disease is *endemic* in this part of the world; more than 80 percent of the population are at one time or another affected by it.

endorse \in-'dȯrs, en-\ v. APPROVE; SUPPORT. Everyone waited to see which one of the rival candidates for the city council the mayor would *endorse*. (secondary meaning) //endorsement, n.

energize \'e-nər-ˌjīz\ v. INVIGORATE; MAKE FORCEFUL AND ACTIVE. Rather than exhausting Maggie, dancing *energized* her.

enervate \'e-nər-ˌvāt\ v. WEAKEN. She was slow to recover from her illness; even a short walk to the window *enervated* her. //enervation, n.

engender \in-'jen-dər, en-\ v. CAUSE; PRODUCE. To receive praise for real accomplishments *engenders* self-confidence in a child.

engross \in-'grōs, en-\ v. OCCUPY FULLY. John was so *engrossed* in his studies that he did not hear his mother call.

enhance \in-'han(t)s, en-\ v. ADVANCE; IMPROVE. You can *enhance* your chances of being admitted to the college of your choice by learning to write well; an excellent essay will *enhance* any application.

enigmatic \ˌe-(ˌ)nig-'ma-tik *also* ˌē-(ˌ)nig-\ adj. OBSCURE; PULLING. Many have sought to fathom the *enigmatic* smile of the Mona Lisa. //enigma, n.

enmity \'en-mə-tē\ n. ILL WILL; HATRED. At Camp David, President Carter labored to bring an end to the *enmity* that prevented the peaceful coexistence of Egypt and Israel.

enormity \i-'nȯr-mə-tē\ n. HUGENESS (IN A BAD SENSE). He did not realize the *enormity* of his crime until he saw what suffering he had caused.

enrapture \in-'rap-chər, en-\ v. PLEASE INTENSELY. The audience was *enraptured* by the freshness of the voices and the excellent orchestration.

ensconce \in-'skän(t)s\ v. SETTLE COMFORTABLY. Now that the children were *ensconced* safely in their private school, the jet-setting parents decided to leave for Europe.

enthrall \in-'thrȯl, en-\ v. CAPTURE; ENSLAVE. From the moment he saw her picture, he was *enthralled* by her beauty.

entice \in-'tīs, en-\ v. LURE; ATTRACT; TEMPT. Would the mayor's attempts to *entice* the members of the International Olympic Committee to select his city as the site of the 2020 Olympic Games succeed? Only time would tell.

entity \'en-tə-tē, ˌe-nə-\ n. REAL BEING. As soon as the Charter was adopted, the United Nations became an *entity* and had to be considered as a factor in world diplomacy.

entomology \ˌen-tə-'mä-lə-jē\ n. STUDY OF INSECTS. Kent found *entomology* the most annoying part of his biology course; studying insects bugged him.

entrance \in-'tran(t)s, en-\ v. PUT UNDER A SPELL; CARRY AWAY WITH EMOTION. Shafts of sunlight on a wall could *entrance* her and leave her spellbound.

entreat \in-'trēt, en-\ v. PLEAD; ASK EARNESTLY. She *entreated* her father to let her stay out until midnight.

entrepreneur \ˌäⁿ-trə-p(r)ə-'nər, -'n(y) u̇r\ n. BUSINESS-MAN; CONTRACTOR. Opponents of our present tax program argue that it discourages *entrepreneurs* from trying new fields of business activity.

enunciate \ē-'nən(t)-sē-ˌāt\ v. SPEAK DISTINCTLY. Stop mumbling! How will people understand you if you do not *enunciate* clearly?

ephemeral \i-ˈfem-rəl, -ˈfēm-; -ˈfe-mə-, -ˈfē-\ adj.
SHORT-LIVED; FLEETING. The mayfly is an *ephemeral*
creature: its adult life lasts little more than a day.

epic \ˈe-pik\ n. LONG HEROIC POEM, NOVEL, OR SIMILAR WORK
OF ART. Kurosawa's film *Seven Samurai* is an *epic*
portraying the struggle of seven warriors to destroy a
band of robbers. //also adj.

epic \ˈe-pik\ adj. UNUSUALLY GREAT IN SIZE OR EXTENT;
HEROIC; IMPRESSIVE. The task of renovating the decrepit
subway system was one of truly *epic* dimensions: it
would cost millions of dollars and involve thousands
of laborers working night and day.

epicure \ˈe-pi-ˌkyur\ n. CONNOISSEUR OF FOOD AND DRINK.
Epicures frequent this restaurant because it features
exotic wines and dishes. //epicurean, adj.

epigram \ˈe-pə-ˌgram\ n. WITTY THOUGHT OR SAYING, USUALLY
SHORT. Poor Richard's *epigrams* made Benjamin
Franklin famous.

epilogue \ˈe-pə-ˌlòg, -ˌläg\ n. SHORT SPEECH AT CONCLUSION
OF DRAMATIC WORK. The audience was so disappointed
in the play that many did not remain to hear the
epilogue.

epitaph \ˈe-pə-ˌtaf\ n. INSCRIPTION IN MEMORY OF A DEAD
PERSON. In his will, he dictated the *epitaph* he wanted
placed on his tombstone.

epithet \ˈe-pə-ˌthet *also* -thət\ n. DESCRIPTIVE WORD OR
PHRASE. So many kings of France were named Charles
that modern students need *epithets* to tell them apart:
it's easy to distinguish Charles the Wise, for example,
from the very different Charles the Fat.

epitome \i-ˈpi-tə-mē\ n. PERFECT EXAMPLE OR EMBODIMENT.
Singing "I am the very model of a modern Major-
General," Major-General Stanley proclaimed himself
the *epitome* of an officer and a gentleman. //epito-
mize, v.

epoch \ˈe-pək, ˈe-ˌpäk\ n. PERIOD OF TIME. The glacial
epoch lasted for thousands of years.

equanimity \\,ē-kwə-'ni-mə-tē, ,e-kwə-\\ n. CALMNESS OF TEMPERAMENT; COMPOSURE. Even the inevitable strains of caring for an ailing mother did not disturb Betty's *equanimity*.

equestrian \\i-'kwes-trē-ən\\ n. RIDER ON HORSEBACK. These paths in the park are reserved for *equestrians* and their steeds. //also adj.

equilibrium \\,ē-kwə-'li-brē-əm, ,e-\\ n. BALANCE. After the divorce, he needed some time to regain his *equilibrium*.

equitable \\'e-kwə-tə-bəl\\ adj. FAIR; IMPARTIAL. I am seeking an *equitable* solution to this dispute, one that will be fair and acceptable to both sides. //equity, n.

equivocal \\i-'kwi-və-kəl\\ adj. AMBIGUOUS; INTENTIONALLY MISLEADING. Rejecting the candidate's *equivocal* comments on tax reform, the reporters pressed him to state clearly where he stood on the issue.

equivocate \\i-'kwi-və-,kāt\\ v. LIE; MISLEAD; ATTEMPT TO CONCEAL THE TRUTH. No matter how bad the news is, give it to us straight. Above all, don't *equivocate*.

erode \\i-'rōd\\ v. EAT AWAY. The limestone was *eroded* by the dripping water until only a thin shell remained. //erosion, n.

erratic \\i-'ra-tik\\ adj. ODD; UNPREDICTABLE. Investors become anxious when the stock market appears *erratic*.

erroneous \\i-'rō-nē-əs, e-\\ adj. MISTAKEN; WRONG. I thought my answer was correct, but it was *erroneous*.

erudite \\'er-ə-dīt, 'er-yə-\\ adj. LEARNED; SCHOLARLY. Unlike much scholarly writing, Huizinga's prose was entertaining as well as *erudite*, lively as well as learned. //erudition, n.

escapade \\'es-kə-,pād\\ n. PRANK; FLIGHTY CONDUCT. The headmaster could not regard this latest *escapade* as a boyish joke and expelled the young man.

esoteric \,e-sə-'ter-ik, -'te-rik\ adj. KNOWN ONLY TO THE CHOSEN FEW. Stories in *The New Yorker* often include allusions to obscure people and events, references so *esoteric* that only true New Yorkers can understand them.

espionage \'es-pē-ə-,näzh, -,näj, -nij \ n. SPYING. In order to maintain its power, the government developed a system of *espionage* that penetrated every household.

espouse \is-'paùz *also* -'paùs\ v. ADOPT; SUPPORT. She was always ready to *espouse* a worthy cause.

esteem \i-'stēm\ v. RESPECT; VALUE; JUDGE. Jill *esteemed* Jack's taste in music, but she deplored his taste in clothes. //also n.

estranged \i-'stränjd\ adj. SEPARATED; ALIENATED. The *estranged* wife sought a divorce. //estrangement, n.

ethereal \i-'thir-ē-əl\ adj. LIGHT; HEAVENLY. In Shakespeare's *The Tempest*, the spirit Ariel is an *ethereal* creature, too airy and unearthly for our mortal world.

etymology \,e-tə-'mä-lə-jē\ n. STUDY OF WORD PARTS. A knowledge of *etymology* can help you on many English tests: if you know what the roots and prefixes mean, you can determine the meanings of unfamiliar words.

Each of the questions below consists of a word in capital letters, followed by five words or phrases. Choose the word or phrase that is most similar in meaning to the word in capital letters and write the letter of your choice on your answer paper.

241. **ENERVATE** (A) weaken (B) sputter (C) arrange (D) scrutinize (E) agree

242. **ENHANCE** (A) improve (B) doubt (C) scuff (D) gasp (E) agree

243. **ENMITY** (A) promise (B) hatred (C) seriousness (D) humility (E) kindness

244. **ENUNCIATE** (A) pray (B) request (C) deliver (D) wait (E) pronounce

245. **EPHEMERAL** (A) sensuous (B) passing (C) popular (D) distasteful (E) temporary

246. **EPIC** (A) flat (B) decisive (C) heroic (D) rough (E) frightening

247. **EQUANIMITY** (A) calmness (B) stirring (C) volume (D) identity (E) luster

248. **EQUILIBRIUM** (A) balance (B) peace (C) inequity (D) directness (E) urgency

249. **EQUITABLE** (A) able to leave (B) able to learn (C) fair (D) preferable (E) rough

250. **EQUIVOCAL** (A) mistaken (B) quaint (C) azure (D) ambiguous (f) universal

251. **ERRATIC** (A) unromantic (B) free (C) popular (D) unpredictable (E) unknown

252. **ERRONEOUS** (A) incorrect (B) dignified (C) curious (D) abrupt (E) round

253. **ERUDITE** (A) professional (B) stately (C) short (D) unknown (E) scholarly

254. **ESOTERIC** (A) consistent (B) specialized (C) permanent (D) extensive (E) ambivalent

255. **ESTRANGED** (A) long-lasting (B) separated (C) ill (D) critical (E) false

eulogy \'yü-lə-jē\ n. PRAISE. Instead of delivering a spoken *eulogy* at Genny's funeral service, Jeff sang a song he had written in her honor. //eulogize, v; eulogistic, adj.

euphemism \'yü-fə-ˌmi-zəm\ n. MILD EXPRESSION IN PLACE OF AN UNPLEASANT ONE. The Nazis did not describe their slaughter of the Jews as genocide; instead, they used a *euphemism*, calling it "the final solution."

euphonious \yü-'fō-nē-əs\ adj. PLEASING IN SOUND. *Euphonious* when spoken, the Italian language is particularly pleasing to the ear when sung.

evanescent \ˌe-və-'ne-sᵊnt\ adj. FLEETING; VANISHING. For a brief moment, the entire skyline was bathed in an orange-red hue in the *evanescent* rays of the sunset.

evasive \i-'vā-siv, -ziv, ē-\ adj. NOT FRANK; ELUDING. The witness's *evasive* answers convinced the judge that she was withholding important evidence. //evade, v.

evocative \i-'vä-kə-tiv\ adj. TENDING TO CALL UP (EMOTIONS, MEMORIES). Scent can be remarkably *evocative*: the aroma of pipe tobacco *evokes* the memory of my father; a whiff of talcum powder calls up images of my daughter as a child. //evoke, v.

exacerbate \ig-'za-sər-ˌbāt\ v. WORSEN; EMBITTER; AGGRAVATE. When acacias are in bloom, the increase of pollen in the air *exacerbates* Richard's asthma.

exalt \ig-'zȯlt\ v. RAISE IN RANK OR DIGNITY; PRAISE. The rock star Mick Jagger was *exalted* to the rank of knighthood by the Queen; he now is known as Sir Mick Jagger.

exasperate \ig-'zas-pə-ˌrāt\ v. VEX; ENRAGE. Johnny often *exasperates* his mother with his pranks.

exculpate \'ek-(ˌ)skəl-ˌpāt, (ˌ)ek-\ v. CLEAR FROM BLAME. The defense lawyer sought evidence that would *exculpate* her client, but the case for his guilt was too strong.

execute \'ek-si-ˌkyüt\ v. PUT INTO EFFECT; CARRY OUT. The choreographer wanted to see how well she could *execute* a pirouette. (secondary meaning) //execution, n.

exemplary \ig-'zem-plə-rē\ adj. SERVING AS A MODEL; OUTSTANDING. At commencement, the Dean praised Ellen for her *exemplary* behavior as class president.

exertion \ig-'zər-shən\ n. EFFORT; EXPENDITURE OF MUCH PHYSICAL WORK. The *exertion* involved in unscrewing the rusty bolt left her exhausted.

exhaustive \ig-'zȯ-stiv \ adj. THOROUGH; COMPREHENSIVE. We have made an *exhaustive* study of all published SAT tests and are happy to share our research with you.

exhort \ig-'zȯrt \ v. URGE. The evangelist *exhorted* all the sinners in the audience to repent.

exigency \'ek-sə-jən(t)-sē, ig-'zi-jən(t)-\ n. URGENT SITUATION; PRESSING NEEDS. The *exigencies* of war gave impetus to funding computer research in general and particularly to funding the development of code-breaking machines.

exonerate \ig-'zä-nə-ˌrāt, eg-\ v. ACQUIT; EXCULPATE. The defense team feverishly sought fresh evidence that might *exonerate* their client.

exorbitant \ig-'zȯr-bə-tənt\ adj. EXCESSIVE. The people grumbled at his *exorbitant* prices but paid them because he had a monopoly.

exorcise \'ek-ˌsȯr-ˌsīz, -sər-\ v. DRIVE OUT EVIL SPIRITS. By incantation and prayer, the medicine man sought to *exorcise* the evil spirits that had taken possession of the young warrior.

exotic \ig-'zä-tik\ adj. NOT NATIVE; STRANGE. To the migrant worker's daughter, even an ordinary drink like ginger ale seemed *exotic*.

expatriate \ek-'spā-trē-ˌāt\ n. EXILE; SOMEONE WHO HAS WITHDRAWN FROM HIS NATIVE LAND. Henry James was an American *expatriate* who settled in England.

expedient \ik-'spē-dē-ənt\ adj. SUITABLE; PRACTICAL; POLITIC. A pragmatic politician, he was guided by what was *expedient* rather than by what was ethical. //expediency, n.

expedite \'ek-spə-ˌdīt\ v. HASTEN. Because we are on a tight schedule, we hope that you will be able to *expedite* the delivery of our order.

expeditious \ˌek-spə-'di-shəs\ adj. RAPID AND EFFICIENT. The more *expeditious* your response is, the happier we will be.

expertise \'ek-(ˌ)spər-'tēz, -'tēs\ n. SPECIALIZED KNOWLEDGE; EXPERT SKILL. Although she was knowledgeable in a number of fields, she was hired for her particular *expertise* in computer programming.

expiate \'ek-spē-ˌāt\ v. MAKE AMENDS FOR (A SIN). In *Les Miserables*, Jean Valjean tried to *expiate* his crimes by performing acts of charity.

explicit \ik-'spli-sət\ adj. TOTALLY CLEAR; DEFINITE; CLEARLY DEFINED. Don't just hint around that you are dissatisfied; be *explicit* about what is bothering you.

exploit \'ek-ˌsploit, ik-'\ n. DEED OR ACTION, PARTICULARLY A BRAVE DEED. Raoul Wallenberg was noted for his *exploits* in rescuing Jews from Hitler's forces.

exploit \ik-'sploit, 'ek-ˌ\ v. MAKE USE OF, SOMETIMES UNJUSTLY. Cesar Chavez fought attempts to *exploit* migrant farmworkers in California. //exploitation, n.

expunge \ik-'spənj\ v. CANCEL; REMOVE. If you behave, I will *expunge* this notation from your record.

expurgate \'ek-spər-ˌgāt\ v. REMOVE OFFENSIVE PARTS OF A BOOK. The editors felt that certain passages in the book had to be *expurgated* before it could be used in the classroom.

extant \'ek-stənt; ek-'stant, 'ek-ˌ\ adj. STILL IN EXISTENCE. Although the book is long out of print, some copies are still *extant*.

extemporaneous \(ˌ)ek-ˌstem-pə-ˈrā-nē-əs\ adj. NOT PLANNED; IMPROMPTU. Departing from his prepared speech, the candidate made a few *extemporaneous*, off-the-cuff remarks.

extol \ik-ˈstōl\ v. PRAISE; GLORIFY. The president *extolled* the astronauts, calling them the pioneers of the space age.

extort \ik-ˈstȯrt\ v. WRING FROM; GET MONEY BY THREATS, ETC. The blackmailer *extorted* money from his victim.

extradition \ˌek-strə-ˈdi-shən\ n. SURRENDER OF PRISONER BY ONE STATE TO ANOTHER. The lawyers opposed the *extradition* of their client on the grounds that for more than five years he had been a model citizen.

extraneous \ek-ˈstrā-nē-əs\ adj. NOT ESSENTIAL; EXTERNAL. It was time to forget about *extraneous* concerns and to focus on the essentials of what needed to be done.

extricate \ˈek-strə-ˌkāt\ v. FREE; DISENTANGLE. Icebreakers were needed to *extricate* the trapped whales from the icy floes that closed them in.

extrovert \ˈek-strə-ˌvərt\ n. PERSON INTERESTED MOSTLY IN EXTERNAL OBJECTS AND ACTIONS. A good salesman is usually an *extrovert* who likes to mingle with people.

exuberance \ig-ˈzü-b(ə-)rən(t)s\ n. JOYFUL ENTHUSIASM; UNRESTRAINED VIGOR AND JOY; OVERFLOWING ABUNDANCE. I was bowled over by the *exuberance* of Amy's welcome. What an enthusiastic greeting! //exuberant, adj.

exult \ig-ˈzəlt\ v. REJOICE. We *exulted* when our team won the victory.

fabricate \ˈfa-bri-ˌkāt\ v. BUILD; LIE. If we *fabricate* the buildings in this project out of standardized sections, we can reduce construction costs considerably. Because of Jack's tendency to *fabricate*, Jill had trouble believing a word he said. //fabrication, n.

facade \fə-ˈsäd\ n. SUPERFICIAL OR FALSE APPEARANCE; FRONT (OF BUILDING). Becky's outward show of confidence was just a *facade* she assumed to hide her insecurity.

facetious \fə-'sē-shəs\ adj. HUMOROUS; JOCULAR. Tolstoy criticized George Bernard Shaw for the *facetious* tone of his play *Arms and the Man*, saying that one should not speak jestingly about war, an inherently serious subject.

facile \'fa-səl\ adj. READY OR FLUENT; EASILY ACCOMPLISHED; SUPERFICIAL. Words came easily to Jonathan: he was a *facile* speaker and prided himself on being ready to make a speech at a moment's notice.

facilitate \fə-'si-lə-ˌtāt\ v. MAKE LESS DIFFICULT; HELP BRING ABOUT. Rest and proper nourishment should *facilitate* the patient's recovery.

facsimile \fak-'si-mə-lē\ n. COPY. Many museums sell *facsimiles* of the works of art on display.

faction \'fak-shən\ n. PARTY; CLIQUE; DISSENSION. The quarrels and bickering of the two small *factions* within the club disturbed the majority of the members.

faculty \'fa-kəl-tē\ n. MENTAL OR PHYSICAL POWERS; TEACHING STAFF. As he grew old, Professor Twiggly feared he might lose his *faculties* and become unfit to teach. However, while he was in full possession of his *faculties*, the school couldn't kick him off the *faculty*.

Each of the questions below consists of a word in capital letters, followed by five words or phrases. Choose the word or phrase that is most similar in meaning to the word in capital letters and write the letter of your choice on your answer paper.

256. **EUPHONIOUS**   (A) harmonious   (B) lethargic   (C) literary   (D) significant   (E) merry

257. **EVASIVE**   (A) secretive   (B) correct   (C) empty   (D) fertile   (E) watchful

258. **EXALT**   (A) scandalize   (B) encourage   (C) avoid   (D) praise   (E) vanish

259. **EXASPERATE**   (A) confide   (B) formalize   (C) irritate   (D) betray   (E) bargain

260. **EXCULPATE**   (A) exonerate   (B) prevail   (C) acquire   (D) ravish   (E) accumulate

261. **EXECUTE**   (A) disobey   (B) endure   (C) prefer   (D) carry out   (E) fidget

262. **EXEMPLARY**   (A) innumerable   (B) philosophic   (C) physical   (D) model   (E) meditative

263. **EXHORT**   (A) decipher   (B) sadden   (C) integrate   (D) admit   (E) urge

264. **EXIGENCY**   (A) state of neglect   (B) refusal to consent   (C) urgency   (D) gain   (E) rebuke

265. **EXONERATE**   (A) forge   (B) clear from blame   (C) record   (D) doctor   (E) reimburse

266. **EXORBITANT**   (A) extravagant   (B) partisan   (C) military   (D) barbaric   (E) counterfeit

267. **EXTEMPORANEOUS**   (A) impromptu   (B) hybrid   (C) humiliating   (D) statesmanlike   (E) picturesque

268. **EXTRANEOUS**   (A) modern   (B) decisive   (C) unnecessary   (D) effective   (E) expressive

269. **EXTRICATE**   (A) punish   (B) release   (C) excel   (D) lubricate   (E) gesticulate

270. **EXULT**   (A) popularize   (B) enlarge   (C) summarize   (D) irritate   (E) rejoice

fallacious \fə-'lā-shəs\ adj. LOGICALLY UNSOUND; MISLEAD-ING. Paradoxically, *fallacious* reasoning does not always yield erroneous results: even though your logic may be faulty, the answer you get may nevertheless be correct.

fallible \'fa-lə-bəl\ adj. LIABLE TO ERR. I know I am *fallible*, but I feel confident that I am right this time.

fallow \'fa-(ˌ)lō\ adj. PLOWED BUT NOT SOWED; UNCULTIVATED. Farmers have learned that it is advisable to permit land to lie *fallow* every few years.

falter \'fȯl-tər\ v. HESITATE. When told to dive off the high board, she did not *falter*, but proceeded at once.

fanaticism \fə-'na-tə-ˌsi-zəm\ n. EXCESSIVE ZEAL; EXTREME DEVOTION TO A BELIEF OR CAUSE. When Islamic funda-mentalists demanded the death of Salman Rushdie because his novel questioned their faith, world opin-ion condemned them for their *fanaticism*. //fanatic, adj., n.

fanciful \'fan(t)-si-fəl\ adj. WHIMSICAL; VISIONARY. Martin had a *fanciful* notion to paint his toenails purple.

fantastic \fan-'tas-tik, fən-\ adj. UNREAL; GROTESQUE; WHIMSICAL. Special effects and animation techniques allow moviemakers to show *fantastic* creatures such as giants, elves, and dwarves interacting with ordi-nary human beings.

farce \'färs\ n. BROAD COMEDY; MOCKERY. Nothing went right; the entire interview degenerated into a *farce*. //farcical, adj.

fastidious \fa-'sti-dē-əs, fə-\ adj. DIFFICULT TO PLEASE; SQUEAMISH. Barry was such a *fastidious* eater that he would eat a sandwich only if his mother first cut off every scrap of crust.

fatalism \'fā-tə-ˌli-zəm\ n. BELIEF THAT EVENTS ARE DETER-MINED BY FORCES BEYOND ONE'S CONTROL. With *fatalism*, he accepted the hardships that beset him. //fatalistic, adj; fatalist n.

fatuous \'fa-chü-əs, -tyü-\ adj. FOOLISH; INANE. It is *fatuous* for publishers to believe that a few flashy quotes on a dust jacket cover will dazzle readers so much that they won't notice that the book itself is not worth the paper it is printed on.

fawning \'fo-niŋ, 'fä-\ adj. OBSEQUIOUS; SERVILE; BOOT-LICK-ING. In *Pride and Prejudice*, Mr. Collins is the arche-typal *fawning* clergyman, wholly dependent for his living on the goodwill of his patron, Lady Catherine, whom he flatters shamelessly. //fawn, v.

feasible \'fē-zə-bəl\ adj. PRACTICAL. Without additional funding, it may not be *feasible* to build a new stadium for the Yankees on New York's West Side.

fecundity \fi-'kən-də-tē, fe-\ n. FERTILITY; FRUITFULNESS. Rabbits are noted for their *fecundity*: in the absence of natural predators, they multiply, well, like rabbits, as the Australians learned to their dismay. //fecund, adj.

feign \'fān\ v. PRETEND. Bobby *feigned* illness, hoping that his mother would let him stay home from school.

feint \'fānt\ n. TRICK; SHIN; SHAM BLOW. The boxer was fooled by his opponent's *feint* and dropped his guard. //also v.

felicitous \fi-'li-sə-təs\ adj. APT; SUITABLY EXPRESSED; WELL CHOSEN. Tyndale's greatest achievement as a transla-tor was that he struck a *felicitous* balance between the demands of biblical scholarship and the need for simplicity of expression. //felicity, n.

felon \'fe-lən\ n. PERSON CONVICTED OF A GRAVE CRIME. A convicted *felon* loses the right to vote.

ferment \'fər-ˌment *also* (ˌ)fər-'\ n. AGITATION; COMMOTION. With the breakup of the Soviet Union, much of Eastern Europe was in a state of *ferment*.

fervor \'fər-vər\ n. GLOWING ARDOR; ENTHUSIASM. At the protest rally, the students cheered the strikers and booed the Dean with equal *fervor*. //fervid, fervent, adj.

festive \'fes-tiv\ adj. JOYOUS; CELEBRATORY. Their wedding in the park was a *festive* occasion.

fetid \'fe-təd\ adj. MALODOROUS; FOUL-SMELLING. When a polecat is alarmed, the scent gland under its tail emits a *fetid* secretion used for territorial marking.

fetter \'fe-tər\ v. SHACKLE. The prisoner was *fettered* to the wall.

fiasco \fē-'as-(ˌ)kō *also* -'äs-\ n. TOTAL FAILURE. Tanya's attempt to look sophisticated by smoking was a *fiasco:* she lit the wrong end of the cigarette and choked when she tried to inhale.

fickle \'fi-kəl\ adj. CHANGEABLE; FAITHLESS. As soon as Romeo saw Juliet, he forgot all about his old girlfriend Rosaline. Was Romeo *fickle*?

fictitious \fik-'ti-shəs\ adj. IMAGINARY. Autobiographical memoirs are supposed to be true to life; for this reason, many readers become indignant when they learn that incidents shown in a memoir are actually *fictitious*.

fidelity \fə-'de-lə-tē, fī-\ n. LOYALTY. Iago wickedly manipulates Othello, arousing his jealousy and causing him to question his wife's *fidelity*.

finale \fə-'na-lē, fi-'nä-\ n. CONCLUSION. It is not until we reach the *finale* of this play that we can understand the author's message.

finesse \fə-'nes\ n. DELICATE SKILL. The *finesse* and adroitness with which the surgeon wielded her scalpel impressed the observers in the operating theater.

finite \'fī-ˌnīt\ adj. LIMITED. Though Bill really wanted to win the pie-eating contest, the capacity of his stomach was *finite*, and he had to call it quits after eating only seven cherry pies.

firebrand \'fi(-ə)r-,brand\ n. HOTHEAD; TROUBLEMAKER. The police tried to keep track of all the local *firebrands* when the president came to town.

fitful \'fit-fəl\ adj. SPASMODIC; INTERMITTENT. After several *fitful* attempts, he decided to postpone the start of the project until he felt more energetic.

flaccid \'fla-səd *also* 'flak-səd\ adj. FLABBY. His sedentary life had left him with *flaccid* muscles.

flagging \'fla-giŋ\ adj. WEAK; DROOPING. The encouraging cheers of the crowd lifted the team's *flagging* spirits. //flag, v.

flagrant \'flā-grənt *also* 'fla-\ adj. CONSPICUOUSLY WICKED. The governor's appointment of his brother-in-law to the state Supreme Court was a *flagrant* violation of the state laws against nepotism.

flair \'fler\ n. TALENT. She has an uncanny *flair* for discovering new artists before the public has become aware of their existence.

flamboyant \flam-'bòi-ənt\ adj. STRIKINGLY BOLD OR BRILLIANT; ORNATE. Modern architecture has discarded the *flamboyant* trimming on buildings and emphasizes simplicity of line.

flaunt \'flȯnt, 'flänt\ v. DISPLAY OSTENTATIOUSLY. Mae West saw nothing wrong with showing off her considerable physical charms, saying, "Honey, if you've got it, *flaunt* it!"

fleck \flek\ v. SPOT. Jackson Pollack's coveralls, *flecked* with paint, bore witness to the sloppiness of the spatter school of art.

fledgling \'flej-liŋ\ adj. INEXPERIENCED. The folk dance club set up an apprentice program to allow *fledgling* dance callers a chance to polish their skills. //also n.

fleece \'flēs\ n. WOOL COAT OF A SHEEP. They shear sheep of their *fleece*, which they then comb into separate strands of wool.

fleece \\'flēs\ v. ROB; PLUNDER. The tricksters *fleeced* him of his inheritance.

flick \\'flik\ n. LIGHT STROKE AS WITH A WHIP. The horse needed no encouragement; one *flick* of the whip was all the jockey had to apply to get the animal to run at top speed.

flinch \\'flinch\ v. HESITATE; SHRINK. He did not *flinch* in the face of danger but fought back bravely.

Each of the questions below consists of a word in capital letters, followed by five words or phrases. Choose the word or phrase that is most similar in meaning to the word in capital letters and write the letter of your choice on your answer paper.

271. **FANCIFUL** (A) imaginative (B) knowing (C) elaborate (D) quick (E) lusty

272. **FATUOUS** (A) fatal (B) natal (C) terrible (D) silly (E) tolerable

273. **FEASIBLE** (A) theoretical (B) impatient (C) constant (D) present (E) workable

274. **FECUNDITY** (A) prophecy (B) futility (C) fruitfulness (D) need (E) dormancy

275. **FEIGN** (A) deserve (B) condemn (C) condone (D) amend (E) pretend

276. **FELICITOUS** (A) apt (B) divergent (C) catastrophic (D) futile (E) inherent

277. **FERMENT** (A) stir up (B) fill (C) ferret (D) mutilate (E) banish

278. **FIASCO** (A) cameo (B) mansion (C) pollution (D) disaster (E) gamble

279. **FICKLE** (A) fallacious (B) tolerant (C) changeable (D) hungry (E) stupid

280. **FINESSE** (A) fatness (B) skill (C) itch (D) cancellation (E) resentment

281. **FINITE** (A) bounded (B) established (C) affirmative (D) massive (E) finicky

282. **FLAG** (A) reverse (B) harvest (C) distract (D) droop (E) resent

283. **FLAIR** (A) conflagration (B) inspiration (C) bent (D) egregiousness (E) magnitude

284. **FLAMBOYANT** (A) old-fashioned (B) gaudy (C) impulsive (D) cognizant (E) eloquent

285. **FLEDGLING** (A) weaving (B) bobbing (C) beginning (D) studying (E) flaying

WORD LIST 20
flippant–gadfly

flippant \\'fli-pənt\\ adj. LACKING PROPER SERIOUSNESS. When Mark told Mona he loved her, she dismissed his earnest declaration with a *flippant* "Oh, you say that to all the girls!" //flippancy, n.

floe \\'flō\\ n. MASS OF FLOATING ICE. The ship made slow progress as it battered its way through the ice *floes*.

florid \\'flȯr-əd, 'flär-\\ adj. OVERLY ORNATE; FLOWERY; REDDISH. He was an old-fashioned orator, known for his overblown rhetoric and his *florid* prose.

flourish \\'flər-ish, 'flə-rish\\ v. GROW WELL; PROSPER. The orange trees *flourished* in the sun.

flout \\'flaůt\\ v. REJECT; MOCK. The painter Julian Schnabel is known for works that *flout* the conventions of high art; rather than painting on canvas, he paints on velvet or even linoleum.

fluctuate \\'flək-chə-,wāt, -chü-,āt\\ v. WAVER. The temperature *fluctuated* so much, we seemed to be putting our jackets on one minute and taking them off the next.

fluency \\'flü-ən(t)-sē\\ n. SMOOTHNESS OF SPEECH. Because English was not Nguyen's native language, we did not expect him to converse with such *fluency*. //fluent, adj.

fluster \\'fləs-tər\\ v. CONFUSE. The teacher's sudden question *flustered* him and he stammered his reply.

flux \\'fləks\\ n. FLOWING; SERIES OF CHANGES. While conditions are in such a state of *flux*, l do not wish to commit myself too deeply in this affair.

foible \\'fȯi-bəl\\ n. WEAKNESS; SLIGHT FAULT. We can overlook the *foibles* of our friends; no one is perfect.

foil \\'fȯi(-ə)l\\ n. CONTRAST. In *Star Wars*, dark, evil Darth Vader is a perfect *foil* for fairhaired, naive Luke Skywalker.

foil \\'fȯi(-ə)l\\ v. DEFEAT; FRUSTRATE. In the end, Skywalker is able to *foil* Vader's diabolical schemes.

foment \'fō-,ment, fō-'\ v. STIR UP; INSTIGATE. Cynical even for a politician, he *fomented* conflicts among his fellow committee members to consolidate his own position.

foolhardy \'fül-,här-dē\ adj. RASH. Don't be *foolhardy*. Get the advice of a reputable investment counselor before buying junk bonds.

forbearance \ fȯr-'ber-ən(t)s, fər-\ n. ABSTINENCE; PATIENCE. John is still weak from his illness and some-what irritable; be patient with him and treat him with *forbearance*. //forbear, v.

foreboding \ fȯr-'bō-diŋ\ n. PREMONITION OF EVIL. Suspecting no conspiracies against him, Caesar gently ridiculed his wife's *forebodings* about the Ides of March.

forensic \fə-'ren(t)-sik, -'ren-zik\ adj. SUITABLE TO DEBATE OR TO COURTS OF LAW. In her best *forensic* manner, the lawyer addressed the jury.

foresight \'fȯr-,sīt\ n. ABILITY TO FORESEE FUTURE HAPPEN-INGS, PRUDENCE. A wise investor, she had the *foresight* to buy land just before the current real estate boom.

formality \fȯr-'ma-lə-tē\ n. ADHERENCE TO ESTABLISHED RULES OR PROCEDURES. Signing this is a mere *formality*; it does not obligate you in any way.

formidable \'fȯr-mə-də-bəl; fȯr-'mi-, fər-'mi-\ adj. INSPIR-ING FEAR OR APPREHENSION; DIFFICULT; AWE-INSPIRING. In the film *Meet the Parents*, the hero is understandably nervous around his fiancée's father, a *formidable* CIA agent.

forte \'fȯrt; *often* 'fȯr-,tā, fȯr-'tā *or* 'fȯr-tē\ n. STRONG POINT OR SPECIAL TALENT. l am not eager to play this rather serious role, for my *forte* is comedy.

fortitude \'fȯr-tə-,tüd, -,tyüd\ n. BRAVERY; COURAGE. He was awarded the medal for his *fortitude* in the battle.

fortuitous \fȯr-'tü-ə-təs, -'tyü-, fər-\ adj. ACCIDENTAL; BY CHANCE. Although he pretended their encounter was *fortuitous*, he had actually been hanging around her usual haunts for the past two weeks, hoping she would turn up.

foster \'fȯs-tər, 'fäs-\ v. REAR; ENCOURAGE. According to the legend, Romulus and Remus were *fostered* by a she-wolf, who raised the abandoned infants as her own. //also adj.

fracas \'frā-kəs, 'fra-\ n. BRAWL, MELEE. The military police stopped the *fracas* in the bar and arrested the belligerents.

frail \'frāl\ adj. WEAK. The delicate child seemed too *frail* to lift the heavy carton. //frailty, n.

franchise \'fran-,chīz\ n. RIGHT GRANTED BY AUTHORITY. The city issued a *franchise* to the company to operate surface transit lines on the streets for 99 years. //also v.

frantic \'fran-tik\ adj. WILD. At the time of the collision, many people became *frantic* with fear.

fraudulent \'frȯ-jə-lənt\ adj. CHEATING; DECEITFUL. The government seeks to prevent *fraudulent* and misleading advertising.

fray \'frā\ n. BRAWL. The three musketeers were in the thick of the *fray*.

frenetic \fri-'ne-tik\ adj. FRENZIED; FRANTIC. Unaccustomed to the *frenetic* pace of urban life, Tom found himself too exhausted to enjoy his new cosmopolitan lifestyle.

frenzied \'fren-zēd\ adj. MADLY EXCITED. As soon as they smelled smoke, the *frenzied* horses milled about in their stalls.

fret \'fret\ v. TO BE ANNOYED OR VEXED. To *fret* over your poor grades is foolish; instead, decide to work harder in the future.

friction \'frik-shən\ n. CLASH IN OPINION; RUBBING AGAINST. Rubbing two sticks against each other, the Boy Scout tried to use *friction* to create a spark.

frigid \\'fri-jəd\\ adj. INTENSELY COLD. Alaska is in the *frigid* zone.

fritter \\'fri-tər\\ v. WASTE. He could not apply himself to any task and *frittered* away his time in idle conversation.

frivolous \\'fri-və-ləs\\ adj. LACKING IN SERIOUSNESS; SELF-INDULGENTLY CAREFREE. Though Nancy enjoyed Bill's *frivolous*, lighthearted companionship, she sometimes wondered whether he could ever be serious. //frivolity, n.

frugality \\frü-'ga-lə-tē\\ n. THRIFT; ECONOMY. In economically hard times, anyone who does not learn to practice *frugality* risks bankruptcy. //frugal, adj.

fruition \\frü-'i-shən\\ n. BEARING OF FRUIT; FULFILLMENT; REALIZATION. After years of scrimping and saving, her dream of owning her own home finally came to *fruition*. //fruitful, adj.

frustrate \\'frəs-ˌtrāt\\ v. THWART; DEFEAT. Constant partisan bickering *frustrated* the governor's efforts to persuade the Legislature to approve his proposed budget. //frustration, n.

furtive \\'fər-tiv\\ adj. STEALTHY; SNEAKY. The boy gave a *furtive* look at his classmate's test paper.

fusion \\'fyü-zhən\\ n. UNION; COALITION; BLENDING. So-called rockabilly music represents a *fusion* of country music and blues that became rock 'n' roll.

futile \\'fyü-təl, 'fyü-ˌtī(-ə)l\\ adj. INEFFECTIVE; FRUITLESS. It is *futile* for me to try to get any work done around here while the telephone is ringing every 30 seconds.

gadfly \\'gad-ˌflī\\ n. ANIMAL-BITING FLY; AN IRRITATING PERSON. Like a *gadfly* he irritated all the guests at the hotel; within 48 hours, everyone regarded him as an annoying busybody.

Each of the questions below consists of a word in capital letters, followed by five words or phrases. Choose the word or phrase that is most similar in meaning to the word in capital letters and write the letter of your choice on your answer paper.

286. **FLORID**   (A) ruddy   (B) rusty   (C) ruined
     (D) patient   (E) poetic

287. **FLUENT**   (A) scanty   (B) radical   (C) orthodox
     (D) glib   (E) magnificent

288. **FOIL**   (A) bury   (B) frustrate   (C) defeat
     (D) desire   (E) gain

289. **FOMENT**   (A) spoil   (B) instigate   (C) interrogate
     (D) spray   (E) maintain

290. **FOOLHARDY**   (A) strong   (B) unwise   (C) brave
     (D) futile   (E) erudite

291. **FORBEARANCE**   (A) patience   (B) contest
     (C) range   (D) intuition   (E) amnesty

292. **FORMIDABLE**   (A) dangerous   (B) outlandish
     (C) grandiloquent   (D) impenetrable   (E) venerable

293. **FOSTER**   (A) speed   (B) fondle   (C) become infected
     (D) raise   (E) roll

294. **FRANCHISE**   (A) subway   (B) kiosk   (C) license
     (D) reason   (E) fashion

295. **FRITTER**   (A) sour   (B) chafe   (C) dissipate
     (D) cancel   (E) abuse

296. **FRUGALITY**   (A) foolishness   (B) extremity
     (C) indifference   (D) enthusiasm   (E) economy

297. **FRUITFUL**   (A) dizzy   (B) empty   (C) diverse
     (D) productive   (E) dreamy

298. **FRUSTRATION**   (A) hindrance   (B) emotion
     (C) flux   (D) complexity   (E) resignation

299. **FURTIVE**   (A) underhanded   (B) coy   (C) brilliant
     (D) quick   (E) abortive

300. **GADFLY**   (A) humorist   (B) nuisance   (C) scholar
     (D) bum   (E) thief

Each of the questions below consists of a sentence from which one word is missing. Choose the most appropriate replacement from among the five choices.

1. Though she claimed to be _____, the smirk on her face belied her sincerity.
   (A) discrete   (B) contrite   (C) disingenuous
   (D) effusive   (E) dogmatic

2. She received the "Employee of the Month" award for her _____ performance on the job.
   (A) evasive   (B) exemplary   (C) dubious
   (D) duplicitous   (E) contentious

3. There will never be a _____ dictionary of the English language because language continues to evolve over time.
   (A) defunct   (B) deducible   (C) dynamic
   (D) definitive   (E) eminent

4. The tooth marks on his paper _____ his story of his dog's misconduct.
   (A) convoluted   (B) denoted   (C) emanated
   (D) corroborated   (E) fabricated

5. I was disappointed when I learned that the impressive buildings at the theme park were merely empty _____.
   (A) facades   (B) exertions   (C) expedients
   (D) dross   (E) delusions

6. His enigmatic _____ fascinated his fellow students and provided the basis for numerous fantastic rumors.
   (A) demeanor   (B) criterion   (C) denouement
   (D) diminution   (E) fecundity

7. A procrastinator to the end, James studied for exams in short bursts of _____ activity.
   (A) florid   (B) discerning   (C) culpable
   (D) evasive   (E) frenetic

8. Thomas Hobbes and John Locke argue that government is necessary because men cannot be _____ judges in their own cases.
   (A) disjointed   (B) disinterested   (C) eccentric
   (D) eminent   (E) evanescent

9. Dr. Frankenstein's lack of _____ prevented him from considering what he would do with his creature once he brought it to life.
   (A) foibles   (B) fidelity   (C) foresight
       (D) erudition   (E) enmity

10. Though some believe that young children lack the capacity to _____, most parents will attest that their children are perfectly able to disguise their feelings.
    (A) distend   (B) contest   (C) cower
        (D) demure   (E) dissemble

11. The _____ of the town near the nuclear weapons test site exhibited an unusually high rate of leukemia and other cancers.
    (A) fusions   (B) denizens   (C) contortions
        (D) covenants   (E) counterparts

12. Before we spend money on this project, I would like _____, rather than theoretical, evidence that it is effective.
    (A) empirical   (B) egregious   (C) contextual
        (D) diffident   (E) extant

13. Despite having grown up in a bohemian, nonconformist household, Thelma was a _____ soul drawn to a more traditional way of life.
    (A) detached   (B) disgruntled   (C) conventional
        (D) farcical   (E) foolhardy

14. He felt that his affair with his secretary was a mere _____, but his wife felt that it was grounds for a divorce.
    (A) foible   (B) feint   (C) egoism
        (D) discretion   (E) disclosure

15. Scientists may suppose that large dinosaurs lived in swamps, but without substantiation that notion is mere _____.
    (A) contingency   (B) default   (C) digression
        (D) efficacy   (E) conjecture

gait \'gāt\ n. MANNER OF WALKING OR RUNNING; SPEED. The lame man walked with an uneven *gait*.

galaxy \'ga-lǝk-sē\ n. LARGE, ISOLATED SYSTEM OF STARS, SUCH AS THE MILKY WAY; ANY COLLECTION OF BRILLIANT PERSONALITIES. Science fiction stories speculate about the possible existence of life in other *galaxies*.

gall \'gȯl\ v. ANNOY; CHAFE. Their taunts *galled* him.

galleon \'ga-lē-ǝn\ n. LARGE SAILING SHIP. The Spaniards pinned their hopes on the *galleon*, the large warship; the British, on the smaller and faster pinnace.

galvanize \'gal-vǝ-ˌnīz\ v. STIMULATE BY SHOCK; STIR UP; REVITALIZE. News that the prince was almost at their door *galvanized* the ugly stepsisters into a frenzy of combing and primping.

gamely \'gām-lē\ adv. IN A SPIRITED MANNER; WITH COURAGE. Because he had fought *gamely* against a much superior boxer, the crowd gave him a standing ovation when he left the arena.

gamut \'ga-mǝt\ n. ENTIRE RANGE. In a classic put-down of actress Katharine Hepburn, the critic Dorothy Parker wrote that the actress ran the *gamut* of emotions from A to B.

gape \'gāp\ v. OPEN WIDELY. The huge pit *gaped* before him; if he stumbled, he would fall in.

garbled \'gär-bǝld\ adj. MIXED UP; BASED ON FALSE OR UNFAIR SELECTION; JUMBLED; DISTORTED. A favorite party game involves passing a whispered message from one person to another; by the time it reaches the last player, the message has become totally *garbled*.

gargantuan \gär-'gan(t)-sh(ǝ-)wǝn\ adj. HUGE; ENORMOUS. The *gargantuan* wrestler was terrified of mice.

garish \'ger-ish\ adj. OVERBRIGHT IN COLOR; GAUDY. She wore a rhinestone necklace with a *garish* red and gold dress trimmed with sequins.

garner \\'gär-nər\ v. GATHER; STORE UP. In her long career as an actress, Katharine Hepburn *garnered* many awards, including the coveted Oscar.

garnish \\'gär-nish\ v. DECORATE. Parsley was used to *garnish* the boiled potato. //also n.

garrulous \\'ger-ə-ləs, 'ga-rə- *also* 'ger-yə-\ adj. TALKATIVE; WORDY. My uncle Henry can out-talk any three people I know. He is the most *garrulous* person in Cayuga County. //garrulity, n.

gauche \\'gōsh\ adj. CLUMSY; BOORISH; COARSE AND UNCOUTH. Compared to the sophisticated young ladies in their elegant gowns, tomboyish Jo felt *gauche* and out of place.

gaudy \\'gȯ-dē, 'gä-\ adj. FLASHY; SHOWY. The newest Trump skyscraper is typically *gaudy*, covered in gilded panels that gleam in the sun.

gaunt \\'gȯnt, 'gänt\ adj. LEAN AND ANGULAR; BARREN. His once round face looked surprisingly *gaunt* after he had lost weight.

genealogy \\,jē-nē-'ä-lə-jē *also* -'a-lə-\ n. RECORD OF DESCENT; LINEAGE. He was proud of his *genealogy* and constantly referred to the achievements of his ancestors.

generality \\,je-nə-'ra-lə-tē\ n. VAGUE STATEMENT. This report is filled with *generalities*; you must be more specific in your statements.

generic \\jə-'ner-ik, -'ne-rik\ adj. CHARACTERISTIC OF A CLASS OR SPECIES. Susan knew so many computer programmers who spent their spare time playing fantasy games that she began to think that playing Dungeons and Dragons was a *generic* trait.

genesis \\'je-nə-səs\ n. BEGINNING; ORIGIN. Tracing the *genesis* of a family is the theme of *Roots*.

geniality \\,jē-nē-'a-lə-tē, jēn-'yal-\ n. CHEERFULNESS; KINDLINESS; SYMPATHY. Kindly Mr. Fezziwig who tried to make Scrooge and all his other employees happy exemplifies the spirit of *geniality*.

genre \'zhän-rə, 'zhäⁿ-; 'zhäⁿr; 'jän-rə\ n. PARTICULAR VARI-
ETY OF ART OR LITERATURE. Both a short story writer
and poet, Langston Hughes proved himself equally
skilled in either *genre*.

genteel \jen-'tēl\ adj. WELL-BRED; ELEGANT; FREE FROM VUL-
GARITY. Hoping to be accepted by polite society, she
cultivated a *genteel* manner and strove to appear the
epitome of respectability.

gentility \jen-'ti-lə-tē\ n. THOSE OF GENTLE BIRTH; REFINE-
MENT. Although the family fortune was long gone, her
family remained proud of its *gentility* and refinement.

germane \(ˌ)jər-'mān\ adj. PERTINENT; BEARING UPON THE
CASE AT HAND. The lawyer objected that the testimony
being offered was not *germane* to the case at hand.

germinal \'jərm-nəl, 'jer-mə-nəl\ adj. IN THE EARLIEST
STAGE OF DEVELOPMENT; CREATIVE. Such an idea is *germinal*; I am certain that it will influence thinkers and
philosophers for many generations.

germinate \'jər-mə-ˌnāt\ v. CAUSE TO SPROUT; SPROUT.
After the seeds *germinate* and develop their permanent leaves, the plants may be removed from the cold
frames and transplanted to the garden.

gesticulation \je-ˌsti-kyə-'lā-shən\ n. MOTION; GESTURE.
We were still too far-off to make out what Mother
was shouting, but from her animated *gesticulations*
we could tell she wanted us to hurry home instantly.
//gesticulate, v.

ghastly \'gast-lē\ adj. HORRIBLE. The murdered man was
a *ghastly* sight.

gibberish \'ji-b(ə-)rish, 'gi-\ n. NONSENSE; BABBLING. Did
you hear that fool boy spouting *gibberish* about mon-
sters from outer space? //gibber, v.

gibe \'jīb\ v. MOCK; TAUNT; SCOFF AT. The ugly stepsisters
constantly *gibed* at Cinderella, taunting her about her
ragged clothes.

giddy \'gi-dē\ adj. LIGHT-HEARTED; DIZZY. The silly, *giddy* young girls rode ride after ride on the Tilt-a-Whirl until they were *giddy* and sick.

gist \'jist\ n. ESSENCE. She was asked to give the *gist* of the essay in two sentences.

glib \'glib\ adj. FLUENT; FACILE; SLICK. Keeping up a steady patter to entertain his customers, the kitchen gadget salesman was a *glib* speaker, never at a loss for words.

gloat \'glōt\ v. VIEW WITH SMUG SATISFACTION; EXPRESS MALICIOUS PLEASURE. Noted for his sportsmanlike behavior in the ring, Joe Louis never *gloated* over his white opponents whom he had defeated.

glossary \'glä-se-rē\ n. BRIEF EXPLANATION OF WORDS USED IN THE TEXT. I have found the *glossary* in this book very useful; it has eliminated many trips to the dictionary.

glossy \'glä-sē, 'glȯ-\ adj. SMOOTH AND SHINING. I want this photograph printed on *glossy* paper, not matte.

glower \'glaù(-ə)r, ÷'glō(-ə)r\ v. SCOWL. The angry boy *glowered* at his father.

glut \'glət\ v. OVERSTOCK; FILL TO EXCESS. The Canadian fur trade proved so successful that the flood of furs coming down to Montréal *glutted* the market in France. //also n.

glutton \'glə-tən\ n. SOMEONE WHO EATS TOO MUCH. When Mother saw that Bobby had devoured all the cookies, she called him a little *glutton*. //gluttonous, adj.

gnarled \'när(-ə)ld\ adj. TWISTED. The weather-beaten old sailor was as *gnarled* and bent as an old oak tree.

goad \'gōd\ v. URGE ON. Mother was afraid that Ben's wild friends would *goad* him into doing something that would get him into trouble with the law. //also n.

gory \'gȯr-ē\ adj. BLOODY. The audience shuddered as they listened to the details of the *gory* massacre.

gossamer \'gä-sə-mər *also* 'gäz-mər, 'gä-zə-\ adj. SHEER; LIKE COBWEBS; GAUZY; DELICATE. Hired to illustrate a book of fairy tales, Jody peopled her illustrations with *gossamer*-winged sprites and gnarled, dwarflike gnomes. //also n.

Each of the questions below consists of a word in capital letters followed by five words or phrases. Choose the word or phrase that is most similar in meaning to the word in capital letters and write the letter of your choice on your answer paper.

301. **GAMUT**   (A) speed   (B) range   (C) origin
(D) refinement   (E) gesture

302. **GARISH**   (A) sordid   (B) flashy   (C) prominent
(D) lusty   (E) thoughtful

303. **GARNER**   (A) prevent   (B) assist   (C) collect
(D) compute   (E) consult

304. **GARNISH**   (A) paint   (B) garner   (C) adorn
(D) abuse   (E) banish

305. **GARRULITY**   (A) credulity   (B) senility
(C) loquaciousness (D) speciousness (E) artistry

306. **GARRULOUS**   (A) arid   (B) hasty   (C) sociable
(D) quaint   (E) talkative

307. **GAUCHE**   (A) rigid   (B) swift   (C) awkward
(D) tacit   (E) needy

308. **GAUDY**   (A) transparent   (B) showy   (C) clean
(D) clumsy · (E) pious

309. **GAUNT**   (A) victorious   (B) tiny   (C) stylish
(D) haggard   (E) nervous

310. **GENTILITY**   (A) falsity   (B) trick   (C) masculinity
(D) refinement   (E) stinginess

311. **GERMANE**   (A) bacteriological   (B) Middle European
(C) prominent   (D) warlike   (E) relevant

312. **GERMINAL**   (A) creative   (B) excused   (C) sterilized
(D) primitive   (E) strategic

313. **GIST**   (A) chaff   (B) summary   (C) expostulation
(D) expiation   (E) chore

314. **GLIB**   (A) slimy   (B) fashionable   (C) antiquated
(D) articulate   (E) anticlimactic

315. **GLUTTON**   (A) fury   (B) giant   (C) overeater
(D) miser   (E) alien

gourmet \\'gūr-ˌmā, gūr-'\\ n. CONNOISSEUR OF FOOD AND DRINK. The *gourmet* stated that this was the best onion soup she had ever tasted.

grandiloquent \\gran-'di-lə-kwənt\\ adj. POMPOUS; BOMBASTIC; USING HIGH-SOUNDING LANGUAGE. Impressed by the importance of the occasion and by his own importance as well, the speaker adopted a lofty, *grandiloquent* style.

grandiose \\'gran-dē-ˌōs, ˌgran-dē-'\\ adj. PRETENTIOUS; HIGH-FLOWN; RIDICULOUSLY EXAGGERATED; IMPRESSIVE. The aged matinee idol still had *grandiose* notions of his supposed importance in the theatrical world.

graphic \\'gra-fik\\ adj. PERTAINING TO THE ART OF DELINEATING; VIVIDLY DESCRIBED. The description of the winter storm was so *graphic* that you could almost feel the hailstones.

gratify \\'gra-tə-ˌfī\\ v. PLEASE. Serena's parents were *gratified* by her successful performance at Wimbledon.

gratis \\'gra-təs, 'grā-\\ adj. FREE. The company offered to give one package *gratis* to every purchaser of one of their products. //also adj.

gratuitous \\grə-'tü-ə-təs, -'tyü-\\ adj. GIVEN FREELY; UNWARRANTED; UNCALLED FOR. Quit making *gratuitous* comments about my driving; no one asked you for your opinion.

gravity \\'gra-və-tē\\ n. SERIOUSNESS. We could tell we were in serious trouble from the *gravity* of her expression. (secondary meaning) //grave, adj.

gregarious \\gri-'ger-ē-əs\\ adj. SOCIABLE. Typically, party-goers are *gregarious*; hermits are not.

grimace \\'gri-məs, gri-'mās\\ n. A FACIAL DISTORTION TO SHOW FEELING SUCH AS PAIN, DISGUST, ETC. Even though he remained silent, his *grimace* indicated his displeasure. //also v.

grotesque \grō-'tesk\ adj. FANTASTIC; COMICALLY HIDEOUS. On Halloween people enjoy wearing *grotesque* costumes.

grovel \'grä-vəl, 'grə-\ v. CRAWL OR CREEP ON GROUND; REMAIN PROSTRATE. Because Mr. Wickfield was never harsh to his employees, he could not understand why Uriah always cringed and *groveled* as if he expected a beating.

grudging \'grə-jiŋ\ adj. UNWILLING; RELUCTANT; STINGY. We received only *grudging* support from the mayor despite his earlier promises of aid.

gruff \'grəf\ adj. ROUGH-MANNERED. Although he was blunt and *gruff* with most people, he was always gentle with children.

guffaw \(ˌ)gə-'fò, 'gə-,\ n. BOISTEROUS LAUGHTER. The loud *guffaws* that came from the closed room indicated that the members of the committee had not yet settled down to serious business. //also v.

guile \'gī(-ə)l\ n. DECEIT; DUPLICITY; WILINESS; CUNNING. Iago used considerable *guile* to trick Othello into believing that Desdemona had been unfaithful to him.

guileless \'gī(-ə)l-ləs\ adj. WITHOUT DECEIT. He is naive, simple, and *guileless*; he cannot be guilty of fraud.

gullible \'gə-lə-bəl\ adj. CREDULOUS; EASILY DECEIVED. Overly *gullible* people have only themselves to blame if they fall for con artists repeatedly. As the saying goes, "Fool me once, shame on you. Fool me twice, shame on me."

gustatory \'gəs-tə-ˌtòr-ē\ adj. AFFECTING THE SENSE OF TASTE. The Thai restaurant offered an unusual *gustatory* experience for those used to a bland cuisine.

gusto \'gəs-(ˌ)tō\ n. ENJOYMENT; ENTHUSIASM. He accepted the assignment with such *gusto* that I feel he would have been satisfied with a smaller salary.

gusty \'gəs-tē\ adj. WINDY. The *gusty* weather made sailing precarious.

hackneyed \'hak-nēd\ adj. COMMONPLACE; TRITE. When the reviewer criticized the movie for its *hackneyed* plot, we agreed; we had seen similar stories hundreds of times before.

haggard \'ha-gərd\ adj. WASTED AWAY; GAUNT. After his long illness, he was pale and *haggard*.

haggle \'ha-gəl\ v. ARGUE ABOUT PRICES. I prefer to shop in a store that has a one-price policy because, whenever I *haggle* with a shopkeeper, I am never certain that I paid a fair price for the articles I purchased.

hallowed \'ha-(,)lōd, 'ha-ləd\ adj. BLESSED; CONSECRATED; VENERATED. General Douglas MacArthur wrote, "Duty, honor, country: those three *hallowed* words reverently dictate what you ought to be, what you can be, what you will be."

hallucination \hə-,lü-sə-'nā-shən\ n. DELUSION; FALSE PERCEPTION. Trippers (people who take psychedelic drugs such as LSD) often undergo *hallucinations*.

hamper \'ham-pər\ v. OBSTRUCT. The new mother didn't realize how much the effort of caring for an infant would *hamper* her ability to keep an immaculate house.

haphazard \(,)hap-'ha-zərd\ adj. RANDOM; BY CHANCE; UNSYSTEMATIC; AIMLESS. In place of a systematic family policy, America has a *haphazard* patchwork of institutions and programs created in response to immediate crises.

hapless \'ha-pləs\ adj. UNFORTUNATE. This *hapless* creature had never known a moment's pleasure.

harangue \hə-'raŋ\ n. INTENSE VERBAL ATTACK; DIATRIBE. In a lengthy *harangue*, the principal berated the students who had trashed the school cafeteria.

harass \hə-'ras; 'her-əs, 'ha-rəs\ v. TO ANNOY BY REPEATED ATTACKS. When he could not pay his bills as quickly as he had promised, he was *harassed* by his creditors.

harbinger \\'här-bən-jər\ n. FORERUNNER. The crocus is an early *harbinger* of spring.

harbor \\'här-bər\ v. PROVIDE A REFUGE FOR; HIDE. The church *harbored* illegal aliens who were political refugees.

harping \\'här-piŋ\ n. TIRESOME DWELLING ON A SUBJECT. After he had reminded me several times about what he had done for me, I told him to stop *harping* on my indebtedness to him. //harp, v.

haughtiness \\'hȯ-tē-nəs, 'hä-\ n. PRIDE; ARROGANCE. When Elizabeth realized that Darcy considered himself too good to dance with his social inferiors, she took great offense at his *haughtiness*.

hazardous \\'ha-zər-dəs\ adj. DANGEROUS. Your occupation is too *hazardous* for insurance companies to consider your application.

hazy \\'hā-zē\ adj. SLIGHTLY OBSCURE. In *hazy* weather, you cannot see the top of this mountain.

heckler \\'he-k(ə-)lər\ n. PERSON WHO HARASSES OTHERS. The *heckler* kept interrupting the speaker with rude remarks. //heckle, v.

hedonism \\'hē-də-ˌni-zəm\ n. BELIEF THAT PLEASURE IS THE SOLE AIM IN LIFE. Buddhist philosophy teaches us to steer a middle course between the extremes of pleasure-loving *hedonism* and self-denying asceticism.

heed \\'hēd\ v. PAY ATTENTION TO; CONSIDER. We hope you *heed* our advice and get a good night's sleep before the test. //also n.

heedless \\'hēd -ləs\ adj. NOT NOTICING; DISREGARDING. He drove on, *heedless* of the danger warnings placed at the side of the road.

herbivorous \ˌ(h)ər-'biv-rəs, -'bi-və-\ adj. GRAIN-EATING. Some *herbivorous* animals have two stomachs for digesting their food. //herbivore, n.

heresy \\'her-ə-sē, 'he-rə-\ n. OPINION CONTRARY TO POPULAR BELIEF; OPINION CONTRARY TO ACCEPTED RELIGION.

Galileo's assertion that the Earth moved around the sun directly contradicted the religious teachings of his day; as a result, he was tried for *heresy*. //heretic, n.

hermetic \(ˌ)hər-'me-tik\ adj. SEALED BY FUSION SO AS TO BE AIRTIGHT. After you sterilize the bandages and place them in a container, close the container using a *hermetic* seal to prevent contamination by airborne bacteria.

hermitage \'hər-mə-tij\ n. HOME OF A HERMIT. Even in his remote *hermitage* he could not escape completely from the world.

heterogeneous \ˌhe-tə-rə-'jē-nē-əs, ˌhe-trə-, -nyəs\ adj. DISSIMILAR; MIXED. This year's entering class is a remarkably *heterogeneous* body: it includes students from 40 different states and 26 foreign countries.

hiatus \hī-'ā-təs\ n. GAP; PAUSE. Except for a brief two-year *hiatus*, during which she enrolled in the Peace Corps, Ms. Clements has devoted herself to her medical career.

Each of the questions below consists of a word in capital letters, followed by five words or phrases. Choose the word or phrase that is most similar in meaning to the word in capital letters and write the letter of your choice on your answer paper.

316. **GRANDIOSE**   (A) false   (B) ideal   (C) proud
    (D) impressive   (E) functional

317. **GRATUITOUS**   (A) undeserved   (B) frank
    (C) ingenuous   (D) frugal   (E) pithy

318. **GREGARIOUS**   (A) friendly   (B) anticipatory
    (C) glorious   (D) horrendous   (E) similar

319. **GRUDGING**   (A) suggestive   (B) doubtful
    (C) untidy   (D) reluctant   (E) bearish

320. **GULLIBLE**   (A) credulous   (B) fickle
    (C) tantamount   (D) easy   (E) stylish

321. **GUSTO**   (A) noise   (B) panic   (C) atmosphere
    (D) gloom   (E) enthusiasm

322. **GUSTY**   (A) windy   (B) noisy   (C) fragrant
    (D) routine   (E) gloomy

323. **HACKNEYED**   (A) carried   (B) cliched   (C) banned
    (D) timely   (E) oratorical

324. **HAGGARD**   (A) shrewish   (B) inspired
    (C) wasted away   (D) maidenly   (E) vast

325. **HALLOWED**   (A) wasteful   (B) mournful
    (C) subsequent   (D) puerile   (E) holy

326. **HAPHAZARD**   (A) safe   (B) indifferent
    (C) accidental   (D) tense   (E) conspiring

327. **HAPLESS**   (A) cheerful   (B) consistent
    (C) unfortunate   D) considerate   (E) shapely

328. **HERBIVORE**   (A) plant-eater   (B) drought
    (C) oasis   (D) panic   (E) harvester

329. **HERETIC**   (A) sophist   (B) nonbeliever
    (C) interpreter   (D) pacifist   (E) owner

330. **HETEROGENEOUS**   (A) orthodox   (B) pagan
    (C) unlikely   (D) mixed   (E) banished

hibernate \'hī-bər-ˌnāt\ v. SLEEP THROUGHOUT THE WINTER. Bears are one of the many species of animals that *hibernate*. //hibernation, n.

hierarchy \'hī-(ə-)ˌrär-kē *also* 'hi(-ə)r-ˌär-\ n. ARRANGEMENT BY RANK OR STANDING; AUTHORITARIAN BODY DIVIDED INTO RANKS. To be low man on the totem pole is to have an inferior place in the *hierarchy*. //hierarchical, adj.

hilarity \hi-'ler-ə-tē\ n. BOISTEROUS MIRTH. Unable to contain their *hilarity* any longer, they broke into great guffaws and whoops of laughter.

hindrance \'hin-drən(t)s\ n. BLOCK; OBSTACLE. Stalled cars along the highway are a *hindrance* to traffic that tow trucks should remove without delay. //hinder, v.

histrionic \ˌhis-trē-'ä-nik\ adj. THEATRICAL; OVERLY DRAMATIC. Forever making *histrionic* gestures or striking a theatrical pose, Maurice was a bit too melodramatic for Maureen's taste. //histrionics, n.

hoard \'hȯrd\ v. STOCKPILE; ACCUMULATE FOR FUTURE USE. Whenever there are rumors of a food shortage, many people are tempted to *hoard* food. //also n.

hoary \'hȯr-ē\ adj. WHITE WITH AGE. Old Father Time was *hoary* and wrinkled with age.

hoax \'hōks\ n. TRICK; PRACTICAL JOKE; DECEPTION; FRAUD. Consider the case of Piltdown man, a scientific forgery that managed to fool the experts for nearly half a century, when the *hoax* was finally unmasked. //also v.

homage \'ä-mij, 'hä-\ n. HONOR; TRIBUTE. In her speech she tried to pay *homage* to a great man.

homily \'hä-mə-lē\ n. SERMON; SERIOUS WARNING. His speeches were always *homilies*, advising his listeners to repent and reform.

homogeneous \ˌhō-(ˌ)mō-'jē-nē-əs, -nyəs\ adj. OF THE SAME KIND. Because the student body at their daughter's prep school was so *homogeneous*, Sarah and James decided to send her to a school that offered greater cultural diversity. //homogeneity, n.

hone \'hōn\ v. SHARPEN. To make shaving easier, he *honed* his razor with great care.

horde \'hȯrd\ n. CROWD. Just before Christmas the stores are filled with *hordes* of shoppers.

horticultural \'hȯr-tə-ˌkəl-chə-rəl\ adj. PERTAINING TO CULTIVATION OF GARDENS. When Michael retired, he began to plant herbs and decorative shrubs and started reading *horticultural* magazines.

hover \'hə-vər, 'hä-\ v. HANG ABOUT; WAIT NEARBY. The police helicopter *hovered* above the accident.

hubris \'hyü-brəs\ n. ARROGANCE; EXCESSIVE SELF-CONCEIT. Filled with *hubris*, Lear refused to heed his friends' warnings.

hue \'hyü\ n. COLOR; ASPECT. The aviary contained birds of every possible *hue*.

humane \hyü-'mān, yü-\ adj. MARKED BY KINDNESS OR CONSIDERATION. It is ironic that the *Humane* Society sometimes must show its compassion toward mistreated animals by killing them to put them out of their misery.

humdrum \'həm-ˌdrəm\ adj. DULL; MONOTONOUS. After his years of adventure, he could not settle down to a *humdrum* existence.

humid \'hyü-məd, 'yü-\ adj. DAMP. Miami's *humid* climate aggravated Martha's asthma, so she decided to move to Arizona.

humility \hyü-'mi-lə-tē, yü-\ n. HUMBLENESS OF SPIRIT. Despite his fame as a Nobel Prize winner, Bishop Tutu spoke with a *humility* and lack of self-importance that immediately won over his listeners.

husband \'həz-bənd\ v. USE SPARINGLY; CONSERVE; SAVE. Marathon runners must *husband* their energy so that they can keep going for the entire distance. //husbandry, n.

hyperbole \hī-'pər-bə-(,)lē\ n. EXAGGERATION; OVERSTATE-MENT. As far as I am concerned, Apple's claims about its new computer are pure *hyperbole*; no machine is that good! //hyperbolic, adj.

hypercritical \,hī-pər-'kri-ti-kəl\ adj. INCLINED TO JUDGE TOO HARSHLY; OVERCRITICAL. Discouraged by a *hypercritical* teacher who seemed to take delight in pointing out her every mistake, Isabel nearly gave up painting.

hypochondriac \,hī-pə-'kän-drē-,ak\ n. PERSON UNDULY WORRIED ABOUT HIS HEALTH; WORRIER WITHOUT CAUSE ABOUT ILLNESS. Molière's play *The Imaginary Invalid* tells the tale of a *hypochondriac* miser who not only deludes himself that he is sick but even wants his daughter to marry a doctor so that he can get free medical care.

hypocritical \,hi-pə-'kri-ti-kəl\ adj. PRETENDING TO BE VIR-TUOUS; DECEIVING. It was *hypocritical* of Martha to say nice things about my poetry to me and then make fun of my verses behind my back. //hypocrisy, n.

hypothetical \,hī-pə-'the-ti-kəl\ adj. BASED ON ASSUMP-TIONS OR HYPOTHESES. Suppose you are accepted by Harvard, Stanford, and Yale. Which school would you choose to attend? Remember, this is only a *hypotheti-cal* question. //hypothesis, n.

icon \'ī-,kän\ n. RELIGIOUS IMAGE; IDOL. The *icons* on the walls of the church were painted in the 13th century.

iconoclastic \(,)ī-,kä-nə-'klas-tik\ adj. ATTACKING CHERISHED TRADITIONS. Deeply *iconoclastic*, Jean Genet deliber-ately set out to shock conventional theatergoers with his radical plays. //iconoclasm, n.; iconoclast, n.

ideology \,ī-dē-'ä-lə-jē, ,i-\ n. DOCTRINE OR BODY OF IDEAS OF A GROUP OF PEOPLE. People who had grown up believ-ing in the communist *ideology* found it hard to adjust to capitalism.

idiom \'i-dē-əm\ n. EXPRESSION WHOSE MEANING AS A WHOLE DIFFERS FROM THE MEANINGS OF ITS INDIVIDUAL WORDS; DIS-TINCTIVE STYLE. The phrase "to lose one's marbles" is an *idiom*: if I say that Joe has lost his marbles, I'm not asking you to find them for him.

idiosyncrasy \‚i-dē-ə-ˈsin-krə-sē\ n. PECULIARITY; ECCEN-TRICITY. One of Richard Nixon's little *idiosyncrasies* was his liking for ketchup on cottage cheese. //idio-syncratic, adj.

idolatry \ī-ˈdä-lə-trē\ n. WORSHIP OF IDOLS; EXCESSIVE ADMI-RATION. Blind to her son's faults, Helen adored him with a love that bordered on *idolatry*.

idyllic \ī-di-lik\ adj. CHARMINGLY CAREFREE; SIMPLE. Far from the city, she led an *idyllic* existence in her rural retreat.

ignoble \ig-ˈnō-bəl\ adj. UNWORTHY; NOT NOBLE. A true knight, Sir Galahad never stooped to perform an *ignoble* deed.

ignominious \‚ig-nə-ˈmi-nē-əs\ adj. DISGRACEFUL; SHAMEFUL. To lose the ping-pong match to a trained chimpanzee! How could Percy endure such an *ignominious* defeat? //ignominy, n.

illimitable \(‚)i(l)-ˈli-mə-tə-bəl\ adj. INFINITE. Man, having explored the far corners of the earth, is now reaching out into *illimitable* space.

illusion \i-ˈlü-zhən\ n. MISLEADING VISION. It is easy to create an optical *illusion* in which lines of equal length appear different. //illusive, adj.

illusory \i-ˈlüs-rē, -ˈlüz-; -ˈlü-sə-, -zə-\ adj. DECEPTIVE; NOT REAL. Unfortunately, the costs of running the lemon-ade stand were so high that Tom's profits proved *illusory*.

immaculate \i-ˈma-kyə-lət\ adj. SPOTLESS; FLAWLESS; ABSOLUTELY CLEAN. Ken and Jessica were wonderful tenants who left the apartment in *immaculate* condi-tion when they moved out.

imminent \ˈi-mə-nənt\ adj. IMPENDING; NEAR AT HAND. Rosa was such a last-minute worker that she could never start writing a paper until the deadline was *imminent*.

Each of the questions below consists of a word in capital letters, followed by five words or phrases. Choose the word or phrase that is most similar in meaning to the word in capital letters and write the letter of your choice on your answer paper.

331. **HIBERNATE**   (A) be musical   (B) be dormant   (C) locate   (D) suffer   (E) reveal

332. **HILARITY**   (A) mirth   (B) heartiness   (C) weakness   (D) casualty   (E) paucity

333. **HOARY**   (A) scaly   (B) aged   (C) erudite   (D) quiet   (E) long

334. **HOMAGE**   (A) regret   (B) foreignness   (C) expectation   (D) quietness   (E) tribute

335. **HONE**   (A) enlarge   (B) take away   (C) sharpen   (D) exit   (E) restore

336. **HUMANE**   (A) kind   (B) proud   (C) tranquil   (D) cheerful   (E) perfect

337. **HUMID**   (A) productive   (B) special   (C) moist   (D) oafish   (E) genuine

338. **HUMILITY**   (A) discord   (B) degradation   (C) wakefulness   (D) lack of pride   (E) excessive desire

339. **HUSBAND**   (A) be dormant   (B) hang about   (C) use sparingly   (D) sharpen   (E) trick

340. **HYPERBOLE**   (A) velocity   (B) climax   (C) curve   (D) exaggeration   (E) expansion

341. **HYPERCRITICAL**   (A) overly exacting   (B) false   (C) extreme   (D) inarticulate   (E) cautious

342. **HYPOTHETICAL**   (A) rational   (B) fantastic   (C) wizened   (D) opposed   (E) assumed

343. **IDIOSYNCRATIC**   (A) eccentric   (B) pacific   (C) noteworthy   (D) western   (E) witty

344. **IGNOBLE**   (A) produced by fire   (B) unworthy   (C) given to questioning   (D) huge   (E) known

345. **ILLUSORY**   (A) deceptive   (B) not certain   (C) not obvious   (D) not coherent   (E) not brilliant

immobility \ˌi-(ˌ)mō-'bi-lə-tē\ n. STATE OF BEING UNABLE TO MOVE. To avoid detection by predators, many animals resort to *immobility*, freezing in place. //immobilize, v.

immune \i-'myün\ adj. RESISTANT TO; FREE OR EXEMPT FROM. Fortunately, Florence had contracted chicken-pox as a child and was *immune* to it when her baby broke out in spots.

immutable \(ˌ)i(m)- 'myü-tə-bəl\ adj. UNCHANGEABLE. All things change over time; nothing is *immutable*.

impair \im-'per\ v. WORSEN; DIMINISH IN VALUE. Drinking alcohol can *impair* your ability to drive safely; if you're going to drink, don't drive.

impartial \(ˌ)im-'pär-shəl\ adj. NOT BIASED; FAIR. Knowing that she could not be *impartial* about her own child, Jo refused to judge any match in which Billy was competing.

impasse \'im-ˌpas, im-'\ n. PREDICAMENT FROM WHICH THERE IS NO ESCAPE. The negotiators reported that they had reached an *impasse* in their talks and had little hope of resolving the deadlock swiftly.

impassive \(ˌ)im-'pa-siv\ adj. WITHOUT FEELING; NOT AFFECTED BY PAIN. The American Indian has been incorrectly depicted as an *impassive* individual, undemonstrative and stoical.

impeach \im-'pēch\ v. CHARGE WITH CRIME IN OFFICE; INDICT. The angry congressman wanted to *impeach* the president for his misdeeds.

impeccable \(ˌ)im-'pek-ə-bəl\ adj. FAULTLESS. The uncrowned Queen of the fashion industry, Diana was acclaimed for her *impeccable* taste.

impecunious \ˌim-pi-'kyü-nyəs, -nē-əs\ adj. WITHOUT MONEY. Although Scrooge claimed he was too *impecunious* to give alms, he easily could have afforded to be charitable.

impede \im-'pēd\ v. HINDER; BLOCK; DELAY. The special prosecutor determined that the Attorney General, though inept, had not intentionally set out to *impede* the progress of the investigation.

impediment \im-'pe-də-mənt\ n. HINDRANCE; STUMBLING BLOCK. She had a speech *impediment* that prevented her speaking clearly.

impending \im-'pen-diŋ\ adj. NEARING; APPROACHING. The entire country was saddened by the news of his *impending* death.

imperious \im-'pir-ē-əs\ adj. DOMINEERING. Jane rather liked a man to be masterful, but Mr. Rochester seemed so bent on getting his own way that he was actually *imperious*!

impermeable \(,)im-'pər-mē-ə-bəl\ adj. IMPERVIOUS; NOT PERMITTING PASSAGE THROUGH ITS SUBSTANCE. Sue chose a raincoat made of Gore-Tex because the material was reportedly *impermeable* to liquids.

impertinent \(,)im-'pər-tə-nənt, -'pərt-nənt\ adj. INSOLENT. His neighbors' *impertinent* curiosity about his lack of dates angered Ted. It was downright rude of them to ask him such personal questions.

imperturbable \,im-pər-'tər-bə-bəl\ adj. CALM; PLACID; COMPOSED. In the midst of the most chaotic battles, the Duke of Wellington remained *imperturbable* and in full command of the situation.

impervious \(,)im-'pər-vē-əs\ adj. IMPENETRABLE; INCA-PABLE OF BEING DAMAGED OR DISTRESSED. Having read so many negative reviews of his acting, the movie star had learned to ignore them, and was now *impervious* to criticism.

impetuous \im-'pech-wəs; -'pe-chə-, -chü-əs\ adj. VIOLENT; HASTY; RASH. "Leap before you look" was the motto suggested by one particularly *impetuous* young man.

impetus \\'im-pə-təs\ n. INCENTIVE; STIMULUS; MOVING FORCE. A new federal highway program would create jobs and give added *impetus* to our economic recovery.

impiety \\(,)im-'pī-ə-tē\ n. IRREVERENCE; WICKEDNESS; LACK OF RESPECT FOR GOD. When members of the youth group draped the church in toilet paper on Halloween, the minister reprimanded them for their *impiety*. //impious, adj.

implacable \\(,)im-'pla-kə-bəl, -'plā-\ adj. INCAPABLE OF BEING PACIFIED. In *A Tale of Two Cities*, Madame Defarge, the *implacable* enemy of the aristocratic Evremondes, is relentless in her efforts to send every last one of them to the guillotine.

implausible \\(,)im-'plȯ-zə-bəl\ adj. UNLIKELY; UNBELIEV-ABLE. Though her alibi seemed *implausible*, it in fact turned out to be true.

implement \\'im-plə-,mənt\ v. PUT INTO EFFECT; SUPPLY WHAT IS NEEDED. The mayor was unwilling to *implement* the plan until she was sure it had the governor's backing. //also n.

implication \\im-plə-'kā-shən\ n. THAT WHICH IS HINTED AT OR SUGGESTED. When Miss Watson said she hadn't seen her purse since the last time Jim was in the house, the *implication* was that she suspected Jim had taken it. //imply, v.

implicit \\im-'pli-sət\ adj. UNDERSTOOD BUT NOT STATED. Jack never came right out and told Jill that he adored her; he believed his love was *implicit* in his actions.

impolitic \\(,)im-'pä-lə-tik\ adj. NOT WISE. I think it is *impolitic* to raise this issue at the present time because the public is too angry.

import \\'im-,pȯrt\ n. SIGNIFICANCE; MEANING. Because Tom knew so little about medical matters, it took a while for the full *import* of the doctor's words to sink in.

importune \\,im-pər-'tün, -'tyün, im-pȯr-,, -chən\ v. BEG PERSISTENTLY; PLEAD. Democratic and Republican phone solicitors *importuned* her for contributions so frequently that she decided to give nothing to either party. //importunate, adj.

imposter \im-'päs-tər\ n. SOMEONE WHO ASSUMES A FALSE IDENTITY. "This man is no doctor! He is a fraud!" cried Holmes, exposing the *imposter*.

impotent \'im-pə-tənt\ adj. WEAK; INEFFECTIVE. Although he wished to break the nicotine habit he found himself *impotent* in resisting the craving for a cigarette.

impoverished \im-'päv-risht, -'pä-və-\ adj. POOR. The typical "rags to riches" story tells the tale of an *impoverished* youth who through his own efforts rises to a position of wealth and prosperity.

impregnable \im-'preg-nə-bəl\ adj. INVULNERABLE. With the introduction of gunpowder in siege warfare, castles that had once seemed *impregnable* were easily breached.

impromptu \im-'präm(p)-(,)tü, -(,)tyü\ adj. WITHOUT PREVIOUS PREPARATION. The judges were amazed that she could make such a thorough, well-supported presentation in an *impromptu* speech.

improvident \(,)im-'prä-və-dənt, -,dent\ adj. THRIFTLESS. He was constantly being warned to mend his *improvident* ways and begin to "save for a rainy day." //improvidence, n.

improvise \'im-prə-,vīz *also* ,im-prə-'\ v. COMPOSE ON THE SPUR OF THE MOMENT. She would sit at the piano and *improvise* for hours on themes from Bach and Handel.

imprudent \(,)im-'prü-d°nt\ adj. LACKING CAUTION; INJUDICIOUS. It is *imprudent* to exercise vigorously and become overheated when you are unwell.

impugn \im-'pyün\ v. DOUBT; CHALLENGE. The club treasurer was furious when the finance committee's report *impugned* the accuracy of his financial records and recommended that he take bonehead math.

inadvertently \,i-nəd-'vər-t°nt-lē\ adv. CARELESSLY; UNINTENTIONALLY; BY OVERSIGHT. Judy's great fear was that she might *inadvertently* omit a question on the exam and mismark her whole answer sheet.

inane \i-'nān\ adj. SILLY; SENSELESS. There is no point to what you're saying. Why are you bothering to make such *inane* remarks? //inanity, n.

inanimate \(,)i-'na-nə-mət\ adj. LIFELESS; DULL; SPIRITLESS. A still life painting is a pictorial representation of *inanimate* objects such as vases or bowls of fruit.

inarticulate \,i-(,)när-'ti-kyə-lət\ adj. SPEECHLESS; PRODUCING INDISTINCT SPEECH. Excruciatingly shy, Roy stammered and became *inarticulate* in the presence of members of the opposite sex.

incandescent \,in-kən-'de-s°nt *also* -(,)kan-\ adj. STRIKINGLY BRIGHT; SHINING WITH INTENSE HEAT. If you leave on an *incandescent* lightbulb, it quickly grows too hot to touch.

incapacitate \,in-kə-'pa-sə-,tāt\ v. DISABLE. During the winter, many people were *incapacitated* by respiratory ailments.

incarcerate \in-'kär-sə-,rāt\ v. IMPRISON. The civil rights workers were willing to be arrested and even *incarcerated* if by their imprisonment they could serve the cause.

incense \in-'sen(t)s\ v. ENRAGE; INFURIATE. Cruelty to defenseless animals *incensed* Kit; the very idea brought tears of anger to her eyes.

incentive \in-'sen-tiv\ n. SPUR; MOTIVE. Mike's strong desire to outshine his big sister was all the *incentive* he needed to do well in school.

inception \in-'sep-shən\ n. START; BEGINNING. She was involved with the project from its *inception*.

incessant \(,)in-'se-sənt\ adj. UNINTERRUPTED. We could not fall asleep because of the crickets' *incessant* chirping, which seemed to go on all night long.

Each of the questions below consists of a word in capital letters, followed by five words or phrases. Choose the word or phrase that is most similar in meaning to the word in capital letters and write the letter of your choice on your answer paper.

346. **IMMOBILIZE**   (A) debate   (B) scour   (C) fix   (D) sanctify   (E) ratify

347. **IMMUTABLE**   (A) silent   (B) unchangeable   (C) articulate   (D) loyal   (E) varied

348. **IMPAIR**   (A) separate   (B) make amends   (C) make worse   (D) falsify   (E) cancel

349. **IMPARTIAL**   (A) fair   (B) combined   (C) high   (D) connecting   (E) lost

350. **IMPASSIVE**   (A) active   (B) emotionless   (C) perfect   (D) anxious   (E) irritated

351. **IMPECCABLE**   (A) unmentionable   (B) quotable   (C) blinding   (D) perfect   (E) hampering

352. **IMPECUNIOUS**   (A) penniless   (B) afflicted   (C) affectionate   (D) affable   (E) afraid

353. **IMPERVIOUS**   (A) impenetrable   (B) perplexing   (C) chaotic   (D) cool   (E) perfect

354. **IMPETUOUS**   (A) rash   (B) inane   (C) just   (D) flagrant   (E) redolent

355. **IMPOLITIC**   (A) campaigning   (B) unwise   (C) aggressive   (D) legal   (E) fortunate

356. **IMPORTUNE**   (A) export   (B) plead   (C) exhibit   (D) account   (E) visit

357. **IMPROMPTU**   (A) prompted   (B) appropriate   (C) extemporaneous   (D) foolish   (E) vast

358. **INADVERTENT**   (A) accidental   (B) repugnant   (C) close to immigration   (D) full   (E) accountable

359. **INANE**   (A) passive   (B) silly   (C) intoxicated   (D) mellow   (E) silent

360. **INCARCERATE**   (A) inhibit   (B) acquit   (C) account   (D) imprison   (E) force

WORD LIST 25

inchoate \in-ˈkō-ət, ˈin-kə-ˌwāt\ adj. RECENTLY BEGUN; RUDIMENTARY; ELEMENTARY. Her blog entries seemed almost *inchoate*, full of ideas struggling to be realized, essays waiting to be born.

incidental \ˌin(t)-sə-ˈden-təl\ adj. NOT ESSENTIAL; MINOR. The scholarship covered his major expenses at college and some of his *incidental* expenses as well.

incipient \in-ˈsi-pē-ənt\ adj. BEGINNING; IN AN EARLY STAGE. I will go to sleep early for I want to break an *incipient* cold.

incisive \in-ˈsī-siv\ adj. CUTTING; SHARP; PENETRATING. The moderator thanked her for her *incisive* comments, which cut straight to the heart of the issue.

incite \in-ˈsīt\ v. AROUSE TO ACTION; GOAD; MOTIVATE. In a fiery speech, Mario *incited* his fellow students to go out on strike to protest the university's hiring policies.

inclement \(ˌ)in-ˈkle-mənt, ˈin-klə-\ adj. STORMY; UNKIND. NASA announced that the scheduled launching of the space shuttle would be postponed because of *inclement* weather.

inclusive \in-ˈklü-siv, -ziv\ adj. TENDING TO INCLUDE ALL. The comedian turned down the invitation to join the Players' Club, saying that any club that would let him in was too *inclusive* for him.

incoherence \ˌin-kō-ˈhir-ən(t)s, -ˈher-\ n. UNINTELLIGIBILITY; LACK OF LOGIC OR RELEVANCE. "This essay makes no sense at all," said the teacher, giving it an F for *incoherence*. //incoherent, adj.

incompatible \ˌin-kəm-ˈpa-tə-bəl\ adj. INHARMONIOUS. The married couple argued incessantly and finally decided to separate because they were *incompatible*. //incompatibility, n.

incongruous \(ˌ)in-ˈkäŋ-grə-wəs\ adj. NOT FITTING; ABSURD. Towering over the nearby houses, the MacMansion looked wholly *incongruous* in the historic neighborhood of small Craftsman bungalows. //incongruity, n.

inconsequential \(ˌ)in-ˌkän(t)-sə-ˈkwen(t)-shəl\ adj. OF TRIFLING SIGNIFICANCE. Brushing off Ali's apologies for having broken the wine glass, Tamara said, "Don't worry about it; it's *inconsequential.*"

incontrovertible \(ˌ)in-ˌkän-trə-ˈvər-tə-bəl\ adj. INDISPUTABLE. The value of the school voucher program remains open to question, for there is no *incontrovertible* evidence that the use of vouchers has improved the education of the students using them, either at private or public schools.

incorrigible \(ˌ)in-ˈkȯr-ə-jə-bəl, -ˈkär-\ adj. UNCORRECTABLE. Though Widow Douglass had hopes of reforming Huck, Miss Watson considered him *incorrigible* and swore he would come to no good end.

incredulity \ˌin-kri-ˈdü-lə-tē, -ˈdyü-\ n. A TENDENCY TO DISBELIEF. Edison's invention of the phonograph was greeted with *incredulity*: one skeptical French scientist claimed the device was nothing but a clever ventriloquist's trick. //incredulous, adj.

increment \ˈiŋ-krə-mənt, ˈin-\ n. INCREASE. The new contract calls for a 10 percent *increment* in salary for each employee for the next two years.

incriminate \in-ˈkri-mə-ˌnāt\ v. ACCUSE. Rather than *incriminate* himself, the witness refused to answer certain questions, claiming the protection of the Fifth Amendment.

incumbent \in-ˈkəm-bənt\ n. OFFICEHOLDER. Which *incumbent* of the White House had the lowest approval ratings during his presidency? //also adj.

incur \in-ˈkər\ v. BRING UPON ONESELF. His parents refused to pay any future debts he might *incur*.

indefatigable \ˌin-di-ˈfa-ti-gə-bəl\ adj. TIRELESS. Although the effort of taking out the garbage exhausted Dave, when it came to partying, he was *indefatigable*.

indemnify \in-'dem-nə-ˌfī\ v. MAKE SECURE AGAINST LOSS; COMPENSATE FOR LOSS. The city will *indemnify* all home owners whose property is spoiled by this project.

indicative \in-'di-kə-tiv\ adj. SUGGESTIVE; IMPLYING. A lack of appetite may be *indicative* of a major mental or physical disorder.

indict \in-'dīt\ v. CHARGE. If the grand jury *indicts* the suspect, he will go to trial. //indictment, n.

indifferent \in-'di-fərnt, -f(ə-)rənt\ adj. UNMOVED; LACKING CONCERN. Because she felt no desire to marry, she was *indifferent* to his constant proposals.

indigenous \in-'di-jə-nəs\ adj. NATIVE. Cigarettes are made of tobacco, a plant *indigenous* to the New World.

indigent \'in-di-jənt\ adj. POOR. Someone who is truly *indigent* cannot afford to buy a pack of cigarettes. //indigence, n.

indignation \ˌin-dig-'nā-shən\ n. ANGER AT AN INJUSTICE. He felt *indignation* at the ill-treatment of helpless animals. //indignant, adj.

indiscriminate \ˌin-dis-'krim-nət, -'kri-mə-\ adj. CHOOSING AT RANDOM; CONFUSED. She disapproved of her son's *indiscriminate* television viewing and decided to restrict him to educational programs.

indisputable \ˌin-di-'spyü-tə-bəl, (ˌ)in-'dis-pyə-\ adj. TOO CERTAIN TO BE DISPUTED. In the face of these *indisputable* statements, I withdraw my complaint.

indissoluble \ˌin-di-'säl-yə-bəl\ adj. PERMANENT. The *indissoluble* bonds of marriage are all too often being dissolved.

indolent \'in-də-lənt\ adj. LAZY. Couch potatoes who lie back on their sofas watching television are by definition *indolent*. //indolence, n.

indomitable \in-'dä-mə-tə-bəl\ adj. UNCONQUERABLE; UNYIELDING. Focusing on her game despite her personal problems, tennis champion Steffi Graf proved she had an *indomitable* will to win.

indubitable \(,)in-'dü-bə-tə-bəl, -'dyü-\ adj. UNQUESTION-ABLE; UNABLE TO BE DOUBTED. Auditioning for the chorus line, Molly was an *indubitable* hit: the director fired the leading lady and hired Molly in her place!

induce \in-'düs, -'dyüs\ v. PERSUADE; BRING ABOUT. After the quarrel, Gina said nothing could *induce* her to talk to Diego again.

inductive \in-'dək-tiv\ adj. PERTAINING TO INDUCTION OR PROCEEDING FROM THE SPECIFIC TO THE GENERAL. Langdell, who introduced the "case method" in the study of law, believed that the principles of law were best learned by *inductive* study of the actual legal situations (the cases) in which they occurred.

indulgent \in-'dəl-jənt\ adj. HUMORING; YIELDING; LENIENT. Jay's mother was excessively *indulgent* and succeeded in spoiling him rotten. //indulgence, n.

ineffable \(,)i-'ne-fə-bəl\ adj. UNUTTERABLE; CANNOT BE EXPRESSED IN SPEECH. Looking down at her newborn daughter, Ruth felt such *ineffable* joy that, for the first time in her life, she had no words to convey what was in her heart.

ineffectual \,i-nə-'fek-chə(-wə)l, -'feksh-wəl\ adj. NOT EFFECTIVE; WEAK. Because the candidate failed to get across his message to the public, his campaign was *ineffectual*.

inept \i-'nept\ adj. UNSUITED; ABSURD; INCOMPETENT. The *inept* glove-maker was all thumbs.

inequity \(,)i-'ne-kwə-tē\ n. UNFAIRNESS. In demanding equal pay for equal work, women protest the basic *inequity* of a system that gives greater financial rewards to men.

inert \i-'nərt\ adj. INACTIVE; LACKING POWER TO MOVE. "Get up, you lazybones," she yelled at her husband, who lay in bed totally *inert*. //inertia, n.

inevitable \i-'ne-və-tə-bəl\ adj. UNAVOIDABLE. Though death and taxes are both supposedly *inevitable*, some people avoid paying taxes for years.

inexorable \(ˌ)i-'neks-rə-bəl, -'nek-sə-, -'neg-zə-rə-\ adj. UNALTERABLE; RELENTLESS; UNYIELDING. After listening to the pleas for clemency, the judge was *inexorable* and gave the convicted man the maximum punishment allowed by law.

infallible \(ˌ)in-'fa-lə-bəl\ adj. UNERRING. Jane refused to believe that the pope was *infallible*, for she reasoned that all human beings were capable of error and therefore the pope could make errors.

infamous \'in-fə-məs\ adj. NOTORIOUSLY BAD. Charles Manson and Jeffrey Dahmer are both *infamous* killers.

infer \in-'fər\ v. DEDUCE; CONCLUDE. From the students' glazed looks, it was easy for me to *infer* that they were bored out of their minds. //inference, n.

infinitesimal \(ˌ)in-ˌfi-nə-'te-sə-məl, -zə-məl\ adj. EXCEEDINGLY SMALL; SO SMALL AS TO BE ALMOST NONEXISTENT. Making sure that everyone was aware that she was on an extremely strict diet, Melanie said she would have only an *infinitesimal* sliver of pie.

infirmity \in-'fər-mə-tē\ n. WEAKNESS. Her greatest *infirmity* was lack of willpower.

inflated \in-'flā-təd\ adj. EXAGGERATED; POMPOUS; ENLARGED (WITH AIR OR GAS). His claims about the new product were *inflated*; it did not work as well as he had promised.

ingenious \in-'jēn-yəs\ adj. CLEVER. Kit admired the *ingenious* way her iPod shuffled the songs on her play list.

Each of the questions below consists of a word in capital letters followed by five words or phrases. Choose the word or phrase that is most similar in meaning to the word in capital letters and write the letter of your choice on your answer paper.

361. **INCLEMENT** (A) unfavorable (B) abandoned (C) kindly (D) selfish (E) active

362. **INCOMPATIBLE** (A) capable (B) reasonable (C) faulty (D) indifferent (E) discordant

363. **INCONSEQUENTIAL** (A) disorderly (B) insignificant (C) subsequent (D) significant (E) preceding

364. **INCONTROVERTIBLE** (A) insular (B) complaisant (C) crass (D) indisputable (E) false

365. **INCORRIGIBLE** (A) narrow (B) straight (C) inconceivable (D) unreliable (E) unreformable

366. **INCRIMINATE** (A) exacerbate (B) involve (C) intimidate (D) lacerate (E) prevaricate

367. **INDICT** (A) exculpate (B) charge (C) exonerate (D) prepare (E) embarrass

368. **INDIGENT** (A) lazy (B) pusillanimous (C) penurious (D) affluent (E) contrary

369. **INDIGNATION** (A) pomposity (B) bombast (C) obeisance (D) wrath (E) message

370. **INDOLENCE** (A) sloth (B) poverty (C) latitude (D) aptitude (E) anger

371. **INDUBITABLE** (A) flagrant (B) doubtful (C) careful (D) unconquerable (E) unquestionable

372. **INDULGENCE** (A) revelation (B) leniency (C) felony (D) starvation (E) stupidity

373. **INEPT** (A) outward (B) spiritual (C) foolish (D) clumsy (E) abundant

374. **INFALLIBLE** (A) final (B) unbelievable (C) perfect (D) inaccurate (E) inquisitive

375. **INFIRMITY** (A) disability (B) age (C) inoculation (D) hospital (E) unity

ingenue \\'an-jə-ˌnü, 'än-; 'aⁿ-zhə-, 'äⁿ-\ n. A NAIVE GIRL OR YOUNG WOMAN; AN ACTRESS WHO PLAYS SUCH PARTS. Although she was forty, she still insisted that she be cast as an *ingenue* and refused to play more mature roles.

ingenuous \in-'jen-yə-wəs, -yü-əs\ adj. NAIVE; YOUNG; UNSOPHISTICATED. The woodsman had not realized how *ingenuous* Little Red Riding Hood was until he heard that she had gone off for a walk in the woods with the Big Bad Wolf.

ingrate \\'in-ˌgrāt\ n. UNGRATEFUL PERSON. That *ingrate* Bob sneered at the tie that I gave him.

ingratiate \in-'grā-shē-ˌāt\ v. MAKE AN EFFORT TO BECOME POPULAR WITH. In *All About Eve*, the heroine, an aspiring actress, wages a clever campaign to *ingratiate* herself with Margo Channing, an established star.

inherent \in-'hir-ənt, -'her-\ adj. FIRMLY ESTABLISHED BY NATURE OR HABIT. Katya's *inherent* love of justice caused her to champion anyone she considered treated unfairly by society.

inhibit \in-'hi-bət\ v. RESTRAIN; RETARD OR PREVENT. Only two things *inhibited* him from taking a punch at Mike Tyson: Tyson's right jab, and Tyson's left hook. //inhibition, n.

inimical \i-'ni-mi-kəl\ adj. UNFRIENDLY; HOSTILE; DETRIMENTAL. Because candidates from minor parties are often excluded from presidential debates, some critics contend that the current electoral process is undemocratic and *inimical* to viewpoints other than those of the Republican and Democratic parties.

inimitable \(ˌ)i-'ni-mə-tə-bəl\ adj. MATCHLESS; NOT ABLE TO BE IMITATED. We admire Auden for his *inimitable* use of language; he is one of a kind.

iniquitous \i-'ni-kwə-təs\ adj. UNJUST; WICKED. Whether or not King Richard III was responsible for the murder of the two young princes in the Tower, it was an *iniquitous* deed. //iniquity, n.

initiate \i-'ni-shē-ˌāt\ v. BEGIN; ORIGINATE; RECEIVE INTO A GROUP. The college is about to *initiate* a program in reducing math anxiety among students.

injurious \in-'jür-ē-əs\ adj. HARMFUL. Smoking cigarettes can be *injurious* to your health.

inkling \'iŋ-kliŋ\ n. HINT. This came as a complete surprise to me as I did not have the slightest *inkling* of your plans.

innate \i-'nāt, 'i-,\ adj. INBORN. Mozart's parents soon recognized young Wolfgang's *innate* talent for music.

innocuous \i-'nä-kyə-wəs\ adj. HARMLESS. An occasional glass of wine with dinner is relatively *innocuous* and should have no ill effect on you.

innovation \'i-nə-ˌvā-shən\ n. CHANGE; INTRODUCTION OF SOMETHING NEW. Although Richard liked to keep up with the latest technological *innovations*, he did not automatically abandon tried and true techniques in favor of something new. //innovative, adj.

inopportune \(ˌ)in-ˌä-pər-'tün, -'tyün\ adj. UNTIMELY; POORLY CHOSEN. A rock concert is an *inopportune* setting for a quiet conversation.

inordinate \in-'or-dᵊn-ət, -'ord-nət\ adj. UNRESTRAINED; EXCESSIVE. She had an *inordinate* fondness for candy, eating two or three boxes in a single day.

insatiable \(ˌ)in-'sā-shə-bəl\ adj. NOT EASILY SATISFIED; GREEDY. David's appetite for oysters was *insatiable*: he could easily eat four dozen at a single sitting.

inscrutable \in-'skrü-tə-bəl\ adj. IMPENETRABLE; NOT READILY UNDERSTOOD; MYSTERIOUS. Experienced poker players try to keep their expressions *inscrutable*, hiding their reactions to the cards behind the familiar "poker face."

insidious \in-'si-dē-əs\ adj. TREACHEROUS; STEALTHY; SLY. Glaucoma is a particularly *insidious* disease, nicknamed "the sneaky thief of sight" for its ability to damage the visual field severely before becoming apparent.

insinuate \in-ˈsin-yə-ˌwāt, -yü-ˌāt\ v. HINT; IMPLY. When you say I'm looking robust, do you mean to *insinuate* that I'm getting fat?

insipid \in-ˈsi-pəd\ adj. TASTELESS; DULL. Flat prose and flat ginger ale are equally *insipid*: both lack sparkle.

insolent \ˈin-s(ə-)lənt\ adj. IMPUDENTLY DISRESPECTFUL; HAUGHTY AND RUDE. How dare you treat me so rudely? The manager will hear just how *insolent* you have been!

insolvent \(ˌ)in-ˈsäl-vənt\ adj. BANKRUPT; LACKING MONEY TO PAY. When rumors that he was *insolvent* reached his creditors, they began to press him for payment of the money due them. //insolvency, n.

insomnia \in-ˈsäm-nē-ə\ n. WAKEFULNESS; INABILITY TO SLEEP. He refused to join us in a midnight cup of coffee because he claimed it gave him *insomnia*.

instigate \ˈin(t)-stə-ˌgāt\ v. URGE; START; PROVOKE. Delighting in making mischief, Sir Toby sets out to *instigate* a quarrel between Sir Andrew and Cesario.

insubordination \ˌin(t)-sə-ˈbȯr-də-nā-shən\ n. DISOBEDIENCE; REBELLIOUSNESS. At the slightest hint of *insubordination* from the sailors of the *Bounty*, Captain Blight had them flogged; finally, they mutinied. //insubordinate, adj.

insularity \ˌin(t)-sù-ˈla-rə-tē, -syù-, ˌin-shə-ˈla-\ n. NARROW-MINDEDNESS; ISOLATION. The *insularity* of the islanders manifested itself in their suspicion of anything foreign. //insular, adj.

insuperable \(ˌ)in-ˈsü-p(ə-)rə-bəl\ adj. INSURMOUNTABLE; INVINCIBLE; UNBEATABLE. Though the odds against their survival seemed *insuperable*, the *Apollo 13* astronauts reached earth safely.

insurgent \in-'sər-jənt\ adj. REBELLIOUS. Because the *insurgent* forces had occupied the capital and gained control of the railway lines, several of the war correspondents covering the uprising predicted a rebel victory. //also n.

insurrection \,in(t)-sə-'rek-shən\ n. REBELLION; UPRISING. In retrospect, given how badly the British treated the American colonists, the eventual *insurrection* seems inevitable.

integrate \'in-tə-,grāt\ v. MAKE WHOLE; COMBINE; MAKE INTO ONE UNIT. Like the members of the English Arts and Crafts movement, Charles Rennie Mackintosh strove to *integrate* architectural and decorative elements in his work.

integrity \in-'te-grə-tē\ n. UPRIGHTNESS; WHOLENESS. Lincoln, whose personal *integrity* has inspired millions, fought a civil war to maintain the *integrity* of the Republic, that these United States might remain undivided for all time.

intellect \'in-tə-,lekt\ n. HIGHER MENTAL POWERS. A reasonably intelligent man himself, Doctor Watson was in awe of Sherlock Holmes's superior *intellect*.

inter \in-'tər\ v. BURY. They are going to *inter* the body tomorrow at Broadlawn Cemetery. //interment, n.

interloper \,in-tər-'lō-pər, 'in-tər-,\ n. INTRUDER. The merchant thought of his competitors as *interlopers* who were stealing away his trade.

interminable \(,)in-'tərm-nə-bəl, -'tər-mə-\ adj. ENDLESS. Although his speech lasted for only twenty minutes, it seemed *interminable* to his bored audience.

intermittent \,in-tər-'mi-tənt\ adj. PERIODIC; ON AND OFF. Though from time to time *intermittent* cannonfire was audible in the distance, Wellington seemed undisturbed by these occasional reminders of the enemy's proximity.

intervene \,in-tər-'vēn\ v. COME BETWEEN. She *intervened* in the argument between her two sons.

intimate \ˌin-tə-ˈmāt\ v. HINT. Was Dick *intimating* that Jane had bad breath when he asked if she'd like a breath mint?

intimidate \in-ˈti-mə-ˌdāt\ v. INSTILL FEAR IN SOMEONE. I'll learn karate and then those big bullies won't be able to *intimidate* me any more. //intimidation, n.

intractable \(ˌ)in-ˈtrak-tə-bəl\ adj. UNRULY; STUBBORN; UNYIELDING. Charlie Brown's friend Pigpen was *intractable*: he pigheadedly refused to take a bath.

intransigence \in-ˈtran(t)-sə-jən(t)s\ n. REFUSAL OF ANY COMPROMISE; STUBBORNNESS. The negotiating team had not expected such *intransigence* from the striking workers, who rejected any hint of a compromise. //intransigent, adj.

intrepid \in-ˈtre-pəd\ adj. FEARLESS. For her *intrepid* conduct nursing the wounded during the war, Florence Nightingale was honored by Queen Victoria.

intricate \ˈin-tri-kət\ adj. COMPLEX; KNOTTY; TANGLED. Philip spent many hours designing mazes so *intricate* that none of his classmates could solve them. //intricacy, n.

intrinsic \in-ˈtrin-zik, -ˈtrin(t)-sik\ adj. ESSENTIAL; INHERENT; BUILT-IN. Although my grandmother's china has little *intrinsic* value, I shall always treasure it for the memories it evokes.

introspective \ˌin-trə-ˈspek-tiv\ adj. LOOKING WITHIN ONESELF. *Introspective* people, self-conscious souls who forever pore over their actions and behavior looking for flaws, lack the spontaneity and naturalness to be popular hosts or hostesses.

introvert \ˈin-trə-ˌvərt\ n. ONE WHO IS INTROSPECTIVE; INCLINED TO THINK MORE ABOUT ONESELF. Uncommunicative by nature and disinclined to look outside himself, he was a classic *introvert*. //also v.

intrude \in-ˈtrüd\ v. TRESPASS; ENTER AS AN UNINVITED PERSON. She hesitated to *intrude* on their conversation.

intuition \‚in-tü-'i-shən, -tyü-\ n. POWER OF KNOWING
WITHOUT REASONING; IMMEDIATE INSIGHT. Even though
Tony denied that anything was wrong, Tina trusted
her *intuition* that something was bothering him.
//intuitive, adj.

inundate \'i-(‚)nən-‚dāt\ v. OVERFLOW; FLOOD. Until the
great dam was built, the waters of the Nile used to
inundate the river valley like clockwork every year.

invalidate \(‚)in-'va-lə-‚dāt\ v. WEAKEN; DESTROY. The
relatives who received little or nothing sought to
invalidate the will by claiming the deceased had
not been in his right mind when he had signed the
document.

Synonym Test • Word List 26

Each of the questions below consists of a word in capital letters, followed by five words or phrases. Choose the word or phrase that is most similar in meaning to the word in capital letters and write the letter of your choice on your answer paper.

376. **INGENUOUS**   (A) clever   (B) stimulating   (C) naive
   (D) worried   (E) cautious

377. **INIMICAL**   (A) antagonistic   (B) anonymous
   (C) fanciful   (D) accurate   (E) atypical

378. **INNOCUOUS**   (A) not capable   (B) not dangerous
   (C) not eager   (D) not frank   (E) not peaceful

379. **INSINUATE**   (A) resist   (B) suggest   (C) report
   (D) rectify   (E) lecture

380. **INSIPID**   (A) witty   (B) flat   (C) wily
   (D) talkative   (E) lucid

381. **INTEGRATE**   (A) tolerate   (B) unite   (C) flow
   (D) copy   (E) assume

382. **INTER**   (A) bury   (B) amuse   (C) relate
   (D) frequent   (E) abandon

383. **INTERLOPER**   (A) braggart   (B) disputant
   (C) intruder   (D) judge   (E) scholar

384. **INTERMITTENT**   (A) heavy   (B) fleet
   (C) occasional   (D) fearless   (E) responding

385. **INTRACTABLE**   (A) culpable   (B) flexible
   (C) unruly   (D) efficient   (E) base

386. **INTRANSIGENCE**   (A) lack of training
   (B) stubbornness   (C) novelty   (D) timidity
   (E) cupidity

387. **INTREPID**   (A) cold   (B) hot   (C) understood
   (D) callow   (E) courageous

388. **INTRINSIC**   (A) extrinsic   (B) abnormal   (C) quiet
   (D) abandoned   (E) basic

389. **INUNDATE**   (A) abuse   (B) deny   (C) swallow
   (D) treat   (E) flood

390. **INVALIDATE**   (A) weaken   (B) orate   (C) hospitalize
   (D) apply   (E) whisper

invective \in-'vek-tiv\ n. ABUSE. He had expected criticism but not the *invective* that greeted his proposal.

inverse \(ˌ)in-'vərs, 'in-,\ adj. OPPOSITE. There is an *inverse* ratio between the strength of light and its distance.

invert \in-'vərt\ v. TURN UPSIDE DOWN OR INSIDE OUT. When he *inverted* his body in a handstand, he felt the blood rush to his head.

inveterate \in-'ve-t(ə-)rət\ adj. DEEP-ROOTED; HABITUAL. An *inveterate* smoker, Bob cannot seem to break the habit, no matter how hard he tries.

invidious \in-'vi-dē-əs\ adj. DESIGNED TO CREATE ILL WILL OR ENVY; INJURIOUS. The Philadelphia Workingmen's Party claimed that, by dividing Americans into two distinct classes, the rich and the poor, capitalism created *invidious* distinctions and unjust and unnatural inequalities.

invincible \(ˌ)in-'vin(t)-sə-bəl\ adj. UNCONQUERABLE. Superman is *invincible*.

inviolable \(ˌ)in-'vī-ə-lə-bəl\ adj. SECURE FROM CORRUPTION, ATTACK, OR VIOLATION. Batman considered his oath to keep the people of Gotham City safe *inviolable*: nothing on earth could make him break this promise. //inviolability, n.

invoke \in-'vōk\ v. CALL UPON; ASK FOR. She *invoked* her advisor's aid in filling out her financial aid forms.

invulnerable \(ˌ)in-'vəl-n(ə-)rə-bəl, -nər-bəl\ adj. INCAPABLE OF INJURY. Achilles was *invulnerable* except in his heel.

iota \ī-'ō-tə\ n. VERY SMALL QUANTITY. She hadn't an *iota* of common sense.

irascible \i-'ra-sə-bəl\ adj. IRRITABLE; EASILY ANGERED. Pop had what people call a hair-trigger temper: he was a hot-tempered, *irascible* guy.

irate \ī-'rāt, 'ī-,, i-'rāt\ adj. ANGRY. When John's mother found out he had overdrawn his checking account for the third month in a row, she was so *irate* she could scarcely speak to him.

irksome \'ərk-səm\ adj. ANNOYING; TEDIOUS. Frequent fliers find the long waits in airport security lines particularly *irksome*. //irk, v.

ironic ,ī-'rä-nik *also* i-'rä-\ adj. RESULTING IN AN UNEXPECTED AND CONTRARY OUTCOME; SARCASTIC. It is *ironic* that his success came when he least wanted it.

irony \'ī-rə-nē *also* 'ī(-ə)r-nē\ n. HIDDEN SARCASM OR SATIRE; USE OF WORDS THAT CONVEY A MEANING OPPOSITE TO THE LITERAL MEANING. Gradually the audience began to realize that the excessive praise the candidate was lavishing on her opponent was actually *irony*: she was in fact ridiculing the poor fool.

irreconcilable \i-,re-kən-'sī-lə-bəl, -'re-kən-,\ adj. INCOMPATIBLE; NOT ABLE TO BE RESOLVED. Because the separated couple were *irreconcilable*, the marriage counselor recommended a divorce.

irrelevant \i-'re-lə-vənt\ adj. NOT APPLICABLE; UNRELATED; BESIDE THE POINT. In foreign policy Hamilton pragmatically maintained that self-interest should be the nation's only guide; questions of gratitude, benevolence, and moral principle, he believed, were *irrelevant*.

irreparable \i-'re-p(ə-)rə-bəl, 'i(r)-\ adj. NOT ABLE TO BE CORRECTED OR REPAIRED. Your apology cannot atone for the *irreparable* damage you have done to her reputation.

irrepressible \,ir-i-'pre-sə-bəl\ adj. UNABLE TO BE RESTRAINED OR HELD BACK. Our friend Kitty's curiosity was *irrepressible*: no matter how often we warned her that curiosity killed the cat, she still kept on poking her nose into other people's business.

irresolute \i-'re-zə-,lüt, ,i(r)-, -lət\ adj. UNCERTAIN HOW TO ACT; WEAK. Once you have made your decision, don't waver: a leader should never appear *irresolute*.

irreverent \i-'rev-rənt, ,i(r)-, -'re-və-; -'re-vərnt\ adj. LACK-ING PROPER RESPECT. Some audience members were amused by the comedian's *irreverent* remarks about the pope; others felt offended by his lack of respect for their faith.

irrevocable \i-'re-və-kə-bəl, ,i(r)-\ adj. UNALTERABLE. As Sue dropped the "Dear John" letter into the mailbox, she suddenly had second thoughts, but it was too late: her action was *irrevocable*—she could not take it back.

itinerant \ī-'ti-nə-rənt\ adj. WANDERING; TRAVELING. He was an *itinerant* peddler and traveled through Pennsylvania and Virginia selling his wares. //also n.

itinerary \ī-'ti-nə-,rer-ē, ə-\ n. PLAN OF A TRIP. Disliking sudden changes in plans when she traveled abroad, Ethel refused to alter her *itinerary*.

jaded \'jā-did\ adj. DULLED OR SATIATED BY OVERINDUL-GENCE; FATIGUED. He looked for exotic foods to stimu-late his *jaded* appetite.

jargon \'jär-gən, -,gän\ n. LANGUAGE USED BY SPECIAL GROUP; GIBBERISH; TECHNICAL TERMINOLOGY. The com-puter salesmen at the store used a *jargon* of their own that we simply couldn't follow; we had no idea what they were jabbering about.

jaundiced \'jȯn-dəst\ adj. PREJUDICED (ENVIOUS, HOSTILE, OR RESENTFUL); YELLOWED. Because Martha disliked Mary, she looked at Mary's paintings with a *jaundiced* eye, calling them formless smears.

jaunty \'jȯn-tē, 'jän-\ adj. LIGHTHEARTED; ANIMATED; EASY AND CAREFREE. In *An American in Paris*, Gene Kelly sang and danced his way through "I Got Rhythm" in a properly *jaunty* style.

jeopardize \'je-pər-dīz\ v. ENDANGER; IMPERIL; PUT AT RISK. You can't give me a D in chemistry; you'll *jeopardize* my chances of getting into M.I.T. //jeopardy, n.

jettison \ˈje-tə-sən, -zən\ v. THROW OVERBOARD; DISCARD. In order to enable the ship to ride safely through the storm, the captain had to *jettison* much of his cargo.

jingoism \ˈjiŋ-(ˌ)gō-ˌi-zəm\ n. EXTREMELY AGGRESSIVE AND MILITANT PATRIOTISM. Always bellowing "America first!" the congressman epitomized the spirit of *jingoism*: you could almost hear the sabers rattling as he marched down the hall.

jocular \ˈjä-kyə-lər\ adj. SAID OR DONE IN JEST. Although Bill knew the boss hated jokes, he couldn't resist making one *jocular* remark.

jollity \ˈjä-lə-tē\ n. GAIETY; CHEERFULNESS. The festive Christmas dinner was a merry one, and old and young alike joined in the general *jollity*.

jostle \ˈjä-səl\ v. SHOVE; BUMP. In the subway he was *jostled* by the crowds.

jovial \ˈjō-vē-əl, -vyəl\ adj. GOOD-NATURED; MERRY. A frown seemed out of place on his invariably *jovial* face.

jubilation \ˌjü-bə-ˈlā-shən\ n. REJOICING. There was great *jubilation* when the armistice was announced.

judicious \jü-ˈdi-shəs\ adj. SOUND IN JUDGMENT; WISE. At a key moment in his life, he made a *judicious* investment that was the foundation of his later wealth.

juggernaut \ˈjə-gər-ˌnȯt, -ˌnät\ n. IRRESISTIBLE CRUSHING FORCE. Nothing could survive in the path of the *juggernaut*.

juncture \ˈjəŋ(k)-chər\ n. CRISIS; JOINING POINT. At this critical *juncture*, let us think carefully before determining the course we shall follow.

juxtapose \ˈjək-stə-ˌpōz\ v. PLACE SIDE BY SIDE. You'll find it easier to compare the two sketches if you *juxtapose* them.

kindle \ˈkin-dəl\ v. START A FIRE; INSPIRE. Her teacher's praise for her poetry *kindled* a spark of hope inside Maya.

kindred \\'kin-drəd\\ adj. RELATED; BELONGING TO THE SAME FAMILY. Tom Sawyer and Huck Finn were *kindred* spirits, born mischief makers who were always up to some new tomfoolery. //also n.

kinetic \\kə-'ne-tik *also* kī-\\ adj. PRODUCING MOTION. Designers of the electric automobile find that their greatest obstacle lies in the development of light and efficient storage batteries, the source of the *kinetic* energy needed to propel the vehicle.

kleptomaniac \\ˌklep-tə-'mā-nē-ˌak\\ n. PERSON WHO HAS A COMPULSIVE DESIRE TO STEAL. They discovered that the wealthy customer was a *kleptomaniac* when they caught her stealing some cheap trinkets.

labyrinth \\'la-bə-ˌrin(t)th, -rən(t)th\\ n. MAZE. Hiding from Indian Joe, Tom and Becky soon lost themselves in the *labyrinth* of secret underground caves.

laceration \\ˌla-sə-'rā-shən\\ n. TORN, RAGGED WOUND. The stock car driver needed stitches to close up the *lacerations* he suffered in the crash.

lachrymose \\'la-krə -ˌmōs\\ adj. PRODUCING TEARS. His voice has a *lachrymose* quality that is more appropriate at a funeral than a class reunion.

lackadaisical \\ˌla-kə-'dā-zi-kəl\\ adj. LACKING SPIRIT OR ZEST; LISTLESS; LAZY. Because Gatsby had his mind more on his love life than on his finances, he did a very *lackadaisical* job of managing his money.

lackluster \\'lak-ˌləs-tər\\ adj. DULL. We were disappointed by the *lackluster* performance.

laconic \\lə-'kä-nik\\ adj. BRIEF AND TO THE POINT. Many of the characters portrayed by Clint Eastwood are *laconic* types: strong men of few words.

laggard \\'la-gərd\\ adj. SLOW; SLUGGISH. The sailor had been taught not to be *laggard* in carrying out orders. //lag, n., v.

Each of the questions below consists of a word in capital letters, followed by five words or phrases. Choose the word or phrase that is most similar in meaning to the word in capital letters and write the letter of your choice on your answer paper.

391. **IRKSOME**   (A) annoying   (B) lazy   (C) tireless   (D) devious   (E) excessive

392. **IRRELEVANT**   (A) lacking piety   (B) fragile   (C) congruent   (D) not pertinent   (E) varied

393. **IRREPARABLE**   (A) legible   (B) not correctable   (C) proverbial   (D) concise   (E) legal

394. **IRREVERENT**   (A) related   (B) mischievous   (C) respective   (D) disrespectful   (E) violent

395. **JADED**   (A) upright   (B) satiated   (C) aspiring   (D) applied   (E) void

396. **JAUNDICED**   (A) dark   (B) dire   (C) broken   (D) dapper   (E) envious

397. **JAUNTY**   (A) white   (B) inflamed   (C) quickened   (D) aged   (E) perky

398. **JEOPARDIZE**   (A) enervate   (B) discard   (C) endanger   (D) shove   (E) inspire

399. **JETTISON**   (A) discard   (B) submerge   (C) descend   (D) decelerate   (E) repent

400. **JOCULAR**   (A) arterial   (B) bloodless   (C) verbose   (D) jesting   (E) blind

401. **JUDICIOUS**   (A) punitive   (B) wise   (C) criminal   (D) licit   (E) temporary

402. **KINDLE**   (A) outwit   (B) spark   (C) bother   (D) vent   (E) qualify

403. **LACHRYMOSE**   (A) saddening   (B) smooth   (C) passionate   (D) curt   (E) tense

404. **LACKADAISICAL**   (A) monthly   (B) possessing time   (C) spiritless   (D) pusillanimous   (E) intelligent

405. **LACONIC**   (A) milky   (B) concise   (C) wicked   (D) flagrant   (E) derelict

WORD LIST 28
lampoon–loquacious

lampoon \lam-'pün\ v. RIDICULE. When the Puritans were in power, few had dared openly to *lampoon* them; but, with the restoration of the monarchy, Puritans became fair game for the satirical pens of their enemies. //also n.

languid \'laŋ-gwəd\ adj. WEARY; SLUGGISH; LISTLESS. Her siege of illness left her *languid* and pallid. //languor, n.

languish \'laŋ-gwish\ v. LOSE ANIMATION; LOSE STRENGTH. Left at Miss Minchin's school for girls while her father went off to war, Sarah Crewe refused to *languish*; instead, she hid her grief and actively befriended her less fortunate classmates.

lank \'laŋk\ adj. LONG AND THIN. *Lank*, gaunt, Abraham Lincoln was a striking figure.

larceny \'lärs-nē, -sə-nē\ n. THEFT. Because of the prisoner's record, the district attorney refused to reduce the charge from grand *larceny* to petit *larceny*.

largess \lär-'zhes, lär-'jes *also* 'lär-,jes\ n. GENEROUS GIFT; GIFTS; OR THE ACT OF GIVING THE GIFTS. Lady Bountiful distributed *largess* to the poor.

lascivious \lə-'si-vē-əs\ adj. LUSTFUL. In the plays of the commedia dell'arte, the character Pantalone is a *lascivious* old man dreaming lustful dreams about the pretty young wenches he unsuccessfully pursues.

lassitude \'la-sə-,tüd, -,tyüd\ n. LANGUOR; WEARINESS. After a massage and a long soak in the hot tub, I gave in to my growing *lassitude* and lay down for a nap.

latent \'lā-tənt\ adj. POTENTIAL BUT UNDEVELOPED; DORMANT; HIDDEN. Polaroid pictures were once popular at parties because people enjoyed seeing the *latent* photographic image gradually appear before their eyes.

lateral \'la-tə-rəl *also* 'la-trəl\ adj. COMING FROM THE SIDE. In order to get good plant growth, the gardener must pinch off all *lateral* shoots.

latitude \'la-tə-ˌtüd, -ˌtyüd\ n. FREEDOM FROM NARROW LIMITATIONS. I think you have permitted your son too much *latitude* in this matter.

laud \'lòd\ v. PRAISE. The Soviet premier *lauded* the heroic efforts of the rescue workers after the earthquake. //laudable, laudatory, adj.

lavish \'la-vish\ adj. LIBERAL; WASTEFUL; EXTRAVAGANT. Her wealthy suitors wooed her with *lavish* gifts. //also v.

lax \'laks\ adj. CARELESS. We dislike restaurants where the service is *lax* and inattentive.

lechery \'le-chə-rē\ n. GROSS LEWDNESS; LUSTFULNESS. In his youth he led a life of *lechery* and debauchery; he did not mend his ways until middle age. //lecherous, adj.

legacy \'le-gə-sē\ n. A GIFT MADE BY A WILL; ANYTHING HANDED DOWN FROM THE PAST. Part of my *legacy* from my parents is an album of family photographs.

legend \'le-jənd\ n. EXPLANATORY LIST OF SYMBOLS ON A MAP. The *legend* at the bottom of the map made it clear which symbols stood for rest areas along the highway and which stood for public camp sites. (secondary meaning)

leniency \'lē-nē-ən(t)-sē, -nyən(t)-sē\ n. MILDNESS; PERMISSIVENESS. Considering the gravity of the offense, we were surprised by the *leniency* of the sentence.

lethal \'lē-thəl\ adj. DEADLY. It is unwise to leave *lethal* weapons where children may find them.

lethargic \lə-'thär-jik, le-\ adj. DROWSY; DULL. In class, she tried to stay awake and listen to the professor, but the stuffy room made her *lethargic*; she felt as if she was about to nod off. //lethargy, n.

levity \'le-və-tē\ n. LIGHTNESS, FRIVOLITY. Stop giggling and wriggling around in the pew; such *levity* is improper in church.

lewd \'lüd\ adj. LUSTFUL. The dirty old man whispered *lewd* suggestions in the ear of the sweet young thing.

lexicographer \,lek-sə-'kä-grə-fər\ n. COMPILER OF A DICTIONARY. The new dictionary is the work of many *lexicographers* who spent years compiling and editing the work.

lexicon \'lek-sə-,kän *also* -kən\ n. DICTIONARY. I cannot find this word in any *lexicon* in the library.

liability \,lī-ə-'bi-lə-tē\ n. DRAWBACK; DEBTS. Her lack of an extensive vocabulary was a *liability* that she was unable to overcome.

libel \'lī-b(ə-)l\ n. DEFAMATORY STATEMENT; ACT OF WRITING SOMETHING THAT SMEARS A PERSON'S CHARACTER. If Batman wrote that the Joker was a dirty, rotten, mass-murdering criminal, could the Joker sue Batman for *libel*?

libretto \lə-'bre-(,)tō\ n. TEXT OF AN OPERA. The composer of an opera's music is remembered more frequently than the author of its *libretto*.

lilliputian \,li-lə-'pyü-shən\ adj. EXTREMELY SMALL. Tiny and delicate, the model was built on a *lilliputian* scale. //also n.

limber \'lim-bər\ adj. FLEXIBLE. Hours of ballet classes kept him *limber*.

lineage \'li-nē-ij *also* 'li-nij\ n. DESCENT; ANCESTRY. He traced his *lineage* back to Mayflower days.

linguistic \liŋ-'gwis-tik\ adj. PERTAINING TO LANGUAGE. Growing up speaking Spanish and English, Santiago developed *linguistic* skills that proved helpful when he studied French and Latin in high school.

lionize \'lī-ə-,nīz\ v. TREAT AS A CELEBRITY. She enjoyed being *lionized* and adored by the public.

liquidate \'li-kwə-,dāt\ v. SETTLE ACCOUNTS; CLEAR UP. He was able to *liquidate* all his debts in a short period of time.

listless \'list-ləs\ adj. LACKING IN SPIRIT OR ENERGY. We had expected him to be full of enthusiasm and were surprised by his *listless* attitude.

lithe \'līth, 'līth\ adj. FLEXIBLE; SUPPLE; EFFORTLESSLY GRACEFUL. Ballerinas tend to be *lithe* and willowy; sumo wrestlers do not.

litigation \ˌli-tə-'gā-shən\ n. LAWSUIT. Try to settle this dispute without involving any lawyers; I do not want to get bogged down in *litigation*. //litigant, n.; litigate, v.

loath \'lōth, 'lōth\ adj. AVERSE; RELUCTANT. Fearing for their son's safety, the overprotective parents were *loath* to let him go on the class trip.

loathe \'lōth, 'lōth\ v. DETEST. Booing and hissing, the audience showed how much they *loathed* the villain.

lode \'lōd\ n. METAL-BEARING VEIN. If this *lode* that we have discovered extends for any distance, we have found a fortune.

lofty \'lȯf-tē\ adj. VERY HIGH. Though Barbara Jordan's fellow students used to tease her about her *lofty* ambitions, she rose to hold one of the highest positions in the land.

loiter \'lȯi-tər\ v. HANG AROUND; LINGER. The policeman told him not to *loiter* in the alley.

longevity \län-'je-və-tē, lȯn-\ n. LONG LIFE. Researchers in human *longevity* report that Okinawans and inhabitants of South Georgia have achieved extremely great life spans.

loquacious \lō-'kwā-shəs\ adj. TALKATIVE. Though our daughter barely says a word to us these days, put a cell phone in her hand and see how *loquacious* she can be: our phone bills are out of sight!

Each of the questions below consists of a word in capital letters, followed by five words or phrases. Choose the word or phrase that is most similar in meaning to the word in capital letters and write the letter of your choice on your answer paper.

406. **LAMPOON**   (A) darken   (B) mock   (C) abandon   (D) sail   (E) fly

407. **LANGUID**   (A) weariness   (B) length   (C) embarrassment   (D) wine   (E) avarice

408. **LATENT**   (A) trim   (B) forbidding   (C) execrable   (D) early   (E) dormant

409. **LAUDATORY**   (A) dirtying   (B) disclaiming   (C) praising   (D) inflammatory   (E) debased

410. **LAVISH**   (A) hostile   (B) unwashed   (C) timely   (D) decent   (E) plentiful

411. **LAX**   (A) salty   (B) careless   (C) shrill   (D) boring   (E) cowardly

412. **LECHERY**   (A) trust   (B) compulsion   (C) zeal   (D) addiction   (E) lustfulness

413. **LETHARGIC**   (A) convalescent   (B) beautiful   (C) enervating   (D) sluggish   (E) interrogating

414. **LEVITY**   (A) bridge   (B) dam   (C) praise   (D) blame   (E) frivolity

415. **LILLIPUTIAN**   (A) destructive   (B) proper   (C) minuscule   (D) elegant   (E) barren

416. **LIMBER**   (A) graceful   (B) flexible   (C) tangential   (D) timid   (E) weary

417. **LISTLESS**   (A) alone   (B) mundane   (C) positive   (D) enervated   (E) vast

418. **LITHE**   (A) limber   (B) limpid   (C) facetious   (D) insipid   (E) vast

419. **LOATH**   (A) loose   (B) evident   (C) deliberate   (D) reluctant   (E) tiny

420. **LOQUACIOUS**   (A) chatty   (B) sentimental   (C) soporific   (D) soothing   (E) sedate

lucid \'lü-səd\ adj. EASILY UNDERSTOOD; CLEAR; INTELLIGIBLE. Lexy makes an excellent teacher: her explanations of technical points are *lucid* enough for a child to grasp. //lucidity, n.

lucrative \'lü-krə-tiv\ adj. PROFITABLE. He turned his hobby into a *lucrative* profession.

ludicrous \'lü-də-krəs\ adj. RIDICULOUS; LAUGHABLE; ABSURD. Gwen tried to keep a straight face, but Bill's suggestion was so *ludicrous* that she finally had to laugh.

lugubrious \lu̇-'gü-brē-əs *also* -'gyü-\ adj. MOURNFUL. Gloomy Gus walked around with a *lugubrious* expression on his face.

lull \'ləl\ n. MOMENT OF CALM. Not wanting to get wet, they waited under the awning for a *lull* in the rain.

luminous \'lü-mə-nəs\ adj. SHINING; ISSUING LIGHT. The sun is a *luminous* body.

lunar \'lü-nər *also* -ˌnär\ adj. PERTAINING TO THE MOON. American astronaut Neil Armstrong was the first man to set foot on the *lunar* surface.

lurid \'lu̇r-əd\ adj. WILD; SENSATIONAL. Do the *lurid* cover stories in the *Enquirer* actually influence people to buy that trashy tabloid?

luscious \'lə-shəs\ adj. PLEASING TO TASTE OR SMELL. The ripe peach was *luscious*.

lustrous \'ləs-trəs\ n. SHINING; GLOSSY; RADIANT; ILLUSTRIOUS. Rapunzel brushed her shining hair one hundred strokes until it hung down in *lustrous* golden waves. //luster, n.

luxuriant \(ˌ)ləg-'zhu̇r-ē-ənt, (ˌ)lək-'shu̇r-\ adj. ABUNDANT; RICH AND SPLENDID; FERTILE. Lady Godiva's naked body was completely hidden by her *luxuriant* hair.

macabre \mə-'käb; -'kä-brə, -bər; -'käbrə\ adj. GRUESOME; GRISLY; SHOCKINGLY REPELLENT. The city morgue is a *macabre* spot for the uninitiated.

machinations \ˌma-kə-ˈnā-shəns, ma-shə-\ n. EVIL SCHEMES OR PLOTS. Fortunately, Batman saw through the Riddler's wily *machinations* and was able to save Gotham City from destruction by the forces of evil.

maelstrom \ˈmāl-strəm, -ˌsträm\ n. WHIRLPOOL. The canoe was tossed about in the *maelstrom*.

magnanimous \mag-ˈna-nə-məs\ adj. GENEROUS. Philanthropists, by definition, are *magnanimous*; misers, by definition, are not.

magnate \ˈmag-ˌnāt, -nət\ n. PERSON OF PROMINENCE OR INFLUENCE. Growing up in Pittsburgh, Annie Dillard was surrounded by the mansions of the great steel and coal *magnates* who set their mark on that city.

magnitude \ˈmag-nə-ˌtüd, -ˌtyüd\ n. GREATNESS; EXTENT. It is difficult to comprehend the *magnitude* of his crime.

maim \ˈmām\ v. MUTILATE; INJURE. The hospital could not take care of all who had been wounded or *maimed* in the railroad accident.

maladroit \ˌma-lə-ˈdroit\ adj. CLUMSY; BUNGLING. "Oh! My stupid tongue!" exclaimed Jane, embarrassed at having said anything so *maladroit*.

malaise \mə-ˈlāz, ma-, -ˈlez\ n. UNEASINESS; VAGUE FEELING OF ILL HEALTH. Feeling slightly queasy before going onstage, Carol realized that this touch of *malaise* was merely stage fright.

malapropism \ˈma-lə-ˌprä-ˌpi-zəm\ n. COMIC MISUSE OF A WORD. When Mrs. Malaprop criticizes Lydia for being "as headstrong as an allegory on the banks of the Nile," she confuses "allegory" and "alligator" in a typical *malapropism*.

malcontent \ˌmal-kən-ˈtent\ n. PERSON DISSATISFIED WITH EXISTING STATE OF AFFAIRS. He was one of the few *malcontents* in Congress; he constantly voiced his objections to the presidential program. //also adj.

malediction \ˌma-lə-ˈdik-shən\ n. CURSE. When the magic mirror revealed that Snow White was still alive, the wicked queen cried out in rage and uttered dreadful *maledictions*.

malefactor \\'ma-lə-ˌfak-tər\\ n. CRIMINAL. Mighty Mouse will save the day, hunting down *malefactors* and saving innocent mice from peril.

malevolent \\mə-'le-və-lənt\\ adj. WISHING EVIL. Iago is a *malevolent* villain who takes pleasure in ruining Othello.

malicious \\mə-'li-shəs\\ adj. HATEFUL; SPITEFUL. Jealous of Cinderella's beauty, her *malicious* stepsisters expressed their spite by forcing her to perform menial tasks.

malign \\mə-'līn\\ v. SPEAK EVIL OF; DEFAME. Putting her hands over her ears, Rose refused to listen to Betty *malign* her friend Susan.

malignant \\mə-'lig-nənt\\ adj. INJURIOUS; TENDING TO CAUSE DEATH; AGGRESSIVELY MALEVOLENT. Though many tumors are benign, some are *malignant*, growing out of control and endangering the life of the patient.

malingerer \\mə-'liŋ-gər-ər\\ n. ONE WHO FEIGNS ILLNESS TO ESCAPE DUTY. The captain ordered the sergeant to punish all *malingerers* and force them to work. //malinger, v.

malleable \\'ma-lē-ə-bəl, 'mal-yə-bəl, 'ma-lə-bəl\\ adj. CAPABLE OF BEING SHAPED BY POUNDING; IMPRESSIONABLE. Gold is a *malleable* metal, easily shaped into bracelets and rings. Fagin hoped Oliver was a *malleable* lad, easily shaped into a thief.

malodorous \\ˌmal-'ō-də-rəs\\ adj. FOUL-SMELLING. The compost heap was most *malodorous* in summer.

mammal \\'ma-məl\\ n. A VERTEBRATE ANIMAL WHOSE FEMALE SUCKLES ITS YOUNG. Many people regard the whale as a fish and do not realize that it is a *mammal*.

mammoth \\'ma-məth\\ adj. GIGANTIC. To try to memorize every word on this vocabulary list would be a *mammoth* undertaking; take on projects that are more manageable in size.

mandatory \\'man-də-,tȯr-ē\ adj. OBLIGATORY; COMPULSORY. It is *mandatory* that, before graduation, all students must pass the swimming test. //mandate, n., v.

maniacal \mə-'nī-ə-kəl\ adj. RAVING MAD. Though Mr. Rochester had locked his mad wife in the attic, he could still hear her *maniacal* laughter echoing throughout the house.

manifest \\'ma-nə-,fest\ adj. EVIDENT; VISIBLE; OBVIOUS. Digby's embarrassment when he met Madonna was *manifest*: his ears turned bright pink, and he couldn't look her in the eye. //also v.

manipulate \mə-'ni-pyə-,lāt\ v. OPERATE WITH THE HANDS; INFLUENCE SKILLFULLY. Jim Henson understood how to *manipulate* the Muppets; Madonna understands how to *manipulate* men (and publicity).

marred \\'märd\ adj. DAMAGED; DISFIGURED. She had to refinish the *marred* surface of the table. //mar, v.

marsupial \mär-'sü-pē-əl\ n. ONE OF A FAMILY OF MAMMALS THAT NURSE THEIR OFFSPRING IN A POUCH. The most common *marsupial* in North America is the opossum.

martial \\'mär-shəl\ adj. WARLIKE. The sound of *martial* music inspired the young cadet with dreams of military glory.

masochist \\'ma-sə-,kist\ n. PERSON WHO ENJOYS HIS OWN PAIN. The *masochist* begs, "Hit me." The sadist smiles and says, "I won't."

maternal \mə-'tər-nəl\ adj. MOTHERLY. Many animals display *maternal* instincts only while their offspring are young and helpless.

matriarch \\'mā-trē-,ärk\ n. WOMAN WHO RULES A FAMILY OR LARGER SOCIAL GROUP. The *matriarch* ruled her gypsy tribe with a firm hand.

maudlin \\'mȯd-lən\ adj. EFFUSIVELY SENTIMENTAL. Whenever a particularly *maudlin* tearjerker was playing at the movies, Marvin embarrassed himself by weeping copiously.

Each of the questions below consists of a word in capital letters, followed by five words or phrases. Choose the word or phrase that is most similar in meaning to the word in capital letters and write the letter of your choice on your answer paper.

421. **LUGUBRIOUS** (A) frantic (B) mournful (C) burdensome (D) oily (E) militant

422. **LURID** (A) sensational (B) duplicate (C) heavy (D) painstaking (E) intelligent

423. **MACABRE** (A) musical (B) frightening (C) chewed (D) wicked (E) exceptional

424. **MAGNANIMOUS** (A) loquacious (B) generous (C) rudimentary (D) qualitative (E) minimizing

425. **MAGNITUDE** (A) realization (B) fascination (C) enormity (D) gratitude (E) interference

426. **MALADROIT** (A) malicious (B) starving (C) thirsty (D) tactless (E) artistic

427. **MALEDICTION** (A) misfortune (B) hap (C) fruition (D) correct pronunciation (E) curse

428. **MALEFACTOR** (A) quail (B) lawbreaker (C) beneficiary (D) banker (E) female agent

429. **MALEVOLENT** (A) ill willed (B) vacuous (C) ambivalent (D) volatile (E) primitive

430. **MALIGN** (A) intersperse (B) vary (C) emphasize (D) frighten (E) defame

431. **MALLEABLE** (A) flexible (B) blatant (C) brilliant (D) brownish (E) basking

432. **MANIACAL** (A) demoniac (B) saturated (C) insane (D) sanitary (E) handcuffed

433. **MANIFEST** (A) limited (B) obvious (C) faulty (D) varied (E) vital

434. **MARRED** (A) enjoyable (B) simple (C) imperfect (D) agreeable (E) proud

435. **MARTIAL** (A) bellicose (B) celibate (C) divorced (D) quiescent (E) planetary

maverick \'mav-rik, 'ma-və-\ n. REBEL; NONCONFORMIST. To the masculine literary establishment, George Sand with her insistence on wearing trousers and smoking cigars was clearly a *maverick* who fought her proper womanly role.

maxim \'mak-səm\ n. PROVERB; A TRUTH PITHILY STATED. Aesop's story of the hare and the tortoise illustrates the *maxim* "Slow and steady wins the race."

meager \'mē-gər\ adj. SCANTY; INADEQUATE. Still hungry after his *meager* serving of porridge, Oliver Twist asked for a second helping.

meander \mē-'an-dər\ v. TO WIND OR TURN IN ITS COURSE. Needing to stay close to a source of water, he followed every twist and turn of the stream as it *meandered* through the countryside.

meddlesome \'me-dəl-səm\ adj. INTERFERING. He felt his marriage was suffering because of his *meddlesome* mother-in-law.

mediate \'mē-dē-,āt\ v. SETTLE A DISPUTE THROUGH THE SERVICES OF AN OUTSIDER. King Solomon was asked to *mediate* a dispute between two women over which one of them was the mother of a particular child.

mediocre \,mē-dē-'ō-kər\ adj. ORDINARY; COMMONPLACE. We were disappointed because he gave a rather *mediocre* performance in this role.

meditation \,me-də-'tā-shən\ n. REFLECTION; THOUGHT. She reached her decision only after much *meditation*.

medley \'med-lē\ n. MIXTURE. To avoid boring listeners by playing any one tune for too long, bands may combine three or four tunes into a *medley*.

melee \'mā-,lā, mā-'\ n. FIGHT. The captain tried to ascertain the cause of the *melee* that had broken out among the crew members.

mellifluous \me-'li-flə-wəs, mə-\ adj. FLOWING SMOOTHLY; SMOOTH. What a *mellifluous* language Italian is! Even the street vendors' cries sound melodious.

memento \mə-'men-(ˌ)tō, ÷mō-\ n. TOKEN; REMINDER. Take this book as a *memento* of your visit.

mendacious \men-'dā-shəs\ adj. LYING; FALSE. Distrusting Huck from the start, Miss Watson assumed he was *mendacious* and refused to believe a word he said.

mendicant \'men-di-kənt\ n. BEGGAR. "O noble sir, give alms to the poor," cried Aladdin, playing the *mendicant.*

menial \'mē-nē-əl, -nyəl\ adj. SUITABLE FOR SERVANTS; LOWLY AND SOMETIMES DEGRADING. Her wicked step-mother forced Cinderella to do *menial* tasks around the house while her ugly stepsisters lolled about, primping and painting their toenails. //also n.

mentor \'men-ˌtȯr, -tər\ n. TEACHER. During this very try-ing period, she could not have had a better *mentor*, for the teacher was sympathetic and understanding.

mercenary \'mər-sə-ˌner-ē, -ne-rē\ adj. INTERESTED IN MONEY OR GAIN. Andy's every act was prompted by *mercenary* motives; his first question was always "What's in it for me?" //also n.

mercurial \(ˌ)mər-'kyùr-ē-əl\ adj. FICKLE; CHANGING; CAPRI-CIOUS. Quick as quicksilver to change his moods, he was a *mercurial* creature, whose reactions were impossible to predict.

mesa \'mā-sə\ n. HIGH, FLAT-TOPPED HILL. The *mesa*, rising above the surrounding countryside, was the most con-spicuous feature of the area.

mesmerize \'mez-mə-ˌrīz\ *also* 'mes-\ v. HYPNOTIZE. The incessant drone seemed to *mesmerize* him and place him in a trance.

metamorphosis \ˌme-tə-'mȯr-fə-səs\ n. CHANGE OF FORM. In *Miss Congeniality*, the FBI agent heroine under-goes a *metamorphosis* that transforms her from a

classic ugly duckling into a potential beauty queen.
//metamorphose, v.

metaphor \\'me-tə-ˌfȯr *also* -fər\ n. IMPLIED COMPARISON.
"He soared like an eagle" is an example of a simile;
"He is an eagle in flight," a *metaphor*.

mete \\'mēt\ v. MEASURE; DISTRIBUTE. He tried to be impartial in his efforts to *mete* out justice.

methodical \mə-'thä-di-kəl\ adj. SYSTEMATIC. An accountant must be *methodical* and maintain order among
his financial records.

meticulous \mə-'ti-kyə-ləs\ adj. EXCESSIVELY CAREFUL;
PAINSTAKING; SCRUPULOUS. Martha Stewart was a *meticulous* housekeeper, fussing about each and every
detail that went into creating her perfect home.

metropolis \mə-'trä-p(ə-)ləs\ n. LARGE CITY. Every
evening the terminal is filled with thousands of com-
muters traveling from this *metropolis* to their subur-
ban homes.

mettle \\'me-təl\ n. COURAGE; SPIRIT. When challenged by
the other horses in the race, the thoroughbred proved
its *mettle* by its determination to hold the lead.

microcosm \\'mī-krə-ˌkä-zəm\ n. SMALL WORLD; THE WORLD
IN MINIATURE. The village community that Jane Austen
depicts in her novels serves as a *microcosm* of
English society in her time, for in this small world we
see all the social classes meeting and mingling.

mien \\'mēn\ n. DEMEANOR; BEARING. She had the gracious
mien of a queen.

migratory \\'mī-grə-ˌtȯr-ē\ adj. WANDERING. The return of
the *migratory* birds to the northern sections of this
country is a harbinger of spring. //migrate, v.

milieu \mēl-'yə(r), -'yü, -'yœ; 'mēl-ˌyü\ n. ENVIRONMENT;
MEANS OF EXPRESSION. Surrounded by city slickers and
arty bohemians, the country boy felt out of his *milieu*.

militant \\'mi-lə-tənt\ adj. COMBATIVE; BELLICOSE; AGGRES-
SIVE IN SUPPORT OF A CAUSE. Susan B. Anthony was a

militant reformer whose aggressive tactics in support of women's rights sometimes set her at odds with more conservative suffragists. //also n.

millennium \mə-'le-nē-əm\ n. THOUSAND-YEAR PERIOD; PERIOD OF HAPPINESS AND PROSPERITY. I do not expect the *millennium* to come during my lifetime.

mimicry \'mi-mi-krē\ n. IMITATION. Her gift for *mimicry* was so great that her friends said that she should be in the theater.

minuscule \'mi-nəs-ˌkyül *also* mi-'nəs-\ adj. EXTREMELY SMALL. Why should I involve myself with a project with so *minuscule* a chance for success?

minute \mī-'nüt, mə-, -'nyüt\ adj. EXTREMELY SMALL. The twins resembled one another closely; only *minute* differences set them apart.

mire \'mī(-ə)r\ v. ENTANGLE; STICK IN SWAMPY GROUND. Their rear wheels became *mired* in mud. //also n.

mirth \'mərth\ n. MERRIMENT; LAUGHTER. Sober Malvolio found Sir Toby's *mirth* improper.

misanthrope \'mi-sən-ˌthrōp\ n. ONE WHO HATES HUMANITY. In *Gulliver's Travels* Swift portrays human beings as vile, degraded beasts; for this reason, various critics consider him a *misanthrope*. //misanthropic, adj.

misapprehension \(ˌ)mis-ˌa-pri-'hen(t)-shən\ n. ERROR; MISUNDERSTANDING. I am afraid you are suffering from a *misapprehension*, Mr. Collins; I do not want to marry you at all.

misconstrue \ˌmis-kən-'strü\ v. INTERPRET INCORRECTLY; MISJUDGE. She took the passage seriously rather than humorously because she *misconstrued* the author's ironic tone.

miscreant \'mis-krē-ənt\ n. VILLAIN; SCOUNDREL; REPROBATE. Arrested for drunk driving, the councilman wound up in a jail cell in the company of drug dealers and shoplifters and other common *miscreants*.

misdemeanor \,mis-di-'mē-nər\ n. MINOR CRIME. The culprit pleaded guilty to a *misdemeanor* rather than face trial for a felony.

miserly \'mī-zər-lē\ adj. STINGY; MEAN. Transformed by his vision on Christmas Eve, stingy old Scrooge ceased being *miserly* and became a generous, kind old man. //miser, n.

misgivings \,mis-'gi-viŋz\ n. DOUBTS. Hamlet described his *misgivings* to Horatio but decided to fence with Laertes despite his foreboding of evil.

misnomer \,mis-'nō-mər\ n. WRONG NAME; INCORRECT DESIGNATION. His tyrannical conduct proved to all that his nickname, King Eric the Just, was a *misnomer*.

Each of the questions below consists of a word in capital letters, followed by five words or phrases. Choose the word or phrase that is most similar in meaning to the word in capital letters and write the letter of your choice on your answer paper.

436. **MEAGER** (A) inadequate (B) true (C) certain (D) devious (E) carefree

437. **MEDIOCRE** (A) average (B) bitter (C) medieval (D) industrial (E) agricultural

438. **MELEE** (A) heat (B) brawl (C) attempt (D) weapon (E) choice

439. **MELLIFLUOUS** (A) porous (B) honeycombed (C) strong (D) smooth (E) viscous

440. **MENIAL** (A) intellectual (B) clairvoyant (C) servile (D) arrogant (E) laudatory

441. **MENTOR** (A) guide (B) genius (C) talker (D) philosopher (E) stylist

442. **MESMERIZE** (A) remember (B) hypnotize (C) delay (D) bore (E) analyze

443. **METICULOUS** (A) steadfast (B) recent (C) quaint (D) painstaking (E) overt

443. **MICROCOSM** (A) dreamlike state (B) small world (C) scenario (D) quantity (E) total

445. **MILITANT** (A) combative (B) dramatic (C) religious (D) quaint (E) paternal

446. **MIMICRY** (A) comedian (B) quorum (C) majority (D) hazard (E) imitation

447. **MIRTH** (A) dessert (B) laughter (A) train (D) mirror (E) statement

448. **MISANTHROPE** (A) person working solely for money (B) aggressive reformer (C) hater of humankind (D) villain (E) nonconformist

449. **MISCONSTRUE** (A) gamble (B) retract (C) prove useless (D) show off (E) interpret incorrectly

450. **MISDEMEANOR** (A) felony (B) peccadillo (C) indignity (D) fiat (E) illiteracy

Each of the questions below consists of a sentence from which one word is missing. Choose the most appropriate replacement from among the five choices.

1. An exemplary research paper includes specific evidence, rather than _____.
   (A) malapropisms   (B) jargon   (C) irony
   (D) incentives   (E) generalities

2. There is a deep philosophical divide between those who advocate full exploitation of our natural resources and those who champion careful _____ of those same resources.
   (A) husbandry   (B) guile   (C) humility
   (D) indignation   (E) mediation

3. After hatching, the tadpole is gill-breathing and legless and propels itself by means of a tail; later it undergoes a _____ and develops the lungs, legs, and other organs of an adult frog and loses the tail.
   (A) meditation   (B) metamorphosis   (C) malingering
   (D) inundation   (E) incarceration

4. The cult leader was always on the lookout for _____ and impressionable youth.
   (A) grotesque   (B) indefatigable   (C) gullible
   (D) incorrigible   (E) maniacal

5. Please use a coaster under your glass in order to avoid _____ the wood furniture.
   (A) lionizing   (B) invoking   (C) invalidating
   (D) marring   (E) miring

6. The professor's eccentric wardrobe caused endless _____ among his students.
   (A) mirth   (B) manipulation   (C) malaise
   (D) lethargy   (E) instigation

7. An avid reader as a child, Maya Angelou had an _____ appetite for books.
   (A) insular   (B) implicit   (C) insatiable
   (D) impregnable   (E) illusory

8. Made up of immigrants, the population of the United States is far more _____ than that of Japan.
   (A) generic   (B) garish   (C) histrionic
       (D) indigenous   (E) heterogeneous

9. Many children believe that their parents are _____ and are shocked to learn that they can make mistakes.
   (A) indissoluble   (B) intermittent   (C) infallible
       (D) insidious   (E) intractable

10. The young knight was sent on a perilous quest to test his _____.
   (A) mettle   (B) maxim   (C) luster
       (D) latitude   (E) indolence

11. Learning disabilities, such as dyslexia, can significantly _____ a student's academic progress.
   (A) lull   (B) manifest   (C) impede
       (D) mesmerize   (E) meander

12. I planned to _____ all of my possessions in a massive garage sale before embarking on a two-year voyage to circumnavigate the globe.
   (A) lacerate   (B) mete   (C) liquidate
       (D) invert   (E) hamper

13. Young people sometimes fail to grasp the long-term _____ of many of the decisions they face.
   (A) import   (B) guile   (C) innovation
       (D) microcosm   (E) mimicry

14. The dour _____ of the school's headmaster made all of the students dread being called before him.
   (A) insinuation   (B) mien   (C) gentility
       (D) harbinger   (E) histrionics

15. Hamlet's constant equivocation often left him _____ by indecision.
   (A) impoverished   (B) ingenious   (C) kindled
       (D) immobilized   (E) impecunious

misogynist \mə-'sä-jə-nist\ n. HATER OF WOMEN. H. L. Mencken once cynically defined a *misogynist* as a man who hates women as much as women hate one another.

missile \'mi-səl\ n. OBJECT TO BE THROWN OR PROJECTED. Carefully folding his book report into a paper airplane, Beavis threw the *missile* across the classroom at Butthead.

mitigate \'mi-tə-ˌgāt\ v. LESSEN OR MAKE LESS SEVERE; APPEASE. Because solar energy has the power to reduce greenhouse gases, conversion to the use of solar energy may help *mitigate* global warming.

mnemonic \ni-'mä-nik\ adj. PERTAINING TO MEMORY. She used *mnemonic* tricks—simple word associations and mental images—to help remember new vocabulary words.

mobile \'mō-bəl, -ˌbī-əl *also* -ˌbēl\ adj. MOVABLE; NOT FIXED. The *mobile* blood bank operated by the Red Cross visited our neighborhood today. //mobility, n.

mode \'mōd\ n. MANNER OF ACTING OR DOING; METHOD; PREVAILING STYLE. Henry plans to adopt a simpler *mode* of life: he is going to be a mushroom hunter and live off the land.

modicum \'mä-di-kəm *also* 'mō-\ n. LIMITED QUANTITY; MODERATE AMOUNT. In colonial times, the only requirements for teaching in the lower schools were a *modicum* of learning and a willingness to work in what was then an ill-paid, low-prestige occupation.

modulate \'mä-jə-ˌlāt\ v. TONE DOWN IN INTENSITY; REGULATE; CHANGE FROM ONE KEY TO ANOTHER. Always singing at the top of her lungs, the budding Brunhilde never learned to *modulate* her voice. //modulation, n.

molecule \'mä-li-ˌkyül\ n. THE SMALLEST PART OF A HOMOGENEOUS SUBSTANCE. In chemistry, we study how atoms and *molecules* react to form new substances.

mollify \'mä-lə-,fī\ v. SOOTHE. The airline customer service representative tried to *mollify* the angry passenger by offering her a seat in first class.

molt \'mōlt\ v. SHED OR CAST OFF HAIR OR FEATHERS. When Molly's canary *molted*, he shed feathers all over the house.

molten \'mōl-tən\ adj. MELTED. The city of Pompeii was destroyed by volcanic ash rather than by *molten* lava flowing from Mount Vesuvius.

momentous \mō-'men-təs, mə-\ adj. VERY IMPORTANT. When Marie and Pierre Curie discovered radium, they had no idea of the *momentous* impact their discovery would have upon society.

momentum \mō-'men-təm, mə-\ n. QUANTITY OF MOTION OF A MOVING BODY; IMPETUS. The car lost *momentum* as it tried to ascend the steep hill.

monarchy \'mä-nər-kē *also* -,när-\ n. GOVERNMENT UNDER A SINGLE RULER. Though England today is a *monarchy*, there is some question whether it will be one in 20 years, given the present discontent at the prospect of Prince Charles as king.

monastic \mə-'nas-tik\ adj. RELATED TO MONKS. Withdrawing from the world, Thomas Merton joined a contemplative religious order and adopted the *monastic* life.

monetary \'mä-nə-,ter-ē *also* 'mə-\ adj. PERTAINING TO MONEY; FISCAL. Jane held the family purse strings: she made all *monetary* decisions affecting the household.

monolithic \,mä-nə-'li-thik\ adj. SOLIDLY UNIFORM; UNYIELDING. Except where it is under totalitarian state control, journalism has never been a *monolithic* enterprise, but has ranged from sensationalism and scandal to objective reporting and assessment.

monotony \mə-'nä-tə-nē, -'nät-nē\ n. SAMENESS LEADING TO BOREDOM. What could be more deadly dull than the *monotony* of punching numbers into a computer hour after hour?

monumental \,män-yə-'men-təl\ adj. MASSIVE. Writing a dictionary is a *monumental* task; so is reading one.

moodiness \'mü-dē-nəs\ n. FITS OF DEPRESSION OR GLOOM. Her recurrent *moodiness* grew worse and worse until she felt as if she had fallen into a black hole.

moratorium \,mȯr-ə-'tȯr-ē-əm, ,mär-\ n. SUSPENSION OF ACTIVITY; LEGAL DELAY OF OBLIGATION OR OF PAYMENT. If we declare a *moratorium* and delay collection of debts for six months, I am sure the farmers will be able to meet their bills.

morbid \'mȯr-bəd\ adj. GIVEN TO UNWHOLESOME THOUGHT; GLOOMY; CHARACTERISTIC OF DISEASE. People who visit disaster sites in order to peer at the grisly wreckage are indulging their *morbid* curiosity.

moribund \'mȯr-ə-(,)bənd, 'mär-\ adj. AT THE POINT OF DEATH. Hearst took a *moribund*, failing weekly newspaper and transformed it into one of the liveliest, most profitable daily papers around.

morose \mə-'rōs, mȯ-\ adj. ILL-HUMORED; SULLEN; MELAN-CHOLY. Forced to take early retirement, Bill acted *morose* for months; then, all of a sudden, he shook off his sullen mood and was his usual cheerful self.

mortify \'mȯr-tə-,fī\ v. HUMILIATE; PUNISH THE FLESH. She was so *mortified* by her blunder that she ran to her room in tears.

mote \'mōt\ n. SMALL SPECK. The tiniest *mote* in the eye is very painful.

motif \mō-'tēf\ n. THEME. This simple *motif* runs throughout the entire score.

motley \'mät-lē\ adj. MIXED IN NATURE; MADE UP OF MANY COLORS. Captain Ahab had gathered a *motley* crew to sail the vessel: old sea dogs and runaway boys, even a tattooed islander who terrified his shipmates.

mottled \'mä-təld\ adj. SPOTTED; BLOTCHED IN COLORING. When old Falstaff blushed, his face became *mottled*, turning pink and purple and red.

muddle \\'mə-dəl\\ v. CONFUSE; MIX UP. Please don't all try to give me directions at once; if you do, you're sure to *muddle* me. //also n.

muggy \\'mə-gē\\ adj. WARM AND DAMP. August in New York City is often *muggy*.

multiplicity \\,məl-tə-'pli-sə-tē\\ n. STATE OF BEING NUMEROUS. He was appalled by the *multiplicity* of details he had to complete before setting out on his mission.

mundane \\,mən-'dān, 'mən-,\\ adj. WORLDLY AS OPPOSED TO SPIRITUAL; EVERYDAY. Uninterested in spiritual or philosophical discussions, Tom preferred to chat about more *mundane* matters such as the daily weather forecast or the latest basketball results.

munificent \\myu̇-'ni-fə-sənt\\ adj. VERY GENEROUS. The Annenberg Trust made a *munificent* gift that supported art programs in the public schools. //munificence, n.

murky \\'mər-kē\\ adj. DARK AND GLOOMY; THICK WITH FOG; OBSCURE. The *murky* depths of the swamp were so dark that you couldn't tell the vines and branches from the snakes. //murkiness, n.

muse \\'myüz\\ v. PONDER. For a moment he *mused* about the beauty of the scene, but his thoughts soon changed as he recalled his personal problems. //also n.

muster \\'məs-tər\\ v. GATHER; ASSEMBLE. Washington *mustered* his forces at Trenton.

musty \\'məs-tē\\ adj. STALE; SPOILED BY AGE. The attic was dark and *musty*.

mutable \\'myü-tə-bəl\\ adj. SUBJECT TO CHANGE; INCONSTANT. The theory of evolution maintains that species are *mutable*, changing over time through the processes of natural selection and genetic drift.

muted \\'myü-təd\\ adj. SILENT; MUFFLED; TONED DOWN. In the funeral parlor, the mourners' voices had a *muted* quality. //mute, v.

mutinous \\'myü-tə-nəs, 'myüt-nəs\\ adj. UNRULY; REBELLIOUS. The captain had to use force to quiet his *mutinous* crew.

myopic \\mī-'ō-pik, -'ä-\\ adj. NEARSIGHTED; LACKING FORESIGHT. Stumbling into doors despite the thick lenses on his glasses, the nearsighted Mr. Magoo is markedly *myopic*. //myopia, n.

myriad \\'mir-ē-əd\\ n. VERY LARGE NUMBER. *Myriads* of mosquitoes from the swamps invaded our village every twilight. //also adj.

nadir \\'nā-,dir, 'nā-dər\\ n. LOWEST POINT. Although few people realized it, the Dow-Jones averages had reached their *nadir* and would soon begin an upward surge.

naiveté \\nä-,ēv-'tā, -,ē-və-; nä-'ēv-,tā, -'ē-və-; nī-\\ n. SIMPLICITY; ARTLESSNESS. Touched by the *naiveté* of sweet, convent-trained Cosette, Marius pledges himself to protect her innocence. //naive, adj.

narcissist \\'när-sə-sist\\ n. CONCEITED, SELF-CENTERED PERSON. A *narcissist* is his own best friend. //narcissism, adj; narcissistic, adj.

Each of the questions below consists of a word in capital letters, followed by five words or phrases. Choose the word or phrase that is most similar in meaning to the word in capital letters and write the letter of your choice on your answer paper.

451. **MITIGATE**   (A) deserve   (B) lessen   (C) deposit   (D) include   (E) permit

452. **MOLLIFY**   (A) avenge   (B) attenuate   (C) attribute   (D) mortify   (E) appease

453. **MONETARY**   (A) boring   (B) fascinating   (C) fiscal   (D) stationary   (E) scrupulous

454. **MONOLITHIC**   (A) visual   (B) invisible   (C) uniform   (D) anticipatory   (E) obsequious

455. **MONUMENTAL**   (A) singular   (B) massive   (C) statutory   (D) controlling   (E) avenging

456. **MORIBUND**   (A) dying   (B) appropriate   (C) leather bound   (D) answering   (E) undertaking

457. **MOTLEY**   (A) active   (B) disguised   (C) variegated   (D) somber   (E) sick

458. **MUGGY**   (A) attacking   (B) fascinating   (C) humid   (D) characteristic   (E) gelid

459. **MUDDLE**   (A) mix up   (B) hold back   (C) record   (D) print   (E) fertilize

460. **MURKY**   (A) variegated   (B) gloomy   (C) multilateral   (D) polyandrous   (E) frightening

461. **MUNDANE**   (A) global   (B) futile   (C) spatial   (D) heretic   (E) worldly

462. **MUNIFICENT**   (A) grandiose   (B) puny   (C) philanthropic   (D) poor   (E) gracious

463. **MUSTY**   (A) stale   (B) necessary   (C) indifferent   (D) nonchalant   (E) vivid

464. **MYOPIC**   (A) visionary   (B) nearsighted   (C) moral   (D) glassy   (E) blind

465. **NAIVE**   (A) unsophisticated   (B) stupid   (C) loyal   (D) treacherous   (E) unnamed

nebulous \'ne-byə-ləs\ adj. VAGUE; HAZY; CLOUDY. Adam and Phil tried to come up with a clear, intelligible business plan, not some hazy, *nebulous* proposal.

necromancy \,ne-krə-'man(t)-sē\ n. BLACK MAGIC; DEALINGS WITH THE DEAD. The evil sorcerer resorted to *necromancy*, calling on the spirits of the dead to foretell the future.

nefarious \ni-'fer-ē-əs\ adj. VERY WICKED. The villain's crimes, though various, were one and all *nefarious*.

negate \ni-'gāt\ v. CANCEL OUT; NULLIFY; DENY. A sudden surge of adrenaline can *negate* the effects of fatigue; there's nothing like a good shock to wake you up. //negation. n.

negligence \'ne-gli-jən(t)s\ n. NEGLECT; FAILURE TO TAKE REASONABLE CARE. Tommy failed to replace the cover on the well after he fetched his pail of water; because of his *negligence*, Kitty fell in.

nemesis \'ne-mə-səs\ n. AGENT OF VENGEANCE; SOMEONE OR SOMETHING THAT CANNOT BE OVERCOME. Clean-cut and square-jawed, the comic strip detective Dick Tracy was the *nemesis* of a gallery of grotesque criminals whom he pursued relentlessly.

neologism \nē-'ä-lə-,ji-zəm\ n. NEW OR NEWLY COINED WORD OR PHRASE. As we invent new techniques and professions, we must also invent *neologisms* such as "microcomputer" and "astronaut" to describe them.

neophyte \'nē-ə-,fīt\ n. RECENT CONVERT; BEGINNER. This mountain slope contains slides that will challenge experts as well as *neophytes*.

nepotism \'ne-pə-,ti-zəm\ n. FAVORITISM (TO A RELATIVE OR FRIEND). John left his position with the company because he felt that advancement was based on *nepotism* rather than ability.

nettle \'ne-təl\ v. ANNOY; VEX. Do not let him *nettle* you with his sarcastic remarks.

niggardly \'ni-gərd-lē\ adj. MEANLY STINGY; PARSIMONIOUS. The *niggardly* pittance the widow receives from the government cannot keep her from poverty.

nihilist \'nī-(h)ə-ˌlist, 'nē-\ n. ONE WHO BELIEVES TRADITIONAL BELIEFS TO BE GROUNDLESS AND EXISTENCE MEANINGLESS; ABSOLUTE SKEPTIC. In his final days, Hitler revealed himself to be a power-mad *nihilist*, ready to annihilate all of Western Europe, even to destroy Germany itself, in order that his will might prevail. //nihilism, n.

nocturnal \näk-'tər-nəl\ adj. DONE AT NIGHT. Mr. Jones obtained a watchdog to prevent the *nocturnal* raids on his chicken coops.

noisome \'nȯi-səm\ adj. FOUL SMELLING; UNWHOLESOME. The *noisome* atmosphere downwind of the oil refinery not only stank, but it also damaged the lungs of everyone living in the area.

nomadic \nō-'ma-dik\ adj. WANDERING. Several *nomadic* tribes of Indians would hunt in this area each year.

nomenclature \'nō-mən-ˌklā-chər\ n. TERMINOLOGY; SYSTEM OF NAMES. Sharon found her knowledge of Latin and Greek word parts useful in translating medical *nomenclature*.

nominal \'nä-mə-nəl, 'näm-nəl\ adj. IN NAME ONLY; TRIFLING. He offered to drive her to the airport for only a *nominal* fee.

nonchalance \ˌnän-shə-'län(t)s; 'nän-shə-ˌlän(t)s, -lən(t)s\ n. INDIFFERENCE; LACK OF CONCERN OR WORRY. Cool, calm, and collected under fire, James Bond shows remarkable *nonchalance* in the face of danger.

noncommittal \ˌnän-kə-'mi-t°l\ adj. NEUTRAL; UNPLEDGED; UNDECIDED. We were annoyed by his *noncommittal* reply for we had been led to expect definite assurances of his approval.

nonentity \ˌnän-'en-tə-tē, -'e-nə-\ n. NONEXISTENCE; PERSON OF NO IMPORTANCE. Because the two older princes dismissed their youngest brother as a *nonentity*, they never suspected that he was quietly plotting to seize the throne.

nostalgia \nä-'stal-jə, nə- *also* nȯ-, nō-, nə-'stäl-\ n. HOMESICKNESS; LONGING FOR THE PAST. My grandfather seldom spoke of life in the old country; he had little patience with *nostalgia*.

notorious \nō-'tȯr-ē-əs, nə-\ adj. DISREPUTABLE; INFAMOUS; SCANDALOUS; WIDELY KNOWN. To the starlet, any publicity was good publicity; if she couldn't have a good reputation, she's settle for being *notorious*. //notoriety, n.

novelty \'nä-vəl-tē\ n. SOMETHING NEW; NEWNESS. GPS receivers are no longer a *novelty* in automobiles; every rental car we drive these days has one. //novel, adj.

novice \'nä-vəs\ n. BEGINNER. When Grandma got her first cell phone, she was such a complete *novice* that she couldn't even change her ring tone.

noxious \'näk-shəs\ adj. HARMFUL TO HEALTH; MORALLY CORRUPTING. Chemical wastes are *noxious*; bratty kid brothers are merely obnoxious.

nuance \'nü-ˌän(t)s, 'nyü-, -ˌäⁿs; nü-', nyü-'\ n. SHADE OF DIFFERENCE IN MEANING OR COLOR. Jody gazed at the Monet landscape for an hour, appreciating every subtle *nuance* of color in the painting.

nullify \'nə-lə-ˌfī\ v. TO MAKE INVALID. Once the contract was *nullified*, it no longer had any legal force.

numismatist \nü-'miz-mə-tist, nyü-\ n. PERSON WHO COLLECTS COINS. The *numismatist* had a splendid collection of antique coins.

nurture \'nər-chər\ v. NOURISH; EDUCATE; FOSTER. The Head Start program attempts to *nurture* pre-kindergarten children so that they will do well when they enter public school. //also n.

nutrient \'nü-trē-ənt, 'nyü-\ n. NOURISHING SUBSTANCE. As a budding nutritionist, Kim has learned to design diets that contain foods rich in important basic *nutrients*. //also adj.

obdurate \'äb-də-rət, -dyə-; äb-'dur-ət, əb-, -'dyur-\ adj. STUBBORN. Although defeat appeared inevitable, the general was *obdurate* in his refusal to surrender.

obese \ō-'bēs\ adj. FAT. It is advisable that *obese* people try to lose weight.

obfuscate \'äb-fə-ˌskāt; äb-'fəs-ˌkāt, əb-\ v. CONFUSE; MUDDLE. Was the president's spokesman trying to clarify the situation, or was he trying to *obfuscate* the issue so that the voters would never figure out what had been going on?

objective \əb-'jek-tiv, äb-\ adj. NOT INFLUENCED BY EMOTIONS; FAIR. Even though he was her son, she tried to be *objective* about his behavior.

objective \əb-'jek-tiv, äb-\ n. GOAL; AIM. A degree in medicine was her ultimate *objective*.

obligatory \ə-'bli-gə-ˌtȯr-ē, ä- *also* 'ä-bli-gə-\ adj. BINDING; REQUIRED. It is *obligatory* that books borrowed from the library be returned within two weeks.

oblique \ō-'blēk, ə-, -'blīk\ adj. INDIRECT; EVASIVE; SLANTING; DEVIATING FROM THE PERPENDICULAR OR FROM A STRAIGHT LINE. Although the reporters clamored for straight answers from the president's press secretary, he offered only *oblique* answers to their questions.

obliterate \ə-'bli-tə-ˌrāt, ō-\ v. DESTROY COMPLETELY. In the film *Independence Day*, the explosion *obliterated* the White House, vaporizing it completely.

oblivion \ə-'bli-vē-ən, ō-, ä-\ n. OBSCURITY; FORGETFULNESS. After a brief period of popularity, Hurston's works fell into *oblivion*; no one bothered to reprint them or even to read them any more. //oblivious, adj.

obnoxious \äb-'näk-shəs, əb-\ adj. OFFENSIVE. A sneak and a tattletale, Sid was an *obnoxious* little brat.

obscure \äb-'skyu̇r, əb-\ adj. DARK; VAGUE; UNCLEAR. Even
after I read the poem a fourth time, its meaning was
still *obscure.* //obscurity, n.

obscure \äb-'skyu̇r, əb-\ v. DARKEN; MAKE UNCLEAR. At
times he seemed purposely to *obscure* his meaning,
preferring mystery to clarity.

obsequious \əb-'sē-kwē-əs, äb-\ adj. SLAVISHLY ATTENTIVE;
SERVILE; SYCOPHANTIC. Helen valued people who acted
as if they respected themselves; nothing irritated
her more than an *obsequious* waiter or a fawning
salesclerk.

obsession \äb-'se-shən, əb-\ n. COMPULSIVE PREOCCUPA-
TION; FIXED IDEA. Ballet, which had been a hobby,
began to dominate his life; his interest in dancing
became an *obsession.*

Each of the questions below consists of a word in capital letters, followed by five words or phrases. Choose the word or phrase that is most similar in meaning to the word in capital letters and write the letter of your choice on your answer paper.

466. **NEBULOUS**　(A) starry　(B) unclear　(C) cold (D) fundamental　(E) porous

467. **NEFARIOUS**　(A) various　(B) lacking　(C) evil (D) pompous　(E) futile

468. **NEGATION**　(A) postulation　(B) hypothecation (C) denial　(D) violation　(E) anticipation

469. **NEOPHYTE**　(A) novice　(B) satellite　(C) desperado (D) handwriting　(E) violence

470. **NIGGARDLY**　(A) protected　(B) biased　(C) stingy (D) bankrupt　(E) placated

471. **NOCTURNAL**　(A) harsh　(B) marauding (C) patrolling　(D) done at night　(E) fallow

472. **NOISOME**　(A) quiet　(B) dismayed　(C) foul (D) sleepy　(E) inquisitive

473. **NOTORIOUS**　(A) fashionable　(B) infamous (C) inactive　(D) intrepid　(E) invincible

474. **OBDURATE**　(A) stubborn　(B) fleeting　(C) finite (D) fascinating　(E) permanent

475. **OBESE**　(A) skillful　(B) overweight　(C) clever (D) unpredictable　(E) lucid

476. **OBJECTIVE**　(A) elegy　(B) oath of allegiance (C) role model　(D) purpose　(E) approval

477. **OBLIGATORY**　(A) demanding　(B) mandatory (C) facile　(D) friendly　(E) divorced

478. **OBLIVION**　(A) forgetfulness　(B) revenge　(C) peace (D) dialogue　(E) cure

479. **OBSEQUIOUS**　(A) successful　(B) democratic (C) servile　(D) ambitious　(E) lamentable

480. **OBSESSION**　(A) fixed idea　(B) loss　(C) pleasure (D) delusion　(E) feud

obsolete \ˌäb-sə-ˈlēt, ˈäb-sə-,\ adj. OUTMODED; NO LONGER USEFUL; ANTIQUATED. The invention of the pocket calculator made the slide rule used by generations of engineers *obsolete*.

obstinate \ˈäb-stə-nət\ adj. STUBBORN. We tried to persuade him to give up smoking, but he was *obstinate* and refused to change.

obstreperous \əb-ˈstre-p(ə-)rəs, äb-\ adj. BOISTEROUS; NOISY. What do you do when an *obstreperous* horde of drunken policemen carouses through your hotel, crashing into potted plants and singing vulgar songs?

obtrusive \əb-ˈtrü-siv, -ziv\ adj. UNDESIRABLY NOTICEABLE; PROTRUDING. A good waiter stays in the background, always attentive, but never *obtrusive*. //obtrude, v.

obtuse \äb-ˈtüs, əb-, -ˈtyüs\ adj. BLUNT; STUPID. What can you do with someone who is so *obtuse* that he can't even tell that you're insulting him?

obviate \ˈäb-vē-ˌāt\ v. MAKE UNNECESSARY; GET RID OF. In the twentieth century, many people envisioned a paperless society: they believed that electronic communications would *obviate* the need for hard copy.

occult \ə-ˈkəlt, ä-\ adj. MYSTERIOUS; SECRET; SUPERNATURAL. In the sixteenth century, so-called "witch-finders" traveled through England accusing people of witchcraft and other *occult* practices. //also n.

odious \ˈō-dē-əs\ adj. HATEFUL; DISGUSTING; DETESTABLE. Cinderella's ugly stepsisters had the *odious* habit of popping their zits in public. //odium, n.

odyssey \ˈä-də-sē\ n. LONG, EVENTFUL JOURNEY. The refugee's journey from Cambodia was a terrifying *odyssey*.

officious \ə-ˈfi-shəs\ adj. MEDDLESOME; EXCESSIVELY TRYING TO PLEASE. After her long flight, Jill just wanted to nap, but the *officious* bellhop was intent on showing her all the features of the deluxe suite.

ogle \'ō-gəl *also* 'ä-\ v. LOOK AT AMOROUSLY; MAKE EYES AT. At the coffee house, Walter was too shy to *ogle* the pretty girls openly; instead, he peeked out at them from behind the potted ferns.

olfactory \äl-'fak-t(ə-)rē, ōl-\ adj. CONCERNING THE SENSE OF SMELL. A wine taster must have a discriminating palate and a keen *olfactory* sense, for good wine appeals both to the taste buds and to the nose.

oligarchy \'ä-lə-,gär-kē, 'ō-\ n. GOVERNMENT BY A PRIVI-LEGED FEW. One small clique ran the student council: what had been intended as a democratic governing body had turned into an *oligarchy*.

ominous \'ä-mə-nəs\ adj. THREATENING. These clouds are *ominous*; they suggest a severe storm is on the way.

omnipotent \äm-'ni-pə-tənt\ adj. ALL-POWERFUL. Under Stalin, the Soviet government seemed *omnipotent*; no one dared to defy the all-powerful State.

omniscient \äm-'ni-shənt\ adj. ALL-KNOWING. I may not be *omniscient*, but I know a bit more than you do, young man!

omnivorous \äm-'niv-rəs, -'ni-və-\ adj. EATING BOTH PLANT AND ANIMAL FOOD; DEVOURING EVERYTHING. Some animals, including man, are *omnivorous* and eat both meat and vegetables; others are either carnivorous or herbivorous.

onerous \'ä-nə-rəs, 'ō-\ adj. BURDENSOME. He asked for an assistant because his work load was too *onerous*. //onus, n.

opaque \ō-'pāk\ adj. NOT TRANSPARENT. The *opaque* window shade kept the sunlight out of the room. //opacity, n.

opiate \'ō-pē-ət, -,āt\ n. SLEEP PRODUCER; DEADENER OF PAIN. Religion, according to Karl Marx, is the *opiate* of the masses, for it dulls them and makes them submissive to those in power.

opportune \,ä-pər-'tün, -'tyün\ adj. TIMELY; WELL CHOSEN. Sally glanced at her father as he struggled to balance his checkbook; clearly, this would not be an *opportune* moment to ask him for a raise in her allowance.

opportunist \,ä-pər-'tü-nist, -'tyü-\ n. INDIVIDUAL WHO SACRIFICES PRINCIPLES FOR EXPEDIENCY BY TAKING ADVANTAGE OF CIRCUMSTANCES. A born *opportunist*, the vicar of Bray changed his political convictions to suit whoever was in power, switching from fervent monarchist to puritan reformer in order to retain his ecclesiastical living.

optimist \'äp-tə-mist\ n. PERSON WHO LOOKS ON THE GOOD SIDE. The pessimist says the glass is half empty; the *optimist* says it is half full.

optimum \'äp-tə-məm\ adj. MOST FAVORABLE. If you wait for the *optimum* moment to act, you may never begin your project. //also n.

optional \'äp-shnəl, -shə-nəl\ adj. NOT COMPULSORY; LEFT TO ONE'S CHOICE. I was amazed by the range of *optional* accessories available for my iPod. //option, n.

opulence \'ä-pyə-lən(t)s\ n. WEALTH. The glitter and *opulence* of the ballroom took Cinderella's breath away. //opulent, adj.

opus \'ō-pəs\ n. WORK. Do you enjoy Michael Chabon's novels? I just picked up a copy of his latest *opus*.

ordain \or-'dān\ v. COMMAND; ARRANGE; CONSECRATE. The king *ordained* that no foreigner should be allowed to enter the city.

ordinance \'ord-nən(t)s, 'or-də-nən(t)s\ n. DECREE. Passing a red light is a violation of a city *ordinance*.

orient \'or-ē-ənt, -ē-,ent\ v. GET ONE'S BEARINGS; ADJUST. Philip spent his first day in Denver *orienting* himself to the city. //orientation, n.

orifice \\'òr-ə-fəs, 'är-\\ n. MOUTHLIKE OPENING; SMALL OPEN-
ING. The Howe Caverns were discovered when some-
one observed that a cold wind was issuing from an
orifice in the hillside.

ornate \\òr-'nāt\\ adj. EXCESSIVELY OR ELABORATELY DECO-
RATED. The furnishings of homes shown on *Lifestyles
of the Rich and Famous* tended to be highly *ornate*.

ornithology \\,òr-nə-'thä-lə-jē\\ n. STUDY OF BIRDS.
Audubon's studies of American birds greatly influenced the course of *ornithology*.

orthodox \\'òr-thə-,däks\\ adj. TRADITIONAL; CONSERVATIVE
IN BELIEF. Faced with a problem, he preferred to take
an *orthodox* approach rather than shock anyone.
//orthodoxy, n.

oscillate \\'ä-sə-,lāt\\ v. VIBRATE IN A PENDULUM-LIKE WAY;
WAVER. If you stretch a spring and let it go, you will
observe that it *oscillates* or swings back and forth in
a fixed pattern.

ossify \\'ä-sə-,fī\\ v. CHANGE OR HARDEN INTO BONE; BECOME
RIGIDLY CONVENTIONAL AND OPPOSED TO CHANGE. Old men
whose minds have *ossified* fear innovation and cling
to orthodoxy.

ostensible \\ä-'sten(t)-sə-bəl, ə-\\ adj. APPARENT; PROFESSED;
PRETENDED. Cabot sailed from Spain with the *ostensi-
ble* purpose of bringing back spices from the Molucca
Islands; instead, he explored the coastline of South
America.

ostentatious \\,äs-tən-'tā-shəs\\ adj. SHOWY; PRETENTIOUS.
The rich new student tried to attract attention by
making an *ostentatious* display of his wealth.
//ostentation, n.

ostracize \\'äs-trə-,sīz\\ v. EXCLUDE FROM PUBLIC FAVOR; BAN.
As soon as the newspapers carried the story of his
connection with the criminals, his friends began to
ostracize him. //ostracism, n.

oust \'aust\ v. EXPEL; DRIVE OUT. The world wondered if Aquino would be able to *oust* Marcos from office.

overt \ō-'vərt, 'ō-(,)vərt\ adj. OPEN TO VIEW. The counselors to the throne virtually ran the bureaucracy, though they rarely assumed *overt* power for themselves.

pacifist \'pa-sə-fist\ n. ONE OPPOSED TO FORCE; ANTIMILITARIST. Shooting his way through the jungle, Rambo was clearly no *pacifist*. //pacify, v.

Synonym Test • Word List 33

Each of the questions below consists of a word in capital letters, followed by five words or phrases. Choose the word or phrase that is most similar in meaning to the word in capital letters and write the letter of your choice on your answer paper.

481. **OBSOLETE**   (A) heated   (B) desolate   (C) outdated   (D) frightful   (E) automatic

482. **OBSTREPEROUS**   (A) turbid   (B) rowdy   (C) remote   (D) lucid   (E) active

483. **OBTUSE**   (A) sheer   (B) transparent   (C) tranquil   (D) timid   (E) dull

484. **ODIOUS**   (A) fragrant   (B) redolent   (C) fetid   (D) hateful   (E) puny

485. **OGLE**   (A) cry   (B) look   (C) flinch   (D) amend   (E) parade

486. **OMNIPOTENT**   (A) powerful   (B) democratic   (C) despotic   (D) passionate   (E) late

487. **OMNISCIENT**   (A) sophisticated   (B) all-knowing   (C) essential   (D) trivial   (E) isolated

488. **OPIATE**   (A) distress   (B) sleep   (C) pain reliever   (D) laziness   (E) despair

489. **OPPORTUNE**   (A) occasional   (B) fragrant   (C) fragile   (D) timely   (E) neglected

490. **OPTIMIST**   (A) renegade   (B) positive thinker   (C) killjoy   (D) pacifist   (E) benefactor

491. **OPTIMUM**   (A) pessimistic   (B) knowledgeable   (C) minimum   (D) chosen   (E) best

492. **OPTIONAL**   (A) dire   (B) silent   (C) elective   (D) eloquent   (E) ample

493. **OPULENCE**   (A) pessimism   (B) patriotism   (C) potency   (D) passion   (E) luxury

494. **ORNATE**   (A) not reddish   (B) decorative   (C) grave   (D) fragile   (E) not eager

495. **OSTENTATIOUS**   (A) showy   (B) impotent   (C) avid   (D) acrimonious   (E) exaggerated

painstaking \\'pān-,stā-kiŋ\\ adj. SHOWING HARD WORK; TAK-ING GREAT CARE. The new high frequency word list is the result of *painstaking* efforts on the part of our research staff.

palatable \\'pa-lə-tə-bəl\\ adj. AGREEABLE; PLEASING TO THE TASTE. Neither Jack's half-baked opinions nor his overdone steaks were *palatable* to Jill.

palatial \\pə-'lā-shəl\\ adj. MAGNIFICENT. He proudly showed us through his *palatial* home.

palette \\'pa-lət\\ n. BOARD ON WHICH PAINTER MIXES PIG-MENTS. The artist's apprentices had the messy job of cleaning his brushes and *palette*.

pall \\'pȯl\\ v. GROW TIRESOME. The study of word lists can eventually *pall* and put one to sleep.

palliate \\'pa-lē-,āt\\ v. ALLEVIATE; MAKE LESS SEVERE OR INTENSE; EASE PAIN; EXTENUATE. Although we cannot yet cure certain diseases, we can at least *palliate* their symptoms. //palliation, n.

pallid \\'pa-ləd\\ adj. PALE; WAN. Because his occupation required that he work at night and sleep during the day, he had an exceptionally *pallid* complexion.

palpable \\'pal-pə-bəl\\ adj. TANGIBLE; EASILY PERCEPTIBLE. On Super Tuesday as the primary results came in, the tension in the candidate's campaign headquarters was so intense that it seemed almost *palpable*.

paltry \\'pȯl-trē\\ adj. INSIGNIFICANT; PETTY. While NBA stars make an annual average salary of more than $5 million, a player in basketball's minor league may make as little as a *paltry* $15,000.

panacea \\,pa-nə-'sē-ə\\ n. CURE-ALL; REMEDY FOR ALL DISEASES. Some people claim that vitamin C is a *panacea* that can cure everything from cancer to the common cold.

panache \pə-'nash, -'näsh\ n. FLAIR; FLAMBOYANCE. Many performers imitate Noel Coward, but few have his *panache* and sense of style.

pandemonium \,pan-də-'mō-nē-əm\ n. WILD TUMULT. When the ships collided in the harbor, *pandemonium* broke out among the passengers.

panegyric \,pa-nə-'jir-ik, -'jī-rik\ n. FORMAL PRAISE. In England during the Restoration, court poets had the unenviable task of composing *panegyrics* in praise of King Charles II's nonexistent virtues.

panorama \,pa-nə-'ra-mə, -'rä-\ n. COMPREHENSIVE VIEW; UNOBSTRUCTED VIEW IN ALL DIRECTIONS. From Inspiration Point we could see the magnificent *panorama* of the Marin headlands and San Francisco Bay.

pantomime \'pan-tə-,mīm\ n. ACTING WITHOUT DIALOGUE. Artists performing *pantomime* need no words to communicate with their audience; their only language is gesture. //also v.

parable \'pa-rə-bəl\ n. SHORT, SIMPLE STORY TEACHING A MORAL. Plato's *parable* of the cave is a metaphor for ignorance and knowledge, for the chained prisoners within the cave know nothing of the world outside, and see only shadows on the wall before them.

paradigm \'per-ə-,dīm, 'pa-rə- *also* -,dim\ n. MODEL; EXAMPLE; PATTERN. Pavlov's experiment in which he trains a dog to salivate on hearing a bell is a *paradigm* of the conditioned-response experiment in behavioral psychology.

paradox \'per-ə-,däks, 'pa-rə-\ n. SOMETHING APPARENTLY CONTRADICTORY IN NATURE; STATEMENT THAT LOOKS FALSE BUT IS ACTUALLY CORRECT. According to Zeno's *paradox*, an arrow can never reach its target because you can divide the distance it must travel into an infinite number of smaller distances, and therefore the arrow must take an infinite amount of time to hit its mark.

paragon \'per-ə-ˌgän, -gən, 'pa-rə-\ n. MODEL OF PERFEC-TION. Her fellow students loathed Lavinia because the headmistress always pointed her out as a *paragon* of virtue.

parallelism \'pa-rə-ˌle-ˌli-zəm, -lə-ˌli-\ n. STATE OF BEING PARALLEL; SIMILARITY. Although the twins were separated at birth and grew up in very different adoptive families, a striking *parallelism* exists between their lives.

parameter \pə-'ram-ə-tər\ n. BOUNDARY; LIMITING FACTOR; DISTINGUISHING CHARACTERISTIC. According to feminist Andrea Dworkin, men have defined the *parameters* of every subject; now women must redefine the limits of each field.

paranoia \ˌper-ə-'nȯi-ə, ˌpa-rə-\ n. MENTAL DISORDER MARKED BY DELUSIONS OF GRANDEUR OR PERSECUTION. Suffering from *paranoia*, Don claimed everyone was out to get him; ironically, his claim was accurate: even *paranoids* have enemies. //paranoid, paranoiac, adj., n.

paraphernalia \ˌper-ə-fə(r)-'nāl-yə, ˌpa-rə-\ n. EQUIPMENT; ODDS AND ENDS. His desk was cluttered with paper, pen, ink, dictionary, and other *paraphernalia* of the writing craft.

paraphrase \'per-ə-ˌfrāz, 'pa-rə-\ v. RESTATE A PASSAGE IN ONE'S OWN WORDS WHILE RETAINING THOUGHT OF AUTHOR. In 250 words or less, *paraphrase* this article. //also n.

parasite \'per-ə-ˌsīt, 'pa-rə-\ n. ANIMAL OR PLANT LIVING ON ANOTHER; TOADY; SYCOPHANT. The tapeworm is an example of the kind of *parasite* that may infest the human body.

parched \'pärcht\ adj. EXTREMELY DRY; VERY THIRSTY. The *parched* desert landscape seemed hostile to life.

pariah \pə-'rī-ə\ n. SOCIAL OUTCAST. If everyone ostracized the singer Mariah Carey, would she then be Mariah the *pariah*?

parity \'per-ə-tē, 'pa-rə-\ n. EQUALITY; CLOSE RESEMBLANCE. Unfortunately, some doubt exists whether women's salaries will ever achieve *parity* with men's.

parochial \pə-'rō-kē-əl\ adj. NARROW IN OUTLOOK; PROVINCIAL; RELATED TO PARISHES. Although Jane Austen sets her novels in small rural communities, her concerns are universal, not *parochial*.

parody \'per-ə-dē, 'pa-rə-\ n. HUMOROUS IMITATION; SPOOF; TAKEOFF. The show *Forbidden Broadway* presents *parodies* spoofing the year's new productions playing on Broadway.

paroxysm \'pa-rək-,si-zəm *also* pə-'räk-\ n. FIT OR ATTACK OF PAIN, LAUGHTER, RAGE. "Oh, stop! It's too funny! You're killing me!" she cried, going off into *paroxysms* of laughter.

parry \'per-ē, 'pa-rē\ v. WARD OFF A BLOW. Unwilling to injure his opponent in such a pointless clash, D'Artagnan simply tried to *parry* his rival's thrusts.

parsimonious \,pär-sə-'mō-nē-əs\ adj. STINGY; EXCESSIVELY FRUGAL. Criminals are felonious; misers are *parsimonious*. //parsimony, n.

partial \'pär-shəl\ adj. (1) INCOMPLETE. In this issue we have published only a *partial* list of contributors because we lack space to acknowledge everyone. (2) BIASED; HAVING A LIKING FOR SOMETHING. I am extremely *partial* to chocolate eclairs. //partiality, n.

partisan \'pär-tə-zən, -sən, -,zan\ adj. ONE-SIDED; PREJUDICED; COMMITTED TO A PARTY. On certain issues of principle, she refused to take a *partisan* stand, but let her conscience, not her party affiliation, be her guide. //also n.

passive \'pa-siv\ adj. NOT ACTIVE; ACTED UPON. Mahatma Gandhi urged his followers to pursue a program of *passive* resistance and not resort to violence or acts of terrorism.

pastoral \'pas-t(ə-)rəl\ adj. RURAL; SIMPLE AND PEACEFUL; IDYLLIC. Tired of the stress of life in the city, Dale dreamed of moving to the country and enjoying a simple, *pastoral* life.

patent \'pa-tənt, 'pā-\ adj. OPEN FOR THE PUBLIC TO READ; OBVIOUS. It was *patent* to everyone that the witness spoke the truth. //also n.

pathetic \pə-'the-tik\ adj. CAUSING SADNESS, COMPASSION, PITY; TOUCHING. Everyone in the auditorium was weeping by the time he finished his *pathetic* tale about the orphaned boy.

pathological \,pa-thə-'lä-ji-kəl\ adj. PERTAINING TO DISEASE; DISEASED OR MARKEDLY ABNORMAL. Jerome's *pathological* fear of germs led him to wash his hands a hundred times a day.

pathos \'pā-,thäs, -,thòs, -,thōs *also* 'pa-\ n. TENDER SORROW; PITY; QUALITY IN ART OR LITERATURE THAT PRODUCES THESE FEELINGS. The quiet tone of *pathos* that ran through the novel never degenerated into the maudlin or the overly sentimental.

patina \pə-'tē-nə, 'pa-tə-nə\ n. GREEN CRUST ON OLD BRONZE WORKS; TONE SLOWLY TAKEN BY VARNISHED PAINTING. Judging by the *patina* on this bronze statue, we can conclude that this is the work of a medieval artist.

patriarch \'pā-trē-,ärk\ n. FATHER AND RULER OF A FAMILY OR TRIBE. In many primitive tribes, the leader and lawmaker was the *patriarch*.

patrician \pə-'tri-shən\ adj. NOBLE; ARISTOCRATIC. We greatly admired her well-bred, *patrician* elegance. //also n.

patronize \'pā-trə-,nīz, 'pa-\ v. SUPPORT; ACT SUPERIOR TOWARD; BE A CUSTOMER OF. Penniless artists hope to find some wealthy art lover who will *patronize* them. If some condescending wine steward *patronized* me, acting as if I knew nothing about fine wine, I'd refuse to *patronize* his restaurant.

paucity \\'pȯ-sə-tē\\ n. SCARCITY. They closed the restaurant because the *paucity* of customers made it uneconomical to operate.

peccadillo \\,pe-kə-'di-(,)lō\\ n. SLIGHT OFFENSE. Whenever Huck swiped a cookie from the jar, Miss Watson reacted as if he'd committed a major felony and not just a minor *peccadillo*.

Each of the questions below consists of a word in capital letters, followed by five words or phrases. Choose the word or phrase that is most similar in meaning to the word in capital letters and write the letter of your choice on your answer paper.

496. **PAINSTAKING**   (A) intact   (B) appealing   (C) alien   (D) careful   (E) injurious

497. **PALETTE**   (A) pigment board   (B) dark color   (C) bench   (D) spectrum   (E) quality

498. **PALLIATE**   (A) smoke   (B) quicken   (C) substitute   (D) alleviate   (E) sadden

499. **PANDEMONIUM**   (A) chaos   (B) frustration   (C) efficiency   (D) impishness   (E) sophistication

500. **PANEGYRIC**   (A) medication   (B) panacea   (C) rotation   (D) vacillation   (E) praise

501. **PARABLE**   (A) equality   (B) allegory   (C) frenzy   (D) folly   (E) cuticle

502. **PARADOX**   (A) exaggeration   (B) contradiction   (C) hyperbole   (D) invective   (E) poetic device

503. **PARAGON**   (A) exemplar   (B) majority   (C) importance   (D) hatred   (E) clandestine affair

504. **PARANOIA**   (A) fracture   (B) statement   (C) quantity   (D) benefaction   (E) sense of persecution

505. **PARIAH**   (A) village   (B) suburb   (C) outcast   (D) disease   (E) benefactor

506. **PARITY**   (A) duplicate   (B) miniature   (C) golf tee   (D) similarity   (E) event

507. **PARSIMONIOUS**   (A) grammatical   (B) syntactical   (C) effective   (D) stingy   (E) esoteric

508. **PARTIALITY**   (A) completion   (B) equality   (C) bias   (D) divorce   (E) reflection

509. **PASSIVE**   (A) scornful   (B) rural   (C) not active   (D) silly   (E) barbaric

510. **PATENT**   (A) obvious   (B) dutiful   (C) new   (D) rotund   (E) amiable

pecuniary \pi-ˈkyü-nē-ˌer-ē\ adj. PERTAINING TO MONEY. Seldom earning enough to cover their expenses, folk dance teachers work because they love dancing, not because they expect any *pecuniary* reward.

pedagogue \ˈpe-də-ˌgäg\ n. TEACHER; DULL AND FORMAL TEACHER. He could never be a stuffy *pedagogue*; his classes were always lively and filled with humor.

pedantic \pi-ˈdan-tik\ adj. SHOWING OFF LEARNING; BOOKISH. Leavening her decisions with humorous, down-to-earth anecdotes, Judge Judy in no way resembled a *pedantic*, dry-as-dust legal scholar. //pedantry, n.

pedestrian \pə-ˈdes-trē-ən\ adj. ORDINARY; UNIMAGINATIVE. Unintentionally boring, he wrote page after page of *pedestrian* prose.

pejorative \pi-ˈjȯr-ə-tiv, -ˈjär- *also* ˈpe-jə-rə-tiv *or* ˈpē- *or* -ˌrā- *or* ˈpej-rə- *or* ˈpēj-\ adj. NEGATIVE IN CONNOTATION; HAVING A BELITTLING EFFECT. Instead of criticizing Governor Schwarzenegger's policies, the Democrats made *pejorative* comments about the former movie star's acting abilities.

penance \ˈpe-nən(t)s\ n. SELF-IMPOSED PUNISHMENT FOR SIN. The Ancient Mariner said, "I have *penance* done and *penance* more will do," to atone for the sin of killing the albatross.

penchant \ˈpen-chənt\ n. STRONG INCLINATION; LIKING. Dave has a *penchant* for taking risks that more sensible people would avoid: one semester he simultaneously went steady with three girls, two of whom held black belts in karate.

penitent \ˈpe-nə-tənt\ adj. REPENTANT. Although Tweedledee said he was sorry that he had spoiled Tweedledum's new rattle, Tweedledum did not believe that his twin was truly *penitent*. //also n.

pensive \'pen(t)-siv\ adj. DREAMILY THOUGHTFUL; THOUGHT-FUL WITH A HINT OF SADNESS. Michelangelo's statue of Lorenzo de Medici presents the duke in a *pensive* attitude, as if deep in thought.

penurious \pə-'nùr-ē-əs, -'nyùr-\ adj. STINGY; PARSIMONIOUS. Frugal by nature, Scrooge became so tightfisted and mean that even his close relatives called him a *penurious* old miser.

penury \'pen-yə-rē\ n. EXTREME POVERTY. When his pension fund failed, Al feared he would end his days in *penury*.

percussion \pər-'kə-shən\ adj. STRIKING ONE OBJECT AGAINST ANOTHER SHARPLY. The drum is a *percussion* instrument. //also n.

perdition \pər-'di-shən\ n. DAMNATION; COMPLETE RUIN. Praying for salvation, young Steven Daedalus feared his soul was damned to eternal *perdition*.

peremptory \pə-'rem(p)-t(ə-)rē\ adj. DEMANDING AND LEAVING NO CHOICE. From Jack's *peremptory* knock on the door, Jill could tell that he would not give up until she let him in.

perennial \pə-'re-nē-əl\ n. SOMETHING THAT IS CONTINUING OR RECURRENT. These plants are hardy *perennials* and will bloom for many years. //also adj.

perfidious \(,)pər-'fi-dē-əs\ adj. TREACHEROUS; DISLOYAL. When Caesar realized that Brutus had betrayed him, he reproached his *perfidious* friend.

perfunctory \pər-'fəŋ(k)-t(ə-)rē\ adj. SUPERFICIAL; LISTLESS; NOT THOROUGH. Giving the tabletop only a *perfunctory* swipe with her dust cloth, Betty promised herself she'd do a more thorough job tomorrow.

perimeter \pə-'ri-mə-tər\ n. OUTER BOUNDARY. To find the *perimeter* of any quadrilateral, we add the lengths of the four sides.

peripatetic \,per-ə-pə-'te-tik\ adj. WALKING ABOUT; MOVING. As a young man, W. E. B. Du Bois was a *peripatetic* country schoolteacher, wandering the hills in search of a rural community where he could find employment.

peripheral \pə-'ri-f(ə-)rəl\ adj. MARGINAL; OUTER. We lived, not in central London, but in one of those *peripheral* suburbs that spring up on the outskirts of a great city.

periphery \pə-'ri-f(ə-)rē\ n. EDGE, ESPECIALLY OF A ROUND SURFACE. He sensed that there was something just beyond the *periphery* of his vision.

perjury \'pər-jə-rē, 'pərj-rē\ n. FALSE TESTIMONY WHILE UNDER OATH. Rather than lie under oath and risk being indicted for *perjury*, the witness chose to take the Fifth Amendment and refuse to answer any questions on the grounds that he might incriminate himself.

permeate \'pər-mē-ˌāt\ v. PASS THROUGH; SPREAD. The odor of frying onions *permeated* the air. //permeable, adj.

pernicious \pər-'ni-shəs\ adj. VERY DESTRUCTIVE. Crack cocaine has had a *pernicious* effect on urban society: it has destroyed families, turned children into drug dealers, and increased the spread of violent crime.

perpetrate \'pər-pə-ˌtrāt\ v. COMMIT AN OFFENSE; BE RESPONSIBLE FOR. "The Good and Great must ever shun that reckless and abandoned one who stoops to *perpetrate* a pun." (Lewis Carroll)

perpetual \pər-'pe-chə-wəl, -chəl; -'pech-wəl\ adj. EVERLASTING. Big city life is a *perpetual* assault on the senses—constant noise, dirt, traffic jams. The city never sleeps, and neither do you.

perquisite \'pər-kwə-zət\ n. FRINGE BENEFIT; EXTRA MONEY OR SERVICES IN ADDITION TO REGULAR SALARY; RIGHT. Newly hired by Virgin Atlantic, Julie could hardly wait to enjoy the major *perquisite* of her job: free flights to any destination the airline served.

personable \'pərs-nə-bəl, 'pər-sə-nə-bəl\ adj. ATTRACTIVE. Though not as strikingly handsome as a movie star, James was nonetheless a *personable* young man.

perspicacious \‚pər-spə-'kā-shəs\ adj. HAVING INSIGHT; PENETRATING; ASTUTE. "That was absolutely brilliant, Holmes!" cried Watson, as Holmes made yet another *perspicacious* deduction. //perspicacity, n.

perspicuity \‚pər-spə-'kyü-ə-tē\ n. CLEARNESS OF EXPRESSION; FREEDOM FROM AMBIGUITY. One of the outstanding features of this book is the *perspicuity* of its author; her meaning is always clear. //perspicuous, adj.

pert \'pərt\ adj. IMPERTINENT; FORWARD. The matron in charge of the orphanage thought Annie was *pert* and disrespectful.

pertinent \'pər-tə-nənt, 'pərt-nənt\ adj. TO THE POINT; RELEVANT. Virginia Woolf's words on women's rights are as *pertinent* today as they were when she wrote them nearly a century ago.

perturb \pər-'tərb\ v. DISTURB GREATLY. The thought that electricity might be leaking out of the empty lightbulb sockets *perturbed* my aunt so much that at night she crept about the house screwing fresh bulbs in the vacant receptacles. //perturbation, n.

peruse \pə-'rüz\ v. READ WITH CARE. After the fire that burned down her house, Joan closely *perused* her insurance policy to discover exactly what benefits her coverage provided her. //perusal, n.

pervasive \pər-'vā-siv, -ziv\ adj. SPREAD THROUGHOUT; PERMEATING. Despite airing them for several hours, Martha could not rid her clothes of the *pervasive* odor of mothballs that clung to them. //pervade, v.

perversion \pər-'vər-zhən, -shən\ n. CORRUPTION; TURNING FROM RIGHT TO WRONG. Inasmuch as he had no motive for his crimes, we could not understand his *perversion*. //perverse, adj.

perverse \pər-'vərs\ adj. (1) STUBBORNLY WRONGHEADED; (2) WICKED AND PERVERTED. When Jack was in a *perverse* mood, he stubbornly insisted on doing the opposite of whatever Jill asked him. When Hannibal

Lecter was in a *perverse* mood, he nibbled on the flesh of his victims. //perversity, perversion, n.

pessimism \\'pe-sə-ˌmi-zəm *also* 'pe-zə-\\ n. BELIEF THAT LIFE IS BASICALLY BAD OR EVIL; GLOOMINESS. People inclined to *pessimism* view the wineglass as half-empty; people inclined to optimism view it as half-full.

pestilential \\ˌpes-tə-'len(t)-shəl\\ adj. CAUSING PLAGUE; BANEFUL; HARMFUL. Public health officials called for a quarantine to help prevent the spread of yellow fever and other *pestilential* diseases. //pestilence, n.

petrify \\'pe-trə-ˌfī\\ v. TURN TO STONE; PARALYZE WITH FEAR. The sheltered young man was almost too stunned to speak: "The forward manners of some girls today *petrify* me—they absolutely *petrify* me."

petty \\'pe-tē\\ adj. TRIVIAL; UNIMPORTANT; VERY SMALL. She had no major complaints to make about his work, only a few *petty* quibbles.

petulant \\'pe-chə-lənt\\ adj. TOUCHY; PEEVISH. The feverish patient was *petulant* and restless.

phenomena \\fi-'nä-mə-nə, -ˌnä\\ n. OBSERVABLE FACTS; SUBJECTS OF SCIENTIFIC INVESTIGATION. We kept careful records of the *phenomena* we noted in the course of these experiments.

Each of the questions below consists of a word in capital letters, followed by five words or phrases. Choose the word or phrase that is most similar in meaning to the word in capital letters and write the letter of your choice on your answer paper.

511. **PEJORATIVE** (A) insulting (B) legal (C) determining (D) delighting (E) declaiming

512. **PENITENT** (A) logistical (B) philandering (c) sorry (D) vagrant (E) warranted

513. **PENCHANT** (A) distance (B) imminence (C) liking (D) attitude (E) void

514. **PENURIOUS** (A) imprisoned (B) captivated (C) miserly (D) vacant (E) abolished

515. **PERFUNCTORY** (A) official (B) careless (c) insipid (D) vicarious (E) distinctive

516. **PERIPATETIC** (A) worldly (B) disarming (C) wandering (D) seeking (E) inherent

517. **PERIPHERAL** (A) discursive (B) extraneous (C) overcrowded (D) equipped (E) lefthanded

518. **PERMEABLE** (A) perishable (B) effective (C) plodding (D) penetrable (E) lasting

519. **PERNICIOUS** (A) practical (B) comparative (C) harmful (D) tangible (E) detailed

520. **PERPETUAL** (A) continuous (B) standard (C) serious (D) industrial (E) interpretive

521. **PERSPICACIOUS** (A) vengeful (B) consumptive (C) insightful (D) skilled (E) adverse

522. **PERSPICUITY** (A) grace (B) feature (C) review (D) difficulty (E) clearness

523. **PERT** (A) rude (B) perishable (C) moral (D) deliberate (E) stubborn

524. **PERTINENT** (A) understood (B) living (C) discontented (D) puzzling (E) relevant

525. **PETULANT** (A) angry (B) moral (C) declining (D) underhanded (E) peevish

philanthropist \fə-'lan(t)-thrə-pist\ n. LOVER OF MANKIND; DOER OF GOOD. In his role as *philanthropist* and public benefactor, John D. Rockefeller, Sr., donated millions to charity; as an individual, however, he was a tight-fisted old man.

philistine \'fi-lə-ˌstēn; fə-'lis-tən, -ˌtēn; 'fi-lə-stən\ n. NARROW-MINDED PERSON, UNCULTURED AND EXCLUSIVELY INTERESTED IN MATERIAL GAIN. A *philistine* knows the price of everything, but the value of nothing.

phlegmatic \fleg-'ma-tik\ adj. CALM; NOT EASILY DISTURBED; APATHETIC, SLUGGISH. The nurse was a cheerful but *phlegmatic* person, unexcited in the face of sudden emergencies.

phobia \'fō-bē-ə\ n. MORBID FEAR. Her fear of flying was more than mere nervousness; it was a real *phobia*.

pied \'pīd\ adj. VARIEGATED; MULTICOLORED. The *Pied* Piper of Hamelin got his name from the multicolored clothing he wore.

pillage \'pi-lij\ v. PLUNDER. The enemy *pillaged* the quiet village and left it in ruins.

pinnacle \'pi-ni-kəl\ n. PEAK. We could see the morning sunlight illuminate the *pinnacle* while the rest of the mountain lay in shadow.

pious \'pī-əs\ adj. DEVOUT; RELIGIOUS. The challenge for church people today is how to be *pious* in the best sense, that is, to be devout without becoming hypocritical or sanctimonious. //piety, n.

piquant \'pē-kənt, -ˌkänt; 'pi-kwənt\ adj. PLEASANTLY TART-TASTING; STIMULATING. A *piquant* remark stimulates one's interest; a *piquant* sauce stimulates one's appetite. //piquancy, n.

pique \'pēk\ n. IRRITATION; RESENTMENT. The beauty contest competitor showed her *pique* at her loss by refusing to appear with the other contestants at the end of the competition.

pique \'pēk\ v. AROUSE OR PROVOKE; ANNOY. "I know something *you* don't know," taunted Lucy, trying to *pique* Ethel's curiosity.

pithy \'pi-thē\ adj. CONCISE; MEATY; MEANINGFUL; SUBSTANTIAL. While other girls might have gone on and on about how uncool Elton was, Liz summed him up in one *pithy* remark: "He's bogus!"

placate \'plā-ˌkāt, 'pla-\ v. PACIFY; CONCILIATE. The store manager tried to *placate* the angry customer by offering to replace the damaged merchandise or to give her back her money right away.

placid \'pla-səd\ adj. PEACEFUL; CALM. Looking at the storm-tossed waters of the lake, Tom wondered how people had ever come to call it Lake *Placid*.

plagiarize \'plā-jə-ˌrīz *also* -jē-ə-\ v. STEAL ANOTHER'S IDEAS AND PASS THEM OFF AS ONE'S OWN. The teacher could tell that the student had *plagiarized* parts of his essay; she could recognize whole paragraphs straight from *Barron's Book Notes*. //plagiarism, n.

plaintive \'plān-tiv\ adj. MOURNFUL. The dove has a *plaintive* and melancholy call.

platitude \'pla-tə-ˌtüd, -ˌtyüd\ n. TRITE REMARK; COMMONPLACE STATEMENT. In giving advice to his son, old Polonius expressed himself only in *platitudes*; every word out of his mouth was a commonplace.

platonic \plə-'tä-nik, plā-\ adj. PURELY SPIRITUAL; THEORETICAL; WITHOUT SENSUAL DESIRE. Accused of impropriety in his dealings with female students, the professor maintained that he had only a *platonic* interest in the young women involved.

plausible \'plo-zə-bəl\ adj. HAVING A SHOW OF TRUTH BUT OPEN TO DOUBT; SPECIOUS. Your mother made you stay home from school because she needed you to program the VCR? I'm sorry, but you'll have to come up with a more *plausible* excuse than that.

plebeian \pli-'bē-ən\ adj. COMMON; PERTAINING TO THE COMMON PEOPLE; LOW-BROW. A down-to-earth guy who preferred burgers and beer to caviar and champagne, Bob was unashamed of his *plebeian* tastes.

plethora \\'ple-thə-rə\\ n. EXCESS; OVERABUNDANCE. Highly apologetic about her lack of proficiency, she offered a *plethora* of excuses for her shortcomings.

plight \\'plīt\\ n. CONDITION, STATE (ESPECIALLY A BAD STATE OR CONDITION); PREDICAMENT. Many people feel the federal government should do more to alleviate the *plight* of the homeless.

podium \\'pō-dē-əm\\ n. PEDESTAL; RAISED PLATFORM. The audience applauded as the conductor made his way to the *podium*.

poignant \\'pȯi-nyənt\\ adj. KEEN; PIERCING; SEVERE; EMOTIONALLY MOVING. As we watched the tearful reunion of the mother and her children, we were touched by the *poignant* scene.

polemical \\pə-'le-mi-kəl\\ adj. AGGRESSIVE IN VERBAL ATTACK; DISPUTATIOUS. Lexy was a master of *polemical* rhetoric; she should have worn a T-shirt with the slogan "Born to Debate."

politic \\'pä-lə-,tik\\ adj. EXPEDIENT; PRUDENT; WELL DEVISED. It is neither polite nor *politic* to interfere in a fight between friends: at best, they ignore you; at worst, they beat up on you.

polygamist \\pə-'li-gə-mist\\ n. ONE WHO HAS MORE THAN ONE SPOUSE AT A TIME. HBO's sitcom *Big Love* tells the story of a Utah *polygamist* living in the suburbs of Salt Lake City with his three wives and seven children.

pomposity \\päm-'pä-sə-tē\\ n. EXAGGERATED SELF-ESTEEM; EXCESSIVE GRANDNESS IN MANNER OR SPEECH. Although the commencement speaker had some good things to say, we had to laugh at his *pomposity* and general air of self-importance. //pompous, adj.

ponderous \\'pän-d(ə-)rəs\\ adj. WEIGHTY; UNWIELDY. His humor lacked the light touch; his jokes were always *ponderous*.

portent \'pȯr-ˌtent\ n. SIGN; OMEN; FOREWARNING. He regarded the black cloud as a *portent* of evil. //portentous, adj.

portly \'pȯrt-lē\ adj. STOUT; CORPULENT. The salesclerk tactfully referred to the overweight customer as *portly* rather than as obese or fat.

posterity \pä-'ster-ə-tē\ n. DESCENDANTS; FUTURE GENERA-TIONS. We hope to leave a better world to *posterity*.

posthumous \'päs-chə-məs *also* -tə-, -tyə-, -thə-; päst-'hyü-məs, 'pōst-, -'yü-\ adj. AFTER DEATH (AS OF CHILD BORN AFTER FATHER'S DEATH OR BOOK PUBLISHED AFTER AUTHOR'S DEATH). The critics ignored his works during his lifetime; it was only after the *posthumous* publica-tion of his last novel that they recognized his great talent.

postulate \'päs-chə-lət, -ˌlāt\ n. ESSENTIAL PREMISE; UNDER-LYING ASSUMPTION. The basic *postulate* of democracy, set forth in the Declaration of Independence, is that all men are created equal. //also v.

potable \'pō-tə-bəl\ adj. SUITABLE FOR DRINKING. The recent drought in the Middle Atlantic States has emphasized the need for extensive research in ways of making sea water *potable*. //also n.

potent \'pō-tənt\ adj. POWERFUL; PERSUASIVE; GREATLY INFLUENTIAL. Looking at the expiration date on the cough syrup bottle, we wondered whether the medi-cine would still be *potent*. //potency, n.

potential \pə-'ten(t)-shəl\ adj. EXPRESSING POSSIBILITY; LATENT. The cello teacher viewed every new pupil as a *potential* Yo-Yo Ma. //also n.

potion \'pō-shən\ n. DOSE (OF LIQUID). Tristan and Isolde drink a love *potion* in the first act of the opera.

potpourri \ˌpō-pu̇-'rē\ n. HETEROGENEOUS MIXTURE; MEDLEY. He offered a *potpourri* of folk songs from many lands.

practicable \'prak-ti-kə-bəl\ adj. FEASIBLE. The board of directors decided that the plan was *practicable* and agreed to undertake the project.

practical \'prak-ti-kəl\ adj. BASED ON EXPERIENCE; USEFUL. Meg gained some *practical* experience of the legal profession by working as a student intern at a major law firm.

pragmatic \prag-'ma-tik\ adj. PRACTICAL; CONCERNED WITH PRACTICAL VALUES. This coming trip to France should provide me with a *pragmatic* test of the value of my conversational French class.

pragmatist \'prag-mə-tist\ n. PRACTICAL PERSON. No *pragmatist* enjoys becoming involved in a game he can never win.

prattle \'pra-təl\ v. BABBLE. We enjoyed listening to baby Santiago happily *prattle* in English and Spanish about the night and the stars and *la luna*. //also n.

preamble \'prē-,am-bəl, prē-'\ n. INTRODUCTORY STATEMENT. In the *Preamble* to the Constitution, the purpose of the document is set forth.

precarious \pri-'ker-ē-əs\ adj. UNCERTAIN; RISKY. Saying the stock would be a *precarious* investment, the broker advised her client against purchasing it.

precedent \'pre-sə-dənt\ n. SOMETHING PRECEDING IN TIME THAT MAY BE USED AS AN AUTHORITY OR GUIDE FOR FUTURE ACTION. If I buy you a car for your sixteenth birthday, your brothers will want me to buy them cars when they turn sixteen, too; I can't afford to set such an expensive *precedent*. //also adj.

precept \'prē-,sept\ n. PRACTICAL RULE GUIDING CONDUCT. "Love thy neighbor as thyself" is a worthwhile *precept*.

precipice \'pre-s(ə-)pəs\ n. CLIFF; DANGEROUS POSITION. Suddenly Indiana Jones found himself dangling from the edge of a *precipice*.

Synonym Test • Word List 36

Each of the questions below consists of a word in capital letters, followed by five words or phrases. Choose the word or phrase that is most similar in meaning to the word in capital letters and write the letter of your choice on your answer paper.

526. **PHLEGMATIC** (A) calm (B) cryptic (C) practical (D) salivary (E) dishonest

527. **PHOBIA** (A) posture (B) scorn (C) physique (D) fear (E) desire

528. **PIED** (A) motley (B) coltish (C) hairless (D) thoroughbred (E) delicious

529. **PILLAGE** (A) hoard (B) plunder (C) versify (D) denigrate (E) confide

530. **PINNACLE** (A) foothills (B) card game (C) pass (D) taunt (E) peak

531. **PIOUS** (A) historic (B) authoritative (C) multiple (D) fortunate (E) devout

532. **PIQUANT** (A) mutable (B) stimulating (C) aboveboard (D) prejudicial (E) understandable

533. **PIQUE** (A) pyramid (B) revolt (C) resentment (D) struggle (E) inventory

534. **PLACATE** (A) determine (B) transmit (C) pacify (D) allow (E) define

535. **PLAGIARISM** (A) theft of funds (B) theft of ideas (C) belief in God (D) arson (E) ethical theory

536. **PLAINTIVE** (A) mournful (B) senseless (C) persistent (D) rural (E) evasive

537. **PLATITUDE** (A) fatness (B) bravery (C) dimension (D) trite remark (E) strong belief

538. **POLEMICAL** (A) expedient (B) risky (C) powerful (D) disputatious (E) weighty

539. **POLITIC** (A) accurate (B) preferred (C) incidental (D) prudent (E) impoverished

540. **POSTHUMOUS** (A) after dark (B) on awakening (C) in summer (D) after death (E) in winter

precipitate \pri-ˈsi-pə-tət\ adj. HEADLONG; RASH. Though I was angry enough to resign on the spot, I had enough sense to keep myself from quitting a job in such a *precipitate* fashion.

precipitate \pri-ˈsi-pə-ˌtāt\ v. THROW HEADLONG; HASTEN. The removal of American political support appears to have *precipitated* the downfall of the Marcos regime.

precipitous \pri-ˈsi-pə-təs\ adj. STEEP; OVERHASTY. This hill is difficult to climb because it is extremely *precipitous*; one slip, and our descent will be *precipitous* as well.

precise \pri-ˈsīs\ adj. EXACT. If you don't give me *precise* directions and a map, I'll never find your place.

preclude \pri-ˈklüd\ v. MAKE IMPOSSIBLE; ELIMINATE. Because the band had already signed a contract to play in Hollywood on New Year's Eve, that booking *precluded* their accepting the New Year's Eve gig in London they were offered.

precocious \pri-ˈkō-shəs\ adj. ADVANCED IN DEVELOPMENT. Listening to the grown-up way the child discussed serious topics, we couldn't help commenting how *precocious* she was. //precocity, n.

precursor \pri-ˈkər-sər, ˈprē-,\ n. FORERUNNER. Though Gray and Burns share many traits with the Romantic poets who followed them, most critics consider them *precursors* of the Romantic movement, not true Romantics.

predatory \ˈpre-də-ˌtȯr-ē\ adj. LIVING BY FEEDING ON OTHERS; GREEDY AND VORACIOUS. Not just cats, but a wide variety of *predatory* creatures—owls, hawks, weasels, foxes—catch mice for dinner.

predecessor \ˈpre-də-ˌse-sər, ˈprē-; ˌpre-də-ˈ, ˌprē-\ n. FORMER OCCUPANT OF A POST. I hope I can live up to the fine example set by my late *predecessor* in this office.

predilection \ˌpre-də-ˈlek-shən, ˌprē-\ n. PARTIALITY; PREFERENCE. Although Ogden Nash wrote all sorts of poetry over the years, he had a definite *predilection* for limericks.

preeminent \prē-ˈe-mə-nənt\ adj. OUTSTANDING; SUPERIOR. The king traveled to Boston because he wanted the *preeminent* surgeon in the field to perform the operation.

preempt \prē-ˈem(p)t\ v. HEAD OFF; FORESTALL BY ACTING FIRST; APPROPRIATE BEFOREHAND. Hoping to *preempt* any attempts by the opposition to make educational reform a hot political issue, the candidate set out her own plan to revitalize the public schools.

prefatory \ˈpre-fə-ˌtȯr-ē\ adj. INTRODUCTORY. The chairman made a few *prefatory* remarks before he called on the first speaker.

prelude \ˈprel-ˌyüd, ˈprāl-; ˈpre-ˌlüd, ˈprā-\ n. INTRODUCTION; FORERUNNER. I am afraid that this border raid is the *prelude* to more serious attacks.

premeditate \(ˌ)prē-ˈme-də-ˌtāt\ v. PLAN IN ADVANCE. She had *premeditated* the murder for months, reading about common poisons and buying weed killer that contained arsenic.

premonition \ˌprē-mə-ˈni-shən, ˌpre-\ n. FOREWARNING. In horror movies, the hero often has a *premonition* of danger that he foolishly ignores. //premonitory, adj.

preponderance \pri-ˈpän-d(ə-)rən(t)s\ n. SUPERIORITY OF POWER, QUANTITY, ETC. The rebels sought to overcome the *preponderance* of strength of the government forces by engaging in guerrilla tactics. //preponderate, v.

preposterous \pri-ˈpäs-t(ə-)rəs\ adj. ABSURD; RIDICULOUS. The excuse he gave for his lateness was so *preposterous* that everyone laughed.

prerogative \pri-ˈrä-gə-tiv\ n. PRIVILEGE; UNQUESTIONABLE RIGHT. The president cannot levy taxes; that is the *prerogative* of the legislative branch of government.

presage \\'pre-sij *also* pri-'sāj\\ v. FORETELL. The vultures flying overhead *presaged* the discovery of the corpse in the desert.

presentiment \\pri-'zen-tə-mənt\\ n. PREMONITION; FORE-BODING; ANTICIPATORY FEAR; FEELING THAT SOMETHING WILL HAPPEN. Saying goodbye at the airport, Jack had a sudden *presentiment* that this was the last time he would see Jill.

prestige \\pre-'stēzh, -'stēj\\ n. IMPRESSION PRODUCED BY ACHIEVEMENTS OR REPUTATION. The wealthy man sought to obtain social *prestige* by contributing to popular charities. //prestigious, adj.

presumptuous \\pri-'zəm(p)-chə-wəs, -chəs, -shəs\\ adj. ARROGANT; TAKING LIBERTIES; IMPERTINENTLY BOLD. Matilda thought it was somewhat *presumptuous* of the young man to have addressed her without first having been introduced.

pretentious \\pri-'ten(t)-shəs\\ adj. OSTENTATIOUS; OVERLY AMBITIOUS; MAKING UNJUSTIFIED CLAIMS. None of the other prize winners are wearing their medals; isn't it a bit *pretentious* of you to wear yours?

prevail \\pri-'vāl\\ v. INDUCE; TRIUMPH OVER. He tried to *prevail* on her to type his essay for him.

prevalent \\'pre-və-lənt\\ adj. WIDESPREAD; GENERALLY ACCEPTED. A radical committed to social change, Reed had no patience with the conservative views *prevalent* in the America of his day.

prevaricate \\pri-'ver-ə-ˌkāt, -'va-rə-\\ v. LIE. Some people believe that to *prevaricate* in a good cause is justifiable and regard the statement as a "white lie."

prim \\'prim\\ adj. VERY PRECISE AND FORMAL; EXCEEDINGLY PROPER. Never having worked as a governess before, Jane thought it best to assume a very *prim* and proper manner so that her charges would not take liberties with her.

primordial \prī-'mȯr-dē-əl\ adj. EXISTING AT THE BEGIN-
NING (OF TIME); RUDIMENTARY. The Neanderthal Man is
one of our *primordial* ancestors.

pristine \ˌpris-'tēn, pri-'stēn\ adj. CHARACTERISTIC OF EAR-
LIER TIMES; PRIMITIVE; UNSPOILED. This area has been
preserved in all its *pristine* wildness.

privation \prī-'vā-shən\ n. HARDSHIP; WANT. In his youth,
he knew hunger and *privation*.

probe \'prōb\ v. EXPLORE WITH TOOLS. The surgeon *probed*
the wound for foreign matter before suturing it.
//also n.

probity \'prō-bə-tē\ n. UPRIGHTNESS; INCORRUPTIBILITY.
Everyone took his *probity* for granted; his misuse of
funds, therefore, shocked us all.

problematic \ˌprä-blə-'ma-tik\ adj. PERPLEXING; UNSET-
TLED; QUESTIONABLE. Given the many areas of conflict
still awaiting resolution, the outcome of the peace
talks remains *problematic*.

proclivity \prō-'kli-və-tē\ n. INCLINATION; NATURAL TEN-
DENCY. Watching the two-year-old put away his toys
without having been prompted, I was amazed by his
proclivity for neatness.

procrastinate \prə-'kras-tə-ˌnāt, prō-\ v. POSTPONE; DELAY.
Looking at the boxes of receipts and checks he still
had to sort through, Bob was truly sorry that he had
procrastinated for so long and had not filed his taxes
long ago.

prod \'präd\ v. POKE; STIR UP; URGE. If you *prod* him hard
enough, he'll eventually clean his room.

prodigal \'prä-di-gəl\ adj. WASTEFUL; RECKLESS WITH
MONEY. Don't be so *prodigal* spending my hard-earned
money; when you've earned some money yourself,
you can waste it as much as you please! //also n.

prodigious \prə-'di-jəs\ adj. MARVELOUS; ENORMOUS.
Watching the champion weight lifter heave the

weighty barbell to shoulder height and then boost it overhead, we marveled at his *prodigious* strength.

prodigy \\'prä-də-jē\\ n. MARVEL; HIGHLY GIFTED CHILD. Menuhin was a *prodigy*, performing wonders on his violin when he was barely eight years old.

profane \\prō-'fān, prə-\\ v. VIOLATE; DESECRATE. Tourists are urged not to *profane* the sanctity of holy places by wearing immodest garb. //also adj.

profligate \\'prä-fli-gət, -,gāt\\ adj. DISSIPATED; WASTEFUL; LICENTIOUS. We must reverse the *profligate* spending that has characterized this administration's fiscal policy and that has left us with a projected deficit of almost 500 billion dollars. //also n.

profound \\prə-'faůnd, prō-\\ adj. DEEP; NOT SUPERFICIAL; COMPLETE. Freud's remarkable insights into human behavior caused his fellow scientists to honor him as a *profound* thinker. //profundity, n.

profusion \\prə-'fyü-zhən\\ n. LAVISH EXPENDITURE; OVER-ABUNDANT CONDITION. Seldom have I seen food and drink served in such *profusion* as at the wedding feast. //profuse, adj.

progenitor \\prō-'je-nə-tər, prə-\\ n. ANCESTOR. The Roth family, whose *progenitors* emigrated from Germany early in the nineteenth century, settled in Peru, Illinois.

progeny \\'prä-jə-nē\\ n. CHILDREN; OFFSPRING. He was proud of his *progeny* but regarded George as the most promising of all his children.

projectile \\prə-'jek-təl, -,tī(-ə)l\\ n. MISSILE. Man has always hurled *projectiles* at his enemy whether in the form of stones or of highly explosive shells.

proletarian \\,prō-lə-'ter-ē-ən\\ n. MEMBER OF THE WORKING CLASS. The slogan "Workers of the world, unite!" may also be translated as "*Proletarians* of all countries, unite!" //also adj.

prolific \prə-'li-fik\ adj. ABUNDANTLY FRUITFUL. She was a *prolific* writer and wrote as many as three books a year. //proliferate, v.

prolix \prō-'liks, 'prō-(,)\ adj. VERBOSE; DRAWN OUT; TEDIOUSLY WORDY. A *prolix* writer tells his readers everything they *never* wanted to know about his subject. //prolixity n.

promiscuous \prə-'mis-kyə-wəs\ adj. SEXUALLY UNCHASTE; INDISCRIMINATE; HAPHAZARD. In the opera *La Boheme*, we get a picture of the *promiscuous* life led by the young artists of Paris.

Each of the questions below consists of a word in capital letters, followed by five words or phrases. Choose the word or phrase that is most similar in meaning to the word in capital letters and write the letter of your choice on your answer paper.

541. **PRECIPITATE** (A) dull (B) anticipatory (C) incautious (D) considerate (E) welcome

542. **PREFATORY** (A) outstanding (B) magnificent (C) beginning (D) intelligent (E) predatory

543. **PRELUDE** (A) intermezzo (B) diva (C) aria (D) preface (E) duplication

544. **PRESUMPTION** (A) assertion (B) activation (C) motivation (D) proposition (E) arrogance

545. **PRETENTIOUS** (A) ominous (B) calm (C) showy (D) futile (E) volatile

546. **PRIM** (A) formal (B) prior (C) exterior (D) private (E) cautious

547. **PRISTINE** (A) unspoiled (B) condemned (C) irreligious (D) cautious (E) critical

548. **PROBITY** (A) regret (B) assumption (C) honesty (D) extent (E) upswing

549. **PRODIGAL** (A) large (B) wasteful (C) consistent (D) compatible (E) remote

550. **PRODIGIOUS** (A) amazing (B) indignant (C) indifferent (D) indisposed (E) insufficient

551. **PROFANE** (A) desecrate (B) refrain (C) define (D) manifest (E) urge

552. **PROFUSION** (A) ambivalence (B) whimsy (C) abundance (D) thrift (E) complacence

553. **PROLIFIC** (A) hostile (B) productive (C) humble (D) moist (E) youthful

554. **PROLIX** (A) stupid (B) indifferent (C) redundant (D) livid (E) wordy

555. **PROMISCUOUS** (A) indiscriminate (B) unique (C) mortal (D) treacherous (E) generous

promontory \\'prä-mən-ˌtȯr-ē\ n. HEADLANDS. They erected a lighthouse on the *promontory* to warn approaching ships of their nearness to the shore.

prone \\'prōn\ adj. INCLINED TO; PROSTRATE. She was *prone* to sudden fits of anger, during which she would lie *prone* on the floor, screaming and kicking her heels.

propagate \\'prä-pə-ˌgāt\ v. MULTIPLY; SPREAD. Since bacteria *propagate* more quickly in unsanitary environments, it is important to keep hospital rooms clean.

propellants \prə-'pe-lən(t)s\ n. SUBSTANCES THAT PROPEL OR DRIVE FORWARD. The development of our missile program has forced our scientists to seek more powerful *propellants*.

propensity \prə-'pen(t)-sə-tē\ n. NATURAL INCLINATION. Convinced of his own talent, Sol has an unfortunate *propensity* to belittle the talents of others.

propitious \prə-'pi-shəs\ adj. FAVORABLE; KINDLY. Carrie consulted her horoscope to see whether Tuesday would be a *propitious* day to dump her boyfriend.

propound \prə-'pau̇nd\ v. PUT FORTH FOR ANALYSIS. In your discussion, you have *propounded* several questions; let us consider each one separately.

propriety \prə-'prī-ə-tē\ n. FITNESS; CORRECT CONDUCT. Miss Manners counsels her readers so that they may behave with due *propriety* in any social situation and not embarrass themselves.

prosaic \prō-'zā-ik\ adj. COMMONPLACE; DULL. Though the ad writers came up with an imaginative way to publicize the product, the head office rejected it for a more *prosaic*, ordinary slogan.

proscribe \prō-'skrīb\ v. OSTRACIZE; BANISH; OUTLAW. Antony, Octavius, and Lepidus *proscribed* all those who had conspired against Julius Caesar.

proselytize \'prä-s(ə-)lə-,tīz\ v. CONVERT TO A RELIGION OR BELIEF; RECRUIT. Depicting the lives of medical interns, the Pulitzer Prize-winning play *Men in White proselytized* in favor of legalizing abortion.

prostrate \'prä-,strāt\ v. STRETCH OUT FULL ON GROUND. He *prostrated* himself before the idol. //also adj.

protean \'prō-tē-ən, prō-'tē-\ adj. VERSATILE; ABLE TO TAKE ON MANY SHAPES. A remarkably *protean* actor, Alec Guinness could take on any role.

protocol \'prō-tə-,kȯl, -,kōl, -,käl, -kəl\ n. DIPLOMATIC ETIQUETTE. We must run this state dinner according to *protocol* if we are to avoid offending any of our guests.

prototype \'prō-tə-,tīp\ n. ORIGINAL WORK USED AS A MODEL BY OTHERS. The National Air and Space Museum displays the Wright brothers' first plane, the *prototype* of the many American aircraft that came later.

protract \prō-'trakt, prə-\ v. PROLONG. Seeking to delay the union members' vote, the management team tried to *protract* the negotiations endlessly.

protrude \prō-'trüd\ v. STICK OUT. His fingers *protruded* from the holes in his gloves. //protrusion, n.

provident \'prä-və-dənt, -,dent\ adj. DISPLAYING FORESIGHT; THRIFTY; PREPARING FOR EMERGENCIES. In his usual *provident* manner, he had insured himself against this type of loss.

provincial \prə-'vin(t)-shəl\ adj. PERTAINING TO A PROVINCE; LIMITED; UNSOPHISTICATED. As *provincial* governor, Sir Henry administered the Queen's law in his remote corner of Canada. Caught up in local problems, out of touch with London news, he became sadly *provincial*.

provisional \prə-'vizh-nəl, -'vi-zhə-nəl\ adj. TENTATIVE; CONDITIONAL; TEMPORARY. This appointment is *provisional*; only on the approval of the board of directors will it be made permanent.

provoke \prə-'vōk\ v. STIR TO ANGER; CAUSE RETALIATION. In order to prevent a sudden outbreak of hostilities, we must not *provoke* our foe. //provocation, n; provocative, adj.

proximity \präk-'si-mə-tē\ n. NEARNESS. The deer sensed the hunter's *proximity* and bounded away.

prude \'prüd\ n. EXCESSIVELY MODEST PERSON. The X-rated film was definitely not for *prudes*.

prudent \'prü-dᵊnt\ adj. CAUTIOUS; CAREFUL. A miser hoards money not because he is *prudent* but because he is greedy. //prudence, n.

prune \'prün\ v. CUT AWAY; TRIM. With the help of her editor, she was able to *prune* her overlong manuscript into publishable form.

pseudonym \'sü-də-,nim\ n. PEN NAME. Samuel Clemens's *pseudonym* was Mark Twain.

puerile \'pyu̇(-ə)r-əl, -,ī(-ə)l\ adj. CHILDISH; IMMATURE. Throwing tantrums! You should have outgrown such *puerile* behavior years ago.

pugilist \'pyü-jə-list\ n. BOXER. The famous *pugilist* Cassius Clay changed his name to Muhammed Ali.

pugnacious \,pəg-'nā-shəs\ adj. COMBATIVE; DISPOSED TO FIGHT. "Put up your dukes," he cried, making a fist to show how *pugnacious* he was.

pulchritude \'pəl-krə-,tüd, -,tyüd\ n. BEAUTY; COMELINESS. I do not envy the judges who have to select this year's Miss America from this collection of female *pulchritude*.

pulmonary \'pu̇l-mə-,ner-ē, 'pəl-\ adj. PERTAINING TO THE LUNGS. In his researches on *pulmonary* diseases, he discovered many facts about the lungs of animals and human beings.

punctilious \,pəŋk-'ti-lē-əs\ adj. LAYING STRESS ON NICETIES OF CONDUCT, FORM; PRECISE. Percy is *punctilious* about observing the rules of etiquette whenever Miss Manners invites him to stay.

pundit \\'pən-dət\ n. LEARNED HINDU; ANY LEARNED PERSON; AUTHORITY ON A SUBJECT. The film star's political activism has made him the target of conservative *pundits*, who from their position of authority condemn his films for their liberal point of view.

pungent \\'pən-jənt\ adj. STINGING; CAUSTIC. The *pungent* aroma of the smoke made me cough.

punitive \\'pyü-nə-tiv\ adj. PUNISHING. He asked for *punitive* measures against the offender.

puny \\'pyü-nē\ adj. INSIGNIFICANT; TINY; WEAK. The physical fitness expert claimed he could turn a *puny* weakling into an Olympic weightlifter in only six months.

purge \\'pərj\ v. GET RID OF SOMETHING UNWANTED; FREE FROM GUILT; CLEANSE OR PURIFY. When the Communist government *purged* the party, cleansing it of members suspected of capitalist sympathies, they sent the accused dissidents to labor camps in Siberia. //also n.

purport \\'pər-,port\ n. INTENTION; MEANING. If the *purport* of your speech was to arouse the rabble, you succeeded admirably. //also v.

putative \\'pyü-tə-tiv\ adj. SUPPOSED; REPUTED. Although there are some doubts, the *putative* author of this work is Massinger.

pyromaniac \\,pī-rō-'mā-nē-ak\ n. PERSON WITH AN INSANE DESIRE TO SET THINGS ON FIRE. The detectives searched the area for the *pyromaniac* who had set these costly fires.

quack \\'kwak\ n. CHARLATAN; IMPOSTOR. Don't let that *quack* fool you with his extravagant claims; he can't cure you.

quadruped \\'kwä-drə-,ped\ n. FOUR-FOOTED ANIMAL. Most mammals are *quadrupeds*.

quagmire \\'kwag-,mī(-ə)r, 'kwäg-\ n. BOG; MARSH. Up to her knees in mud, Myra wondered how on earth she was going to extricate herself from this *quagmire*.

quail \\'kwāl\\ v. COWER; LOSE HEART. The Cowardly Lion was afraid that he would *quail* in the face of danger.

quaint \\'kwānt\\ adj. ODD; OLD-FASHIONED; PICTURESQUE. Her *quaint* clothes and old-fashioned language marked her as an eccentric.

qualified \\'kwä-lə-ˌfīd\\ adj. LIMITED; RESTRICTED. Unable to give the candidate full support, the mayor gave him only a *qualified* endorsement. (secondary meaning) //qualify, v.

qualms \\'kwämz *also* 'kwȯmz *or* 'kwälmz\\ n. MISGIVINGS. I have no *qualms* about giving this assignment to John; I know he will handle it admirably.

quandary \\'kwän-d(ə-)rē\\ n. DILEMMA. When both Harvard and Stanford accepted Laura, she was in a *quandary* as to which school she should attend.

quarantine \\'kwȯr-ən-ˌtēn, 'kwär-\\ n. ISOLATION OF PERSON OR SHIP TO PREVENT SPREAD OF INFECTION. We will have to place this house under *quarantine* until we determine the exact nature of the disease. //also v.

quarry \\'kwȯr-ē, 'kwär-\\ n. VICTIM; OBJECT OF A HUNT. The police closed in on their *quarry*.

quarry \\'kwȯr-ē, 'kwär-\\ v. DIG INTO. They *quarried* blocks of marble out of the hillside. //also n.

Each of the questions below consists of a word in capital letters, followed by five words or phrases. Choose the word or phrase that is most similar in meaning to the word in capital letters and write the letter of your choice on your answer paper.

556. **PROPITIOUS**   (A) rich   (B) induced   (C) promoted   (D) indicative   (E) favorable

557. **PROSAIC**   (A) pacified   (B) reprieved   (C) pensive   (D) ordinary   (E} rhetorical

558. **PROTEAN**   (A) amateur   (B) catholic   (C) changeable   (D) rapid   (E) unfavorable

559. **PROTRACT**   (A) make circular   (B) lengthen   (C) further   (D) retrace   (E) involve

560. **PROVIDENT**   (A) unholy   (B) foresighted   (C) miserable   (D) disabled   (E) remote

561. **PROVINCIAL**   (A) wealthy   (B) crass   (C) literary   (D) aural   (E) unsophisticated

562. **PROVISIONAL**   (A) thrifty   (B) commonplace   (C) favorable   (D) old-fashioned   (E) tentative

563. **PUERILE**   (A) fragrant   (B) infantile   (C) lonely   (D) feminine   (E) masterly

564. **PUGNACIOUS**   (A) belligerent   (B) feline   (C) mature   (D) angular   (E) inactive

565. **PULCHRITUDE**   (A) beauty   (B) notoriety   (C) bestiality   (D) masculinity   (E) servitude

566. **PUNCTILIOUS**   (A) happy   (B) active   (C) vivid   (D) fussy   (E) futile

567. **PUNGENT**   (A) incomplete   (B) fashionable   (C) articulate   (D) healthy   (E) sharp

568. **PUNITIVE**   (A) large   (B) humorous   (C) punishing   (D) restive   (E) languishing

569. **QUAINT**   (A) poverty-stricken   (B) derivative   (C) posthumous   (D) strange   (E) strident

570. **QUALIFIED**   (A) colonial   (B) quarrelsome   (C) limited   (D) powerful   (E) unremarkable

quell \\'kwel\\ v. PUT DOWN; QUIET. The police used fire hoses and tear gas to *quell* the rioters.

querulous \\'kwer-yə-ləs, -ə-ləs *also* 'kwir-\\ adj. FRETFUL; WHINING. Even the most agreeable toddlers can begin to whine and act *querulous* if they miss their nap.

quibble \\'kwi-bəl\\ v. EQUIVOCATE; PLAY ON WORDS. Do not *quibble*; I want a straightforward and definite answer. //also n.

quiescent \\kwī-'e-sᵊnt\\ adj. AT REST; DORMANT. After this geyser erupts, it will remain *quiescent* for 24 hours.

quip \\'kwip\\ n. TAUNT; WITTY REMARK. You are unpopular because you are too free with your *quips* and sarcastic comments. //also v.

quirk \\'kwərk\\ n. STARTLING TWIST; CAPRICE. By a *quirk* of fate, he found himself working for the man whom he had discharged years before.

quixotic \\kwik-'sä-tik\\ adj. IDEALISTIC BUT IMPRACTICAL. Constantly coming up with *quixotic*, unworkable schemes to save the world, Don has his heart in the right place but his head in the clouds.

quorum \\'kwȯr-əm\\ n. NUMBER OF MEMBERS NECESSARY TO CONDUCT A MEETING. The senator asked for a roll call to determine whether a *quorum* was present.

rabid \\'ra-bəd *also* 'rā-\\ adj. LIKE A FANATIC; FURIOUS. He was a *rabid* follower of the Dodgers and watched them play whenever he could go to the ball park.

rail \\'rāl\\ v. SCOLD; RANT. You may *rail* at him all you want; you will never change him.

ramification \\ˌra-mə-fə-'kā-shən\\ n. BRANCHING OUT; SUBDIVISION. We must examine all the *ramifications* of this problem. //ramify, v.

ramp \\'ramp\\ n. SLOPE; INCLINED PLANE. The house was built with *ramps* instead of stairs in order to enable the man in the wheelchair to move easily from room to room and floor to floor.

rampant \'ram-pənt *also* -,pant\ adj. UNRESTRAINED. The neglected garden was completely overgrown, with *rampant* weeds and unchecked ivy everywhere.

ramshackle \'ram-,sha-kəl\ adj. RICKETY; FALLING APART. The boys propped up the *ramshackle* clubhouse with a couple of boards.

rancid \'ran(t)-səd\ adj. HAVING THE ODOR OF STALE FAT. If not kept refrigerated, butter will quickly spoil and become *rancid*.

rancor \'raŋ-kər, -,kȯr\ n. BITTERNESS; HATRED. Thirty years after the war, she could not let go of the past but was still filled with *rancor* against the foe.

rant \'rant\ v. RAVE; SPEAK BOMBASTICALLY. When he heard that I'd totaled the family car, Dad began to *rant* at me like a complete madman.

rapacious \rə-'pā-shəs\ adj. EXCESSIVELY GRASPING; PLUN-DERING. Hawks and other *rapacious* birds prey on a variety of small animals.

rarefied \'rer-ə-,fīd\ adj. MADE LESS DENSE (OF A GAS). The mountain climbers had difficulty breathing in the *rar-efied* atmosphere. //rarefy, v.

ratify \'ra-tə-,fī\ v. APPROVE FORMALLY; VERIFY. Party leaders doubted that they had enough votes in both houses of Congress to *ratify* the constitutional amendment.

rationalize \'rash-nə-,līz, 'ra-shə-nə-,līz\ v. GIVE A PLAUSI-BLE REASON FOR AN ACTION IN PLACE OF A TRUE, LESS ADMIRABLE ONE; OFFER AN EXCUSE. Jessamyn tried to *rationalize* her purchase of three new Nicole Miller dresses as a long-term investment. //rationalization, n.

raucous \'rȯ-kəs\ adj. HARSH AND SHRILL. The *raucous* crowd of New Year's Eve revelers grew progressively noisier as midnight drew near.

ravage \'ra-vij\ v. PLUNDER; DESPOIL. The marauding army *ravaged* the countryside.

ravenous \'ra-və-nəs, 'rav-nəs\ adj. EXTREMELY HUNGRY. The *ravenous* dog upset several garbage pails in its search for food.

raze \'rāz\ v. DESTROY COMPLETELY. The owners intend to *raze* the hotel and erect an office building on the site.

reactionary \rē-'ak-shə-,ner-ē\ adj. RECOILING FROM PROGRESS; ULTRACONSERVATIVE. Opposing the use of English in worship services, *reactionary* forces in the church fought to reinstate the mass in Latin. //also n.

realm \'relm\ n. KINGDOM; SPHERE. In the animal *realm*, the lion is the king of beasts.

rebuff \ri-'bəf\ v. SNUB; BEAT BACK. She *rebuffed* his invitation so smoothly that he did not realize he had been snubbed.

rebuttal \ri-'bə-təl\ n. REFUTATION; RESPONSE WITH CONTRARY EVIDENCE. The defense lawyer confidently listened to the prosecutor sum up his case, sure that she could answer his arguments in her *rebuttal*. //rebut, v.

recalcitrant \ri-'kal-sə-trənt\ adj. OBSTINATELY STUBBORN. Which animal do you think is more *recalcitrant*, a pig or a mule?

recant \ri-'kant\ v. REPUDIATE; WITHDRAW PREVIOUS STATEMENT. Hoping to make Joan of Arc *recant* her sworn testimony, her English captors tried to convince her that her visions had been sent to her by the Devil.

recapitulate \,rē-kə-'pi-chə-,lāt\ v. SUMMARIZE. Let us *recapitulate* what has been said thus far before going ahead.

recession \ri-'se-shən\ n. WITHDRAWAL; RETREAT. The slow *recession* of the flood waters created problems for the work crews trying to restore power to the area.

recipient \ri-'si-pē-ənt\ n. RECEIVER. Although he had been the *recipient* of many favors, he was not grateful to his benefactor.

reciprocal \ri-'si-prə-kəl\ adj. MUTUAL; EXCHANGEABLE; INTERACTING. The two nations signed a *reciprocal* trade agreement.

reciprocate \ri-'si-prə-ˌkāt\ v. REPAY IN KIND. If they attack us, we shall be compelled to *reciprocate* and bomb their territory. //reciprocity, n.

recluse \'re-ˌklüs, ri-'klüs, 're-ˌklüz\ n. HERMIT. The *recluse* lived in a hut in the forest. //reclusive, adj.

reconcile \'re-kən-ˌsī(-ə)l\ v. MAKE FRIENDLY AFTER QUARREL; CORRECT INCONSISTENCIES. Each month we *reconcile* our checkbook with the bank statement.

recondite \'re-kən-ˌdīt, ri-'kän-\ adj. ABSTRUSE; PROFOUND; SECRET. He read many *recondite* books in order to obtain the material for his scholarly thesis.

reconnaissance \ri-'kä-nə-zən(t)s, -sən(t)s\ n. SURVEY OF ENEMY BY SOLDIERS; RECONNOITERING. If you encounter any enemy soldiers during your *reconnaissance*, capture them for questioning.

recrimination \ri-ˌkri-mə-'nā-shən\ n. COUNTERCHARGES. Loud and angry *recriminations* were her answer to his accusations.

rectify \'rek-tə-ˌfī\ v. CORRECT. I want to *rectify* my error before it is too late.

rectitude \'rek-tə-ˌtüd, -ˌtyüd\ n. UPRIGHTNESS; MORAL VIRTUE. The Eagle Scout was a model of *rectitude*.

recuperate \ri-'kü-pə-ˌrāt, -'kyü-\ v. RECOVER. The doctors were worried because the patient did not *recuperate* as rapidly as they had expected.

recurrent \ri-'kər-ənt, -'kə-rənt\ adj. OCCURRING AGAIN AND AGAIN. These *recurrent* attacks disturbed us and we consulted a physician.

Synonym Test • Word List 39

Each of the questions below consists of a word in capital letters, followed by five words or phrases. Choose the word or phrase that is most similar in meaning to the word in capital letters and write the letter of your choice on your answer paper.

571. **QUELL**   (A) boast   (B) calm   (C) reverse   (D) wet   (E) answer

572. **QUIESCENT**   (A) cold   (B) tranquil   (C) agitated   (D) orderly   (E) rude

573. **QUIXOTIC**   (A) rapid   (B) exotic   (C) longing   (D) timid   (E) idealistic

574. **RANCOR**   (A) ill will   (B) prestige   (C) exotic dance   (D) light snack   (E) diligence

575. **RAUCOUS**   (A) harsh   (B) uncooked   (C) realistic   (D) veracious   (E) anticipating

576. **RAVAGE**   (A) rankle   (B) revive   (C) plunder   (D) pillory   (E) age

577. **RAZE**   (A) shave   (B) heckle   (C) finish   (D) tear down   (E) write

578. **REACTIONARY**   (A) extremely conservative   (B) retrograde   (C) dramatist   (D) militant   (E) chemical

579. **REBUFF**   (A) relinquish   (B) settle   (C) discourage   (D) cancel   (E) avoid

580. **RECALCITRANT**   (A) grievous   (B) secretive   (C) cowardly   (D) thoughtful   (E) inflexible

581. **RECIPROCAL**   (A) irregular   (B) mutual   (C) indifferent   (D) obliged   (E) reviving

582. **RECLUSE**   (A) learned scholar   (B) mocker   (C) hermit   (D) careful worker   (E) daredevil

583. **RECTIFY**   (A) remedy   (B) avenge   (C) create   (D) assemble   (E) attribute

584. **RECUPERATE**   (A) reenact   (B) engage   (C) recapitulate   (D) recover   (E) encounter

585. **RECURRENT**   (A) frequent   (B) bombastic   (C) ambiguous   (D) effervescent   (E) inactive

redolent \'re-də-lənt\ adj. FRAGRANT; ODOROUS; SUGGESTIVE OF AN ODOR. Even though it is February, the air is *redolent* of spring.

redress \ri-'dres\ n. REMEDY; COMPENSATION. Do you mean to tell me that I can get no *redress* for my injuries? //also v.

redundant \ri-'dən-dənt\ adj. SUPERFLUOUS; EXCESSIVELY WORDY; REPETITIOUS. Your composition is *redundant*; you can easily reduce its length. //redundancy, n.

reek \'rēk\ v. EMIT (ODOR). The room *reeked* with stale tobacco smoke. //also n.

refurbish \ri-'fər-bish\ v. RENOVATE; MAKE BRIGHT BY POLISH-ING. The flood left a deposit of mud on everything; it was necessary to *refurbish* our belongings.

refute \ri-'fyüt\ v. DISPROVE. The defense called several respectable witnesses who were able to *refute* the false testimony of the prosecution's only witness. //refutation, n.

regal \'rē-gəl\ adj. ROYAL. Prince Albert had a *regal* manner.

regeneration \ri-,je-nə-'rā-shən, ,rē-\ n. SPIRITUAL REBIRTH. Modern penologists strive for the *regenera-tion* of the prisoners.

regimen \'re-jə-mən *also* 're-zhə-\ n. PRESCRIBED DIET AND HABITS. I doubt whether the results warrant our living under such a strict *regimen*.

rehabilitate \,rē-ə-'bi-lə-,tāt, ,rē-hə-\ v. RESTORE TO PROPER CONDITION. We must *rehabilitate* those whom we send to prison.

reimburse \,rē-əm-'bərs\ v. REPAY. Let me know what you have spent and I will *reimburse* you.

reiterate \rē-'i-tə-,rāt\ v. REPEAT. I shall *reiterate* this message until all have understood it.

rejuvenate \ri-'jü-və-,nāt\ v. MAKE YOUNG AGAIN. The charlatan claimed that his elixir would *rejuvenate* the aged and weary.

relegate \'re-lə-,gāt\ v. BANISH; CONSIGN TO INFERIOR POSITION. If we *relegate* these experienced people to positions of unimportance because of their political persuasions, we shall lose the services of valuably trained personnel.

relevancy \'re-lə-vən(t)-sē\ n. PERTINENCE; REFERENCE TO THE CASE IN HAND. l was impressed by the *relevancy* of your remarks; I now understand the situation perfectly. //relevant, adj.

relinquish \ri-'liŋ-kwish, -'lin-\ v. ABANDON. I will *relinquish* my claims to this property if you promise to retain my employees.

relish \'re-lish\ v. SAVOR; ENJOY. I *relish* a good joke as much as anyone else. //also n.

remedial \ri-'mē-dē-əl\ adj. CURATIVE; CORRECTIVE. Because he was a slow reader, he decided to take a course in *remedial* reading.

reminiscence \,re-mə-'ni-s°n(t)s\ n. RECOLLECTION. Her *reminiscences* of her experiences are so fascinating that she ought to write a book. //reminisce, v.; reminiscent, adj.

remnant \'rem-nənt\ n. REMAINDER. I suggest that you wait until the store places the *remnants* of these goods on sale.

remonstrate \'re-mən-,strāt, ri-'män-\ v. PROTEST. I must *remonstrate* about the lack of police protection in this area.

remorse \ri-'mȯrs\ n. GUILT; SELF-REPROACH. The murderer felt no *remorse* for his crime.

remunerative \ri-'myü-nə-rə-tiv, -,rā-\ adj. COMPENSATING; REWARDING. I find my new work so *remunerative* that I may not return to my previous employment. //remuneration, n.

rend \\'rend\\ v. SPLIT; TEAR APART. In his grief, he tried to *rend* his garments.

render \\'ren-dər\\ v. DELIVER; PROVIDE; REPRESENT. He *rendered* aid to the needy and indigent.

renegade \\'re-ni-ˌgād\\ n. DESERTER; APOSTATE. Because he refused to support his fellow members in their drive, he was shunned as a *renegade*.

renege \\ri-'neg *also* -'nāg, -'nig; rē-\\ v. DENY; GO BACK ON. He *reneged* on paying off his debt.

renounce \\ri-'naun(t)s\\ v. ABANDON; DISCONTINUE; DISOWN; REPUDIATE. Joan of Arc refused to *renounce* her statements even though she knew she would be burned at the stake as a witch.

renovate \\'re-nə-ˌvāt\\ v. RESTORE TO GOOD CONDITION; RENEW. They claim that they can *renovate* worn shoes so that they look like new ones.

renunciation \\ri-ˌnən(t)-sē-'ā-shən\\ n. GIVING UP; RENOUNCING. Do not sign this *renunciation* of your right to sue until you have consulted a lawyer.

reparable \\'re-p(ə-)rə-bəl\\ adj. CAPABLE OF BEING REPAIRED. Fortunately, the damages we suffered in the accident were *reparable* and our car looks brand new.

reparation \\ˌre-pə-'rā-shən\\ n. AMENDS; COMPENSATION. At the peace conference, the defeated country promised to pay *reparations* to the victors.

repellent \\ri-'pe-lənt\\ adj. DRIVING AWAY; UNATTRACTIVE. Mosquitoes find the odor so *repellent* that they leave any spot where this liquid has been sprayed. //also n.

repercussion \\ˌrē-pər-'kə-shən, ˌre-\\ n. REBOUND; REVERBERATION; REACTION. I am afraid that this event will have serious *repercussions*.

repertoire \\'re-pə(r)-ˌtwär\\ n. LIST OF WORKS OF MUSIC, DRAMA, ETC., A PERFORMER IS PREPARED TO PRESENT. The opera company decided to include *Madame Butterfly* in its *repertoire* for the following season.

replenish \ri-'ple-nish\ v. FILL UP AGAIN. The end of rationing enabled us to *replenish* our supply of canned food.

replete \ri-'plēt\ adj. FILLED TO CAPACITY; ABUNDANTLY SUPPLIED. This book is *replete* with humorous situations.

replica \'re-pli-kə\ n. COPY. Are you going to hang this *replica* of the Declaration of Independence in the classroom or in the auditorium?

reprehensible \,re-pri-'hen(t)-sə-bəl\ adj. DESERVING BLAME. Your vicious conduct in this situation is *reprehensible*.

reprieve \ri-'prēv\ n. TEMPORARY STAY. During the 24-hour *reprieve*, the lawyers sought to make the stay of execution permanent. //also v.

reprimand \'re-prə-,mand\ v. REPROVE SEVERELY. I am afraid that my parents will *reprimand* me when I show them my report card. //also n.

reprisal \ri-'prī-zəl\ n. RETALIATION. I am confident that we are ready for any *reprisals* the enemy may undertake.

reproach \ri-'prōch\ n. BLAME; CENSURE. I want my work to be above *reproach* and without error. //also v.

reprobate \'re-prə-,bāt\ n. PERSON HARDENED IN SIN, DEVOID OF A SENSE OF DECENCY. I cannot understand why he has so many admirers if he is the *reprobate* you say he is.

reprove \ri-'prüv\ v. CENSURE; REBUKE. The principal *reproved* the students when they became unruly in the auditorium. //reproof, n.

repudiate \ri-'pyü-dē-,āt\ v. DISOWN; DISAVOW. He announced that he would *repudiate* all debts incurred by his wife.

repugnance \ri-'pəg-nən(t)s\ n. LOATHING. She looked at the snake with *repugnance*.

Each of the questions below consists of a word in capital letters, followed by five words or phrases. Choose the word or phrase that is most similar in meaning to the word in capital letters and write the letter of your choice on your answer paper.

586. **REDUNDANT**   (A) articulate   (B) sinkable
   (C) vaunted   (D) useless   (E) superfluous

587. **REGAL**   (A) oppressive   (B) royal   (C) major
   (D) basic   (E) entertaining

588. **REITERATE**   (A) gainsay   (B) revive   (C) revenge
   (D) repeat   (E) return

589. **RELISH**   (A) desire   (B) nibble   (C) savor
   (D) vindicate   (E) avail

590. **REMORSEFUL**   (A) penitent   (B) lost   (C) foolish
   (D) weak-willed   (E) ambitious

591. **RENEGE**   (A) display   (B) restate   (C) back out
   (D) try again   (E) reiterate

592. **RENUNCIATION**   (A) relinquishing
   (B) willful departure   (C) hard choice
   (D) monologue   (E) swift vengeance

593. **REPELLENT**   (A) propulsive   (B) unattractive
   (C) porous   (D) stiff   (E) elastic

594. **REPERCUSSION**   (A) reaction   (B) restitution
   (C) resistance   (D) magnificence   (E) acceptance

595. **REPLENISH**   (A) polish   (B) repeat   (C) reinstate
   (D) refill   (E) refuse

596. **REPLICA**   (A) museum piece   (B) famous site
   (C) battle emblem   (D) facsimile   (E) replacement

597. **REPRISAL**   (A) reevaluation   (B) assessment
   (C) loss   (D) retaliation   (E) nonsense

598. **REPROVE**   (A) prevail   (B) rebuke   (C) ascertain
   (D) prove false   (E) draw back

599. **REPUDIATE**   (A) besmirch   (B) appropriate
   (C) annoy   (D) reject   (E) avow

600. **REPUGNANCE**   (A) belligerence   (B) tenacity
   (C) renewal   (D) pity   (E) loathing

Comprehensive Test • Word Lists 31–40

Each of the questions below consists of a sentence from which one word is missing. Choose the most appropriate replacement from among the five choices.

1. The politician tried to _____ the angry electorate with promises of reform and tax cuts.
   (A) mortify   (B) obscure   (C) purge
   (D) renounce   (E) placate

2. Though teaching may not be financially _____, it is rewarding in other important ways.
   (A) remunerative   (B) remedial   (C) precipitous
   (D) omnipotent   (E) perfunctory

3. Because I disagreed with the candidate on a few important issues, I could only offer her my _____ support.
   (A) portly   (B) politic   (C) optimum
   (D) qualified   (E) parched

4. Banned from most public areas, tobacco smokers complain that they have become social _____.
   (A) pariahs   (B) nadirs   (C) narcissists
   (D) precepts   (E) pugilists

5. His _____ nature allowed him to remain composed in times of crisis.
   (A) musty   (B) phobic   (C) putative
   (D) phlegmatic   (E) reactionary

6. The violinist accused his unappreciative critics of being
   _____.
   (A) pious   (B) philistine   (C) pithy
   (D) motley   (E) monastic

7. The dentist attempted to _____ his patients' fears by showing distracting videos while he worked on their teeth.
   (A) purport   (B) mollify   (C) nettle
   (D) precipitate   (E) refute

8. Hawthorne's short story tells the tale of a group of aged citizens who attempt to _____ themselves by imbibing a magical elixir.
   (A) rejuvenate   (B) preclude   (C) placate
   (D) pastiche   (E) mute

9. Environmentalists are concerned about the environmental degradation that may take place if the _____ on oil drilling off of California's coast is lifted.
   (A) mnemonic (B) momentum (C) moratorium
        (D) phobia (E) quagmire

10. Slow growth ordinances were passed in order to prevent the _____ village from growing into a sprawling bedroom community.
    (A) plaintive (B) paltry (C) ornate
         (D) quaint (E) reparable

11. High school students are often skeptical of the _____ of their course work to the real world.
    (A) rectitude (B) relevancy (C) obsession
         (D) multiplicity (E) periphery

12. Many felt that it was a _____ of justice when the accused murderer was acquitted of the charges.
    (A) parallel (B) paradigm (C) perversion
         (D) perimeter (E) plagiarism

13. Vinyl records were the _____ of compact discs.
    (A) preponderance (B) novelty (C) momentum
         (D) precursor (E) posterity

14. The aging celebrity followed a punishing _____ of diet and exercise in order to maintain his youthful looks.
    (A) propriety (B) platitude (C) objective
         (D) muse (E) regimen

15. Though he was hired due to _____, he worked so hard that it was clear that he deserved the job based on his own merits.
    (A) nepotism (B) nonchalance (C) neologism
         (D) precedent (E) potential

repulsion \ri-ˈpəl-shən\ n. ACT OF DRIVING BACK; DISTASTE. The *repulsion* of the enemy forces was not accomplished bloodlessly; many of the defenders were wounded in driving the enemy back.

reputed \ri-ˈpyü-tid\ adj. SUPPOSED. He is the *reputed* father of the child. //also v.

rescind \ri-ˈsind\ v. CANCEL. Because of public resentment, the king had to *rescind* his order.

reserve \ri-ˈzərv\ n. SELF-CONTROL; CARE IN EXPRESSING ONESELF. She was outspoken and uninhibited; he was cautious and inclined to *reserve*. (secondary meaning) //reserved, adj.

residue \ˈre-zə-ˌdü, -ˌdyü\ n. REMAINDER; BALANCE. In his will, he requested that after payment of debts, taxes, and funeral expenses, the *residue* be given to his wife.

resigned \ri-ˈzīnd\ adj. UNRESISTING; PATIENTLY SUBMISSIVE. Bob Cratchit was too *resigned* to his downtrodden existence to protest Scrooge's bullying. //resignation, n.

resilient \ri-ˈzil-yənt\ adj. ELASTIC; HAVING THE POWER OF SPRINGING BACK. Steel is highly *resilient* and therefore is used in the manufacture of springs.

resolution \ˌre-zə-ˈlü-shən\ n. DETERMINATION. Nothing could shake his *resolution* to succeed despite all difficulties. //resolved, adj.

resonant \ˈre-zə-nənt, ˈrez-nənt\ adj. ECHOING; RESOUNDING. His *resonant* voice was particularly pleasing. //resonance, n.

respite \ˈres-pət *also* ri-ˈspīt\ n. DELAY IN PUNISHMENT; INTERVAL OF RELIEF; REST. The judge granted the condemned man a *respite* to enable his attorneys to file an appeal.

resplendent \ri-ˈsplen-dənt\ adj. BRILLIANT; LUSTROUS. The toreador wore a *resplendent* costume.

responsiveness \ri-'spän(t)-siv-nəs\ n. STATE OF REACTING
READILY TO APPEALS, ORDERS, ETC. The audience cheered
and applauded, delighting the perfomers by its
responsiveness.

restitution \,res-tə-'tü-shən, -'tyü-\ n. REPARATION; INDEM-
NIFICATION. He offered to make *restitution* for the
window broken by his son.

restive \'res-tiv\ adj. UNMANAGEABLE; FRETTING UNDER
CONTROL. We must quiet the *restive* animals.

restraint \ri-'strānt\ n. CONTROLLING FORCE. She dreamt
of living an independent life, free of all *restraints*.
//restrain, v.

resurgent \ri-'sər-jənt\ adj. RISING AGAIN AFTER DEFEAT,
ETC. The *resurgent* nation surprised everyone by its
quick recovery after total defeat.

retaliate \ri-'ta-lē-,āt\ v. REPAY IN KIND (USUALLY FOR BAD
TREATMENT). Fear that we will *retaliate* immediately
deters our foe from attacking us.

retentive \ri-'ten-tiv\ adj. HOLDING; HAVING A GOOD
MEMORY. The pupil did not need to spend much time
in study as he had a *retentive* mind.

reticence \'re-tə-sən(t)s\ n. RESERVE; UNCOMMUNICATIVE-
NESS; INCLINATION TO BE SILENT. Because of the *reticence* of the key witness, the case against the
defendant collapsed. //reticent, adj.

retinue \'re-tə-,nü, -,nyü\ n. FOLLOWING; ATTENDANTS. The
queen's *retinue* followed her down the aisle.

retort \ri-'tort\ n. QUICK SHARP REPLY. Even when it was
advisable for her to keep her mouth shut, she was
always ready with a quick *retort*. //also v.

retraction \ri-'trak-shən\ n. WITHDRAWAL. He dropped his
libel suit after the newspaper published a *retraction* of
its statement.

retrench \ri-'trench\ v. CUT DOWN; ECONOMIZE. If they
were to be able to send their children to college, they
would have to *retrench*.

retribution \,re-trə-'byü-shən\ n. VENGEANCE; COMPENSA-
TION; PUNISHMENT FOR OFFENSES. The evangelist maintained that an angry deity would exact *retribution*
from the sinners.

retrieve \ri-'trēv\ v. RECOVER; FIND AND BRING IN. The dog
was intelligent and quickly learned to *retrieve* the
game killed by the hunter.

retroactive \,re-(,)trō -'ak-tiv\ adj. MADE EFFECTIVE AS OF
A DATE PRIOR TO ENACTMENT. Because the law was
retroactive to the first of the year, we found she was
eligible for the pension.

retrograde \'re-trə-,grād\ v. GO BACKWARDS; DEGENERATE.
Instead of advancing, our civilization seems to have
retrograded in ethics and culture. //also adj.

retrospective \re-trə-'spek-tiv\ adj. LOOKING BACK ON THE
PAST. It is only when we become *retrospective* that we
can appreciate the tremendous advances made during
this century.

revelry \'re-vəl-rē\ n. BOISTEROUS MERRYMAKING. New
Year's Eve is a night of *revelry*.

reverberate \ri-'vərb-bə-,rāt\ v. ECHO; RESOUND. The
entire valley *reverberated* with the sound of the
church bells.

reverent \'rev-rənt, 're-və-; 're-vərnt\ adj. RESPECTFUL. His
reverent attitude was appropriate in a house of worship. //revere, v.

reverie \'re-və-rē, 'rev-rē\ n. DAYDREAM; MUSING. He was
awakened from his *reverie* by the teacher's question.

revile \ri-'vī-(ə)l\ v. SLANDER; VILIFY. He was avoided by
all who feared that he would *revile* and abuse them if
they displeased him.

revulsion \ri-'vəl-shən\ n. SUDDEN VIOLENT CHANGE OF FEEL-
ING; REACTION. Many people in this country who admired
dictatorships underwent a *revulsion* when they realized what Hitler and Mussolini were trying to do.

rhapsodize \'rap-sə-,dīz\ v. TO SPEAK OR WRITE IN AN EXAG-
GERATEDLY ENTHUSIASTIC MANNER. She greatly enjoyed
her Hawaiian vacation and *rhapsodized* about it for
weeks.

rhetorical \ri-'tòr-i-kəl, -'tär-\ adj. PERTAINING TO EFFEC-
TIVE COMMUNICATION; INSINCERE IN LANGUAGE. To win his
audience, the speaker used every *rhetorical* trick in
the book. //rhetoric, n.

ribald \'ri-bəld *also* 'ri-,bòld, 'rī-,bòld\ adj. WANTON; PRO-
FANE. He sang a *ribald* song that offended many of
the more prudish listeners.

rife \'rīf\ adj. ABUNDANT; CURRENT. In the face of the
many rumors of scandal, which are *rife* at the
moment, it is best to remain silent.

rift \'rift\ n. OPENING; BREAK. The plane was lost in the
stormy sky until the pilot saw the city through a *rift*
in the clouds.

rigor \'ri-gər\ n. SEVERITY. Many settlers could not stand
the *rigors* of the New England winters. //rigorous, adj.

robust \rō-'bəst, 'rō-(,)bəst\ adj. VIGOROUS; STRONG. The
candidate for the football team had a *robust*
physique.

rococo \rə-'kō-(,)kō, rō-kə-'kō\ adj. ORNATE; HIGHLY DECO-
RATED. The *rococo* style in furniture and architecture,
marked by scrollwork and excessive decoration, flourished during the middle of the eighteenth century.

roster \'räs-tər *also* 'ròs- *or* 'rōs-\ n. LIST. They print the
roster of players in the season's program.

rostrum \'räs-trəm *also* 'ròs-\ n. PLATFORM FOR
SPEECH-MAKING; PULPIT. The crowd murmured angrily
and indicated that they did not care to listen to the
speaker who was approaching the *rostrum*.

rote \'rōt\ n. FIXED OR MECHANICAL COURSE OF PROCEDURE;
USE OF MEMORY USUALLY WITH LITTLE THOUGHT TO MEANING
INVOLVED. He recited the passage by *rote* and gave no
indication he understood what he was saying.

rotundity \rō-'tən-də-tē\ n. ROUNDNESS; SONOROUSNESS OF SPEECH. Washington Irving emphasized the *rotundity* of the governor by describing his height and circumference.

rout \'raut\ v. STAMPEDE; DRIVE OUT; DEFEAT DECISIVELY. The reinforcements were able to *rout* the enemy. //also n.

rubble \'rə-bəl\ n. BROKEN FRAGMENTS. Ten years after World War II, some of the *rubble* left by enemy bombings could still be seen.

ruddy \'rə-dē\ adj. REDDISH; HEALTHY LOOKING. His *ruddy* features indicated that he had spent much time in the open.

rudimentary \rü-də-'men-tə-rē, -'men-trē\ adj. NOT DEVELOPED; ELEMENTARY. His dancing was limited to a few *rudimentary* steps.

rueful \'rü-fəl\ adj. REGRETFUL; SORROWFUL; DEJECTED. The artist has captured the sadness of childhood in his portrait of the boy with the *rueful* countenance.

ruffian \'rə-fē-ən\ n. BULLY; SCOUNDREL. The *ruffians* threw stones at the police.

ruminate \'rü-mə-ˌnāt\ v. CHEW THE CUD; PONDER. We cannot afford to wait while you *ruminate* upon these plans.

rummage \'rə-mij\ v. RANSACK; THOROUGHLY SEARCH. When we *rummaged* through the trunks in the attic, we found many souvenirs of our childhood days. //also n.

ruse \'rüs, 'rüz\ n. TRICK; STRATAGEM. You will not be able to fool your friends with such an obvious *ruse*.

rustic \'rəs-tik\ adj. PERTAINING TO COUNTRY PEOPLE; UNCOUTH. The backwoodsman looked out of place in his *rustic* attire.

ruthless \'rüth-ləs *also* 'rüth-\ adj. PITILESS. The escaped convict was a dangerous and *ruthless* murderer.

Each of the questions below consists of a word in capital letters, followed by five words or phrases. Choose the word or phrase that is most similar in meaning to the word in capital letters and write the letter of your choice on your answer paper.

601. **RESILIENT** (A) pungent (B) foolish (C) worthy (D) insolent (E) flexible

602. **RESTIVE** (A) buoyant (B) fidgety (C) remorseful (D) resistant (E) retiring

603. **RETENTIVE** (A) holding (B) accepting (C) repetitive (D) avoiding (E) fascinating

604. **RETICENCE** (A) fatigue (B) fashion (C) treachery (D) reserve (E) magnanimity

605. **RETROGRADE** (A) degenerate (B) inclining (C) evaluating (D) concentrating (E) directing

606. **REVERE** (A) advance (B) respect (C) age (D) precede (E) wake

607. **RIFE** (A) direct (B) plentiful (C) peaceful (D) grim (E) mature

608. **ROBUST** (A) strong (B) violent (C) vicious (D) villainous (E) hungry

609. **ROTUNDITY** (A) promenade (B) nave (C) grotesqueness (D) roundness (E) impropriety

610. **RUDDY** (A) robust (B) hearty (C) witty (D) exotic (E) creative

611. **RUDIMENTARY** (A) pale (B) polite (C) basic (D) asinine (E) quiescent

612. **RUEFUL** (A) trite (B) capital (C) capable (D) regretful (E) zealous

613. **RUFFIAN** (A) rowdy (B) daring person (C) renegade (D) spendthrift (E) zealot

614. **RUSTIC** (A) slow (B) rural (C) corroded (D) mercenary (E) civilian

615. **RUTHLESS** (A) merciless (B) majestic (C) mighty (D) militant (E) maximum

saccharine \'sa-k(ə-)rən, -kə-,rēn, -kə-,rīn\ adj. CLOYINGLY SWEET. She tried to ingratiate herself, speaking sweetly and smiling a *saccharine* smile.

sacrilegious \'sa-krə-,li-jəs *also* -,lē-\ adj. DESECRATING; PROFANE. His stealing of the altar cloth was a very *sacrilegious* act. //sacrilege, n.

sacrosanct \'sa-krō-,saŋ(k)t\ adj. MOST SACRED; INVIOLABLE. The brash insurance salesman invaded the *sacrosanct* privacy of the office of the president of the company.

sadistic \sə-'dis-tik *also* sā- *or* sa-\ adj. INCLINED TO CRUELTY. If we are to improve conditions in this prison, we must first get rid of the *sadistic* warden.

saga \'sä-gə *also* 'sa-\ n. SCANDINAVIAN MYTH; ANY LEGEND. This is a *saga* of the sea and the men who risk their lives on it.

sagacious \sə-'gā-shəs, si-\ adj. KEEN; SHREWD; HAVING INSIGHT. He is much too *sagacious* to be fooled by a trick like that.

salient \'sā-lyənt, -lē-ənt\ adj. PROMINENT. One of the *salient* features of that newspaper is its excellent editorial page.

saline \'sā-,lēn, -,līn\ adj. SALTY. The slightly *saline* taste of this mineral water is pleasant.

salubrious \sə-'lü-brē-əs\ adj. HEALTHFUL. Many people with hay fever move to more *salubrious* sections of the country during the months of August and September.

salutary \'sal-yə-,ter-ē\ adj. TENDING TO IMPROVE; BENEFICIAL; WHOLESOME. The punishment had a *salutary* effect on the boy, as he became a model student.

salvage \'sal-vij\ v. RESCUE FROM LOSS. All attempts to *salvage* the wrecked ship failed. //also n.

sanctimonious \ˌsaŋ(k)-tə-'mō-nē-əs, -nyəs\ adj. DISPLAY-ING OSTENTATIOUS OR HYPOCRITICAL DEVOUTNESS. You do not have to be so *sanctimonious* to prove that you are devout.

sanction \'saŋ(k)-shən\ v. APPROVE; RATIFY. Nothing will convince me to *sanction* the engagement of my daughter to such a worthless young man.

sanguine \'saŋ-gwən\ adj. CHEERFUL; HOPEFUL. Let us not be too *sanguine* about the outcome; something could go wrong.

sarcasm \'sär-ˌka-zəm\ n. SCORNFUL REMARKS; STINGING REBUKE. His feelings were hurt by the *sarcasm* of his supposed friends. //sarcastic, adj.

sardonic \sär-'dä-nik\ adj. DISDAINFUL; SARCASTIC; CYNICAL. The *sardonic* humor of nightclub comedians who satirize or ridicule patrons in the audience strikes some people as amusing and others as rude.

sate \'sāt, 'sat\ v. SATISFY TO THE FULL. Its hunger *sated*, the lion dozed.

satellite \'sa-tə-ˌlīt\ n. SMALL BODY REVOLVING AROUND A LARGER ONE. During the first few years of the Space Age, hundreds of *satellites* were launched by Russia and the United States.

satiate \'sā-sh(ē-)ət\ v. SURFEIT; SATISFY FULLY. The guests, having eaten until they were *satiated*, now listened inattentively to the speakers. //satiety, n.

satirical \sə-'tir-i-kəl\ adj. MOCKING. The humor of cartoonist Gary Trudeau often is *satirical*; through the comments of the Doonesbury characters, Trudeau ridicules political corruption and folly. //satire, n.

saturate \'sa-chə-ˌrāt\ v. SOAK. Their clothes were *saturated* by the rain. //saturation, n.

savor \'sā-vər\ v. HAVE A DISTINCTIVE FLAVOR, SMELL, OR QUALITY; DELIGHT IN. I think your choice of a successor *savors* of favoritism.

scanty \'skan-tē\ adj. MEAGER; INSUFFICIENT. Thinking his helping of food was *scanty*, Oliver Twist asked for more.

scapegoat \'skāp-,gōt\ n. SOMEONE WHO BEARS THE BLAME FOR OTHERS. After the Challenger disaster, NASA searched for *scapegoats* on whom they could cast the blame.

scavenger \'ska-vən-jər\ n. COLLECTOR AND DISPOSER OF REFUSE; ANIMAL THAT DEVOURS REFUSE AND CARRION. The Oakland *Scavenger* Company is responsible for the collection and disposal of the community's garbage.

schism \'si-zəm, 'ski- *also* 'shi-\ n. DIVISION; SPLIT. Let us not widen the *schism* by further bickering.

scintillate \'sin-tə-,lāt\ v. SPARKLE; FLASH. I enjoy her dinner parties because the food is excellent and the conversation *scintillates*.

scoff \'skäf, 'skòf\ v. MOCK; RIDICULE. He *scoffed* at dentists until he had his first toothache.

scrupulous \'skrü-pyə-ləs\ adj. CONSCIENTIOUS; EXTREMELY THOROUGH. I can recommend him for a position of responsibility for I have found him a very *scrupulous* young man.

scrutinize \'skrü-tə-,nīz\ v. EXAMINE CLOSELY AND CRITICALLY. Searching for flaws, the sergeant *scrutinized* every detail of the private's uniform.

scurrilous \'skər-ə-ləs, 'skə-rə-\ adj. OBSCENE; INDECENT. Your *scurrilous* remarks are especially offensive because they are untrue.

scurry \'skər-ē, 'skə-rē\ v. MOVE BRISKLY. The White Rabbit had to *scurry* to get to his appointment on time.

scuttle \'skə-təl\ v. ABANDON PLANS, HOPES; SINK (A VESSEL); HASTEN OR SCURRY. The financial crisis *scuttled* Millicent's dreams of buying her own home.

seclusion \si-'klü-zhən\ n. ISOLATION; SOLITUDE. One moment she loved crowds; the next, she sought *seclusion*.

secular \'se-kyə-lər\ adj. WORLDLY; NOT PERTAINING TO CHURCH MATTERS; TEMPORAL. The church leaders decided not to interfere in *secular* matters.

sedate \si-'dāt\ adj. COMPOSED; GRAVE. The parents were worried because they felt their son was too quiet and *sedate*.

sedentary \'se-dən-,ter-ē\ adj. REQUIRING SITTING. Because he had a *sedentary* occupation, he decided to visit a gymnasium weekly.

sedition \si-'di-shən\ n. RESISTANCE TO AUTHORITY; INSUB- ORDINATION. His words, though not treasonous in themselves, were calculated to arouse thoughts of *sedition*.

sedulous \'se-jə-ləs\ adj. DILIGENT. The young woman was so *sedulous* that she received a commendation for her hard work.

seethe \'sēth\ v. BE DISTURBED; BOIL. The nation was *seething* with discontent as the noblemen continued their arrogant ways.

semblance \'sem-blən(t)s\ n. OUTWARD APPEARANCE; GUISE. Although this book has a *semblance* of wisdom and scholarship, a careful examination will reveal many errors and omissions.

senility \si-'ni-lə-tē *also* se-\ n. OLD AGE; FEEBLEMINDED- NESS OF OLD AGE. Most of the decisions are being made by the junior members of the company because of the *senility* of the president.

sensual \'sen(t)-sh(ə-)wəl, -shəl\ adj. DEVOTED TO THE PLEASURES OF THE SENSES; CARNAL; VOLUPTUOUS. I cannot understand what caused him to drop his *sensual* way of life and become so ascetic.

sententious \sen-'ten(t)-shəs\ adj. TERSE; CONCISE; APHORIS- TIC. After reading so many redundant speeches, I find his *sententious* style particularly pleasing.

Synonym Test • Word List 42

Each of the questions below consists of a word in capital letters, followed by five words or phrases. Choose the word or phrase that is most similar in meaning to the word in capital letters and write the letter of your choice on your answer paper.

616. **SADISTIC** (A) happy (B) quaint (C) cruel (D) vacant (E) fortunate

617. **SAGACIOUS** (A) wise (B) bitter (C) voracious (D) veracious (E) fallacious

618. **SALINE** (A) salacious (B) salty (C) colorless (D) permitted (E) minimum

619. **SALUBRIOUS** (A) salty (B) bloody (C) healthful (D) maudlin (E) temporary

620. **SALUTARY** (A) choleric (B) innovative (C) warranted (D) irritated (E) beneficial

621. **SALVAGE** (A) remove (B) outfit (C) burn (D) save (E) confuse

622. **SANCTIMONIOUS** (A) hypothetical (B) paltry (C) mercenary (D) hypocritical (E) grateful

623. **SATIETY** (A) satisfaction (B) warmth (C) erectness (D) ignorance (E) drunkenness

624. **SCANTY** (A) collected (B) remote (C) invisible (D) scarce (E) straight

625. **SCURRILOUS** (A) savage (B) scabby (C) scandalous (D) volatile (E) major

626. **SECULAR** (A) vivid (B) worldly (C) punitive (D) positive (E) varying

627. **SEDENTARY** (A) vicarious (B) loyal (C) accidental (D) stationary (E) afraid

628. **SEDULOUS** (A) industrious (B) forlorn (C) posthumous (D) shallow (E) oppressive

629. **SENILITY** (A) virility (B) loquaciousness (C) forgetfulness (D) agedness (E) majority

630. **SENTENTIOUS** (A) paragraphed (B) positive (C) posthumous (D) pacific (E) brief

sequester \si-ˈkwes-tər\ v. RETIRE FROM PUBLIC LIFE; SEGREGATE; SECLUDE. Although he had hoped for a long time to *sequester* himself in a small community, he never was able to drop his busy round of activities in the city.

serendipity \ˌser-ən-ˈdi-pə-tē\ n. GIFT FOR FINDING VALUABLE THINGS NOT SEARCHED FOR. Many scientific discoveries are a matter of *serendipity*.

serenity \sə-ˈre-nə-tē\ n. CALMNESS; PLACIDITY. The *serenity* of the sleepy town was shattered by a tremendous explosion.

serrated \ˈser-ˌā-təd, sə-ˈrā-təd\ adj. HAVING A SAWTOOTHED EDGE. The beech tree is one of many plants that have *serrated* leaves.

servile \ˈsər-vəl, -ˌvī(-ə)l\ adj. SLAVISH; CRINGING. Uriah Heep was a very *servile* individual.

severance \ˈsev-rən(t)s, ˈse-və-\ n. DIVISION; PARTITION; SEPARATION. The *severance* of church and state is a basic principle of our government.

severity \sə-ˈver-ə-tē\ n. HARSHNESS; PLAINNESS. The newspapers disapproved of the *severity* of the sentence.

shackle \ˈsha-kəl\ v. CHAIN; FETTER. The criminal's ankles were *shackled* to prevent his escape. //also n.

sham \ˈsham\ v. PRETEND. He *shammed* sickness to get out of going to school. //also n.

shimmer \ˈshi-mər\ v. GLIMMER INTERMITTENTLY. The moonlight *shimmered* on the water as the moon broke through the clouds for a moment. //also n.

shoddy \ˈshä-dē\ adj. SHAM; NOT GENUINE; INFERIOR. You will never get the public to buy such *shoddy* material.

shrewd \ˈshrüd\ adj. CLEVER; ASTUTE. A *shrewd* investor, he took clever advantage of the fluctuations of the stock market.

sibling \'si-bliŋ\ n. BROTHER OR SISTER. We may not enjoy being *siblings*, but we cannot forget that we still belong to the same family.

simile \'si-mə-(,)lē\ n. COMPARISON OF ONE THING WITH ANOTHER, USING THE WORD *LIKE* OR *AS*. "My love is like a red, red rose" is a *simile*.

simulate \'sim-yə-,lāt\ v. PRETEND, FEIGN. He *simulated* insanity in order to avoid punishment for his crime.

sinister \'si-nəs-tər\ adj. EVIL. We must defeat the *sinister* forces that seek our downfall.

sinuous \'sin-yə-wəs, -yü-əs\ adj. WINDING; BENDING IN AND OUT; NOT MORALLY HONEST. The snake moved in a *sinuous* manner.

skeptic \'skep-tik\ n. DOUBTER; PERSON WHO SUSPENDS JUDGMENT UNTIL HE HAS EXAMINED THE EVIDENCE SUPPORTING A POINT OF VIEW. In this matter, I am a *skeptic*; I want proof. //skeptical, adj.

skimp \'skimp\ v. PROVIDE SCANTILY; LIVE VERY ECONOMICALLY. They were forced to *skimp* on necessities in order to make their limited supplies last the winter.

skinflint \'skin-,flint\ n. MISER. The old *skinflint* refused to give her a raise.

skulk \'skəlk\ v. MOVE FURTIVELY AND SECRETLY. He *skulked* through the less fashionable sections of the city in order to avoid meeting any of his former friends.

slacken \'sla-kən\ v. SLOW UP; LOOSEN. As they passed the finish line, the runners *slackened* their pace.

slander \'slan-dər\ n. DEFAMATION; UTTERANCE OF FALSE AND MALICIOUS STATEMENTS. Unless you can prove your allegations, your remarks constitute *slander*. //also v.

sleazy \'slē-zē *also* 'slā-\ adj. FLIMSY; UNSUBSTANTIAL. This is a *sleazy* material; it will not wear well.

sleeper \'slē-pər\ n. SOMETHING ORIGINALLY OF LITTLE VALUE OR IMPORTANCE THAT IN TIME BECOMES VERY VALUABLE. Unnoticed by the critics at its publication, the eventual Pulitzer Prize winner was a classic *sleeper*.

slither \'sli-<u>th</u>ər\ v. SLIP OR SLIDE. During the recent ice storm, many people *slithered* down this hill as they walked to the station.

sloth \'slòth, 'slàth *also* 'slōth\ n. LAZINESS. Such *sloth* in a young person is deplorable; go to work!

slough \'sləf\ v. DISPOSE OR GET RID OF; SHED. Each spring, the snake *sloughs* off its skin.

slovenly \'slə-vən-lē *also* 'slä-\ adj. UNTIDY; CARELESS IN WORK HABITS. Such *slovenly* work habits will never produce good products.

sluggard \'slə-gərd\ n. LAZY PERSON. "You are a *sluggard*, a drone, a parasite," the angry father shouted at his lazy son.

sluggish \'slə-gish\ adj. SLOW; LAZY; LETHARGIC. After two nights without sleep, she felt *sluggish* and incapable of exertion.

smirk \'smərk\ n. CONCEITED SMILE. Wipe that *smirk* off your face! //also v.

smolder \'smōl-dər\ v. BURN WITHOUT FLAME; BE LIABLE TO BREAK OUT AT ANY MOMENT. The rags *smoldered* for hours before they burst into flame.

snicker \'sni-kər\ n. HALF-STIFLED LAUGH. The boy could not suppress a *snicker* when the teacher sat on the tack. //also v.

snivel \'sni-vəl\ v. RUN AT THE NOSE; SNUFFLE; WHINE. Don't you come *sniveling* to me complaining about your big brother.

sobriety \sə-'brī-ə-tē, sō-\ n. SOBERNESS. The solemnity of the occasion filled us with *sobriety*.

sodden \'sä-dən\ adj. SOAKED; DULL, AS IF FROM DRINK. He set his *sodden* overcoat near the radiator to dry.

sojourn \'sō-,jərn, sō-'\ n. TEMPORARY STAY. After his *sojourn* in Florida, he began to long for the colder climate of his native New England home.

solace \'sä-ləs *also* 'sō-\ n. COMFORT IN TROUBLE. I hope you will find *solace* in the thought that all of us share your loss.

solemnity \sə-'lem-nə-tē\ n. SERIOUSNESS; GRAVITY. The minister was concerned that nothing should disturb the *solemnity* of the marriage service. //solemn, adj.

solicitous \sə-'li-sə-təs, -'lis-təs\ adj. WORRIED; CONCERNED. The employer was very *solicitous* about the health of her employees as replacements were difficult to get.

soliloquy \sə-'li-lə-kwē\ n. TALKING TO ONESELF. The *soliloquy* is a device used by the dramatist to reveal a character's innermost thoughts and emotions.

solvent \'säl-vənt, 'sȯl-\ adj. ABLE TO PAY ALL DEBTS. By dint of very frugal living, he was finally able to become *solvent* and avoid bankruptcy proceedings.

Each of the questions below consists of a word in capital letters, followed by five words or phrases. Choose the word or phrase that is most similar in meaning to the word in capital letters and write the letter of your choice on your answer paper.

631. **SERENITY**   (A) clumsiness   (B) holiness
   (C) peacefulness   (D) official   (E) potentate

632. **SERRATED**   (A) worried   (B) embittered
   (C) sawtoothed   (D) fallen   (E) infantile

633. **SERVILE**   (A) moral   (B) puerile   (C) futile
   (D) foul   (E) subservient

634. **SHODDY**   (A) poor quality   (B) barefoot   (C) sunlit
   (D) querulous   (E) garrulous

635. **SIMILE**   (A) gratitude   (B) magnitude
   (C) comparison   (D) aptitude   (E) kindness

636. **SINISTER**   (A) unwed   (B) ministerial   (C) bad
   (D) returned   (E) splintered

637. **SKEPTICAL**   (A) tractable   (B) rash   (C) dramatic
   (D) vain   (E) doubting

638. **SLEAZY**   (A) fanciful   (B) creeping   (C) flimsy
   (D) uneasy   (E) warranted

639. **SLOTH**   (A) penitence   (B) filth   (C) futility
   (D) poverty   (E) laziness

640. **SLOUGH**   (A) toughen   (B) trap   (C) violate
   (D) cast off   (E) depart

641. **SLOVENLY**   (A) half-baked   (B) loved
   (C) inappropriate   (D) messy   (E) rapidly

642. **SOBRIETY**   (A) soberness   (B) aptitude
   (C) scholasticism   (D) monotony   (E) aversion

643. **SOJOURN**   (A) good time   (B) livelihood
   (C) bargain   (D) epitaph   (E) vacation

644. **SOLEMNITY**   (A) seriousness   (B) sunrise
   (C) legality   (D) divorce   (E) iniquity

645. **SOLVENT**   (A) enigmatic   (B) financially sound
   (C) fiducial   (D) puzzling   (E) gilded

WORD LIST 44

somber \'säm-bər\ adj. GLOOMY; DEPRESSING. From the doctor's grim expression, I could tell he had *somber* news.

somnambulist \säm-'nam-byə-‚list\ n. SLEEPWALKER. The most famous *somnambulist* in literature is Lady Macbeth; her monologue in the sleepwalking scene is one of the highlights of Shakespeare's play.

sonorous \sə-'nȯr-əs, 'sä-nə-rəs\ adj. RICH AND FULL IN SOUND; RESONANT. His *sonorous* voice resounded through the hall.

sophisticated \sə-'fis-tə-kā-təd\ adj. WORLDLY; NOT NAIVE; COMPLEX. David's tastes were far too *sophisticated* for him to enjoy a typical barbecue: rather than grill hamburgers over plain charcoal, he grilled quail and crayfish on a bed of mesquite charcoal.

sophistry \'sä-fə-strē\ n. SEEMINGLY PLAUSIBLE BUT FALLACIOUS REASONING. Instead of advancing valid arguments, he tried to overwhelm his audience with a flood of *sophistries*. //sophist, n.

sophomoric \‚säf-'mȯr-ik, -'mär- *also* ‚sȯf- *or* ‚sä-fə- *or* ‚sȯ-fə-\ adj. IMMATURE; SHALLOW. Your *sophomoric* remarks are a sign of your youth and indicate that you have not given much thought to the problem.

soporific \‚sä-pə-'ri-fik\ adj. SLEEP PRODUCER. I do not need a sedative when I listen to one of his *soporific* speeches. //also n.

sordid \'sȯr-dəd\ adj. FILTHY; BASE; VILE. The social worker was angered by the *sordid* housing provided for the homeless.

sparse \'spärs\ adj. NOT THICK; THINLY SCATTERED; SCANTY. He had moved from the densely populated city to the remote countryside where the population was *sparse*.

spasmodic \spaz-'mä-dik\ adj. FITFUL; PERIODIC. The *spasmodic* coughing in the auditorium annoyed the performers.

spawn \\'spȯn, 'spän\\ adj. GIVE BIRTH TO; LAY EGGS. Fish ladders had to be built in the dams to assist the salmon returning to *spawn* in their native streams. //also n.

specious \\'spē-shəs\\ adj. SEEMINGLY REASONABLE BUT INCORRECT. Let us not be misled by such *specious* arguments.

spectrum \\'spek-trəm\\ n. COLORED BAND PRODUCED WHEN BEAM OF LIGHT PASSES THROUGH A PRISM. The visible portion of the *spectrum* includes red at one end and violet at the other.

sphinx-like \\'sfiŋ(k)s-ˌlīk\\ adj. ENIGMATIC; MYSTERIOUS. The Mona Lisa's *sphinx-like* expression has puzzled art lovers for centuries.

sporadic \\spə-'ra-dik\\ adj. OCCURRING IRREGULARLY. Although there are *sporadic* outbursts of shooting, we may report that the major rebellion has been defeated.

spry \\'sprī\\ adj. VIGOROUSLY ACTIVE; NIMBLE. She was eighty years old, yet still *spry* and alert.

spurious \\'spyu̇r-ē-əs\\ adj. FALSE; COUNTERFEIT. The antique dealer hero of Jonathan Gash's mystery novels gives the reader tips on how to tell *spurious* antiques from the real thing.

spurn \\'spərn\\ v. REJECT; SCORN. The heroine *spurned* the villain's advances.

squalid \\'skwä-ləd\\ adj. DIRTY; NEGLECTED; POOR. It is easy to see how crime can breed in such a *squalid* neighborhood. //squalor, n.

squander \\'skwän-dər\\ v. WASTE. The prodigal son *squandered* the family estate.

staccato \\stə-'kä-(ˌ)tō\\ adj. PLAYED IN AN ABRUPT MANNER; MARKED BY ABRUPT SHARP SOUND. His *staccato* speech reminded one of the sound of a machine gun.

stagnant \'stag-nənt\ adj. MOTIONLESS; STALE; DULL. The *stagnant* water was a breeding ground for disease. //stagnate, v., stagnation, n.

staid \'stād\ adj. SOBER; SEDATE. Her conduct during the funeral ceremony was *staid* and solemn.

stalemate \'stāl-ˌmāt\ n. DEADLOCK. Negotiations between the union and the employers have reached a *stalemate*; neither side is willing to budge from previously stated positions.

stamina \'sta-mə-nə\ n. STRENGTH; STAYING POWER. I doubt that she has the *stamina* to run the full distance of the marathon race.

stanza \'stan-zə\ n. DIVISION OF A POEM. Do you know the last *stanza* of "The Star-Spangled Banner"?

static \'sta-tik\ adj. UNCHANGING; LACKING DEVELOPMENT. Nothing had changed at home; things were *static*. //stasis, n.

statute \'sta-(ˌ)chüt, -chət\ n. LAW. We have many *statutes* in our law books that should be repealed. //statutory, adj.

steadfast \'sted-ˌfast *also* -fəst\ adj. LOYAL. I am sure you will remain *steadfast* in your support of the cause.

stereotyped \'ster-ē-ə-ˌtīpt, 'stir-\ adj. FIXED AND UNVARYING REPRESENTATION. My chief objection to the book is that the characters are *stereotyped*.

stigmatize \'stig-mə-ˌtīz\ v. BRAND; MARK AS WICKED. I do not want to *stigmatize* this young offender for life by sending her to prison. //stigma, n.

stilted \'stil-təd\ adj. BOMBASTIC; INFLATED. His *stilted* rhetoric did not impress the college audience; they were immune to bombastic utterances.

stipend \'stī-ˌpend, -pənd\ n. PAY FOR SERVICES. There is a nominal *stipend* for this position.

stoic \'stō-ik\ n. PERSON WHO IS INDIFFERENT TO PLEASURE OR PAIN. The doctor called her patient a *stoic* because he had borne the pain of the examination without whimpering. //also adj.

stoke \\'stōk\\ v. TO FEED PLENTIFULLY. They swiftly *stoked* themselves, knowing they would not have another meal until they reached camp.

stolid \\'stä-ləd\\ adj. DULL; IMPASSIVE. I am afraid that this imaginative poetry will not appeal to such a *stolid* person.

stratagem \\'stra-tə-jəm, -,jem\\ n. DECEPTIVE SCHEME. We saw through his clever *stratagem*.

stratum \\'strā-təm, 'stra-\\ n. LAYER OF EARTH'S SURFACE; LAYER OF SOCIETY. Unless we alleviate conditions in the lowest *stratum* of our society, we may expect grumbling and revolt.

strident \\'strī-dənt\\ adj. LOUD AND HARSH. She scolded him in a *strident* voice.

stringent \\'strin-jənt\\ adj. BINDING; RIGID. I think these regulations are too *stringent*.

strut \\'strət\\ n. POMPOUS WALK. His *strut* as he marched about the parade ground revealed him for what he was: a pompous buffoon. //also v.

strut \\'strət\\ n. SUPPORTING BAR. The engineer calculated that the *strut* supporting the rafter needed to be reinforced. (secondary meaning)

stupor \\'stü-pər, 'styü-\\ n. STATE OF APATHY; DAZE; LACK OF AWARENESS. In his *stupor*, the addict was unaware of the events taking place around him.

stymie \\'stī-mē\\ v. PRESENT AN OBSTACLE; STUMP. The detective was *stymied* by the contradictory evidence in the robbery investigation. //also n.

suavity \\'swä-və-tē\\ n. URBANITY; POLISH. He is particularly good in roles that require *suavity* and sophistication. //suave, adj.

subjective \\(,)səb-'jek-tiv\\ adj. OCCURRING OR TAKING PLACE WITHIN THE SUBJECT; UNDULY EGOCENTRIC,

PERSONAL. Your analysis is highly *subjective*; you have permitted your emotions and your opinions to color your thinking.

subjugate \ˈsəb-ji-ˌgāt\ v. CONQUER; BRING UNDER CONTROL. It is not our aim to *subjugate* our foe; we are interested only in establishing peaceful relations.

sublime \sə-ˈblīm\ adj. EXALTED; NOBLE; UPLIFTING. Mother Teresa has been honored for her *sublime* deeds.

Each of the questions below consists of a word in capital letters, followed by five words or phrases. Choose the word or phrase that is most similar in meaning to the word in capital letters and write the letter of your choice on your answer paper.

646. **SONOROUS** (A) resonant (B) reassuring (C) repetitive (D) resinous (E) sisterly

647. **SOPHOMORIC** (A) unprecedented (B) immature (C) insipid (D) intellectual (E) illusionary

648. **SOPORIFIC** (A) silent (B) caustic (C) memorial (D) sleep inducing (E) springing

649. **SPASMODIC** (A) intermittent (B) fit (C) inaccurate (D) violent (E) physical

650. **SPORADIC** (A) seedy (B) latent (C) vivid (D) inconsequential (E) occasional

651. **SPRY** (A) competing (B) nimble (C) indignant (D) foppish (E) fundamental

652. **SPURIOUS** (A) not genuine (B) angry (C) mitigated (D) interrogated (E) glorious

653. **SQUANDER** (A) fortify (B) depart (C) roam (D) waste (E) forfeit

654. **STACCATO** (A) musical (B) long (C) abrupt (D) sneezing (E) pounded

655. **STAMINA** (A) patience (B) pistils (C) strength (D) fascination (E) patina

656. **STEREOTYPED** (A) banal (B) antique (C) modeled (D) repetitious (E) continued

657. **STILTED** (A) candid (B) pompous (C) modish (D) acute (E) inarticulate

658. **STRINGENT** (A) binding (B) reserved (C) utilized (D) lambent (E) indigent

659. **SUAVITY** (A) ingeniousness (B) indifference (C) urbanity (D) constancy (E) paucity

660. **SUBLIME** (A) unconscious (B) respected (C) exalted (D) sneaky (E) replaced

subliminal \(ˌ)sə-ˈbli-mə-nəl\ adj. BELOW THE THRESHOLD OF CONSCIOUSNESS. We may not be aware of the *subliminal* influences that affect our thinking.

subsequent \ˈsəb-si-kwənt, -sə-ˌkwent\ adj. FOLLOWING; LATER. In *subsequent* lessons, we shall take up more difficult problems.

subside \səb-ˈsīd\ v. SETTLE DOWN; DESCEND; GROW QUIET. The doctor assured us that the fever would eventually *subside*.

subsidiary \səb-ˈsi-dē-ˌer-ē, -ˈsi-də-rē\ adj. SUBORDINATE; SECONDARY. This information may be used as *subsidiary* evidence but is not sufficient by itself to prove your argument. //also n.

subsidy \ˈsəb-sə-dē, -zə-\ n. DIRECT FINANCIAL AID BY GOVERNMENT, ETC. Without this *subsidy*, American ship operators would not be able to compete in world markets. //subsidize, v.

substantiate \səb-ˈstan(t)-shē-ˌāt\ v. VERIFY; SUPPORT. I intend to *substantiate* my statement by producing witnesses.

substantive \ˈsəb-stən-tiv\ adj. ESSENTIAL; PERTAINING TO THE SUBSTANCE. Although the delegates were aware of the importance of the problem, they could not agree on the *substantive* issues.

subterfuge \ˈsəb-tər-ˌfyüj\ n. PRETENSE; EVASION. As soon as we realized that you had won our support by a *subterfuge*, we withdrew our endorsement of your candidacy.

subtlety \ˈsə-təl-tē\ n. NICETY; CUNNING; GUILE; DELICACY. The *subtlety* of his remarks was unnoticed by most of his audience. //subtle, adj.

subversive \səb-ˈvər-siv, -ziv\ adj. TENDING TO OVERTHROW, RUIN, OR UNDERMINE. We must destroy such *subversive* publications.

succinct \(ˌ)sək-'siŋ(k)t, sə-'siŋ(k)t\ adj. BRIEF; TERSE; COMPACT. His remarks are always *succinct* and pointed.

succor \'sə-kər\ n. AID; ASSISTANCE; RELIEF. We shall be ever grateful for the *succor* your country gave us when we were in need. //also v.

succulent \'sə-kyə-lənt\ adj. JUICY; FULL OF RICHNESS. The citrus foods from Florida are more *succulent* to some people than those from California. //also n.

succumb \sə-'kəm\ v. YIELD; GIVE IN; DIE. I *succumb* to temptation whenever it comes my way.

summation \(ˌ)sə-'mā-shən\ n. ACT OF FINDING THE TOTAL; SUMMARY. In his *summation*, the lawyer emphasized the testimony given by the two witnesses.

sumptuous \'səm(p)(t)-shə-wəs, -shəs, -shwəs\ adj. LAVISH; RICH. I cannot recall when I have had such a *sumptuous* Thanksgiving feast.

sunder \'sən-dər\ v. SEPARATE; PART. Northern and southern Ireland are politically and religiously *sundered*.

supercilious \ˌsü-pər-'si-lē-əs, -'sil-yəs\ adj. CONTEMPTUOUS; HAUGHTY. I resent your *supercilious* and arrogant attitude.

superficial \ˌsü-pər-'fi-shəl\ adj. TRIVIAL; SHALLOW. Since your report gave only a *superficial* analysis of the problem, I cannot give you more than a passing grade.

superfluous \sù-'pər-flü-əs\ adj. EXCESSIVE; OVERABUNDANT; UNNECESSARY. Please try not to include so many *superfluous* details in your report; just give me the bare facts. //superfluity, n.

supersede \'sü-pər-ˌsēd\ v. CAUSE TO BE SET ASIDE; REPLACE. This regulation will *supersede* all previous rules.

supplant \sə-'plant\ v. REPLACE; USURP. Ferdinand Marcos was *supplanted* by Corazon Aquino as president of the Philippines.

supple \'sə-pəl *also* 'sü-\ adj. FLEXIBLE; PLIANT. The angler found a *supple* limb and used it as a fishing rod.

supplicate \'sə-plə-ˌkāt\ v. PETITION HUMBLY; PRAY TO GRANT A FAVOR. We *supplicate* Your Majesty to grant him amnesty. //suppliant, adj., n.

supposition \ˌsə-pə-'zi-shən\ n. HYPOTHESIS; THE ACT OF SUPPOSING. I decided to confide in him based on the *supposition* that he would be discreet. //suppose, v.

suppress \sə-'pres\ v. CRUSH; SUBDUE; INHIBIT. After the armed troops had *suppressed* the rebellion, the city was placed under martial law.

surfeit \'sər-fət\ n. OVERINDULGENCE; EXCESSIVE AMOUNT; STATE OF BEING OVERLY FULL. The greedy child stuffed himself with candy to the point of *surfeit*. //also v.

surly \'sər-lē\ adj. RUDE; CROSS. Because of his *surly* attitude, many people avoided his company.

surmise \sər-'mīz, 'sər-ˌ\ v. GUESS. I *surmise* that he will be late for this meeting. //also n.

surmount \sər-'maùnt\ v. OVERCOME. He had to *surmount* many obstacles in order to succeed.

surpass \sər-'pas\ v. EXCEED. Her SAT scores *surpassed* our expectations.

surreptitious \ˌsər-əp-'ti-shəs, ˌsə-rəp-, sə-ˌrep-\ adj. SECRET. News of their *surreptitious* meeting gradually leaked out.

surrogate \'sər-ə-ˌgāt, 'sə-rə-\ n. SUBSTITUTE. For a fatherless child, a male teacher may become a father *surrogate*.

surveillance \sər-'vā-lən(t)s *also* -'väl-yən(t)s *or* -'vā-ən(t)s\ n. WATCHING; GUARDING. The FBI kept the house under constant *surveillance* in the hope of capturing all the criminals at one time.

susceptible \sə-'sep-tə-bəl\ adj. IMPRESSIONABLE; EASILY INFLUENCED; HAVING LITTLE RESISTANCE, AS TO A DISEASE. He was a very *susceptible* young man, and so his parents worried that he might fall into bad company.

sustenance \\'səs-tə-nən(t)s\\ n. MEANS OF SUPPORT, FOOD, NOURISHMENT. In the tropics, the natives find *sustenance* easy to obtain, due to all the fruit trees. //sustain, v.

swelter \\'swel-tər\\ v. BE OPPRESSED BY HEAT. I am going to buy an air-conditioning unit for my apartment as I do not intend to *swelter* through another hot and humid summer.

swindler \\'swin(d)-lər, 'swin-dəl-ər\\ n. CHEAT. She was gullible and trusting, an easy victim for the first *swindler* who came along.

sycophant \\'si-kə-fənt *also* -,fant\\ n. SERVILE FLATTERER. The king believed the flattery of his *sycophants* and refused to listen to his prime minister's warnings. //sycophantic, adj.

symmetry \\'si-mə-trē\\ n. ARRANGEMENT OF PARTS SO THAT BALANCE IS OBTAINED; CONGRUITY. The addition of a second tower will give this edifice the *symmetry* it now lacks.

synchronous \\'siŋ-krə-nəs, 'sin-\\ adj. SIMILARLY TIMED; SIMULTANEOUS WITH. We have many examples of scientists in different parts of the world who have made *synchronous* discoveries. //synchronize, v.

synthesis \\'sin(t)-thə-səs\\ n. COMBINING PARTS INTO A WHOLE. Now that we have succeeded in isolating this drug, our next problem is to plan its *synthesis* in the laboratory. //synthesize, v.

synthetic \\sin-'the-tik\\ adj. ARTIFICIAL; RESUMING FROM SYNTHESIS. During the twentieth century, many *synthetic* products have replaced natural products. //also n.

tacit \\'ta-sət\\ adj. UNDERSTOOD; NOT PUT INTO WORDS. We have a *tacit* agreement based on only a handshake.

taciturn \\'ta-sə-,tərn\\ adj. HABITUALLY SILENT; TALKING LITTLE. New Englanders are reputedly *taciturn* people.

tactile \'tak-təl, -'tī(-ə)l\ adj. PERTAINING TO THE ORGANS OR SENSE OF TOUCH. His callused hands had lost their *tactile* sensitivity.

tainted \'tān-təd\ adj. CONTAMINATED; CORRUPT. Health authorities are always trying to prevent the sale and use of *tainted* food.

tantalize \'tan-tə-,līz\ v. TEASE; TORTURE WITH DISAPPOINT-MENT. Tom loved to *tantalize* his younger brother with candy; he knew the boy was forbidden to have it.

Each of the questions below consists of a word in capital letters, followed by five words or phrases. Choose the word or phrase that is most similar in meaning to the word in capital letters and write the letter of your choice on your answer paper.

661. **SUBLIMINAL**   (A) radiant   (B) indifferent   (C) unconscious   (D) domestic   (E) horizontal

662. **SUBTLE**   (A) senile   (B) experienced   (C) delicate   (D) rapid   (E) partial

663. **SUPERCILIOUS**   (A) haughty   (B) highbrow   (C) angry   (D) inane   (E) philosophic

664. **SUPERFICIAL**   (A) abnormal   (B) portentous   (C) shallow   (D) angry   (E) tiny

665. **SUPERFLUOUS**   (A) acute   (B) extraneous   (C) associate   (D) astronomical   (E) inferior

666. **SUPPLIANT**   (A) intolerant   (B) swallowing   (C) beseeching   (D) finishing   (E) flexible

667. **SURFEIT**   (A) substitute   (B) overabundance   (C) hypothesis   (D) pretense   (E) assistance

668. **SURREPTITIOUS**   (A) secret   (B) snakelike   (C) nightly   (D) abstract   (E) furnished

669. **SUSCEPTIBLE**   (A) vulnerable   (B) reflective   (C) disapproving   (D) confident   (E) past

670. **SWINDLER**   (A) cheat   (B) thrifty shopper   (C) gambler   (D) miser   (E) wanderer

671. **SYCOPHANTIC**   (A) quiet   (B) reclusive   (C) servilely flattering   (D) frolicsome   (E) eagerly awaiting

672. **SYNTHETIC**   (A) simplified   (B) doubled   (C) tuneful   (D) artificial   (E) fiscal

673. **TACIT**   (A) unspoken   (B) allowed   (C) neutral   (D) impertinent   (E) unwanted

674. **TAINTED**   (A) chief   (B) simple   (C) irregular   (D) contaminated   (E) gifted

675. **TANTALIZE**   (A) tease   (B) wax   (C) warrant   (D) authorize   (E) summarize

tantamount \'tan-tə-ˌmaůnt\ adj. EQUAL. Your ignoring their pathetic condition is *tantamount* to murder.

tantrum \'tan-trəm\ n. FIT OF PETULANCE; CAPRICE. The child learned that he could have almost anything if he went into a *tantrum*.

tarry \'ter-ē, 'ta-rē\ v. DELAY; DAWDLE. We can't *tarry* if we want to get to the airport on time.

taut \'tȯt\ adj. TIGHT; READY. The captain maintained that he ran a *taut* ship.

tautological \ˌtȯ-tə-'lä-ji-kəl\ adj. NEEDLESSLY REPETITIOUS. In the sentence "It was visible to the eye," the phrase "to the eye" is *tautological*. //tautology, n.

tedious \'tē-dē-əs, 'tē-jəs\ adj. BORING; TIRING. The repetitious nature of work on the assembly line made Martin's job very *tedious*. //tedium, n.

temerity \tə-'mer-ə-tē\ n. BOLDNESS; RASHNESS. Do you have the *temerity* to argue with me?

temper \'tem-pər\ v. RESTRAIN; BLEND; TOUGHEN. His hard times in the army only served to *temper* his strength.

temperate \'tem-p(ə-)rət\ adj. RESTRAINED; SELF-CONTROLLED; MODERATE. Noted for his *temperate* appetite, he seldom gained weight.

tempo \'tem-(ˌ)pō\ n. SPEED OF MUSIC. I find the conductor's *tempo* too slow for such a brilliant piece of music.

temporal \'tem-p(ə-)rəl\ adj. NOT LASTING FOREVER; LIMITED BY TIME; SECULAR. At one time in our history, *temporal* rulers assumed that they had been given their thrones by divine right.

tenacious \tə-'nā-shəs\ adj. HOLDING FAST. I had to struggle to break his *tenacious* hold on my arm. //tenacity, n.

tenet \'te-nət *also* 'tē-nət\ n. DOCTRINE; DOGMA. The agnostic did not accept the *tenets* of their faith.

tensile \'ten(t)-səl *also* 'ten-ˌsī(-ə)l\ adj. CAPABLE OF BEING STRETCHED. Mountain climbers must know the *tensile* strength of their ropes.

tentative \'ten-tə-tiv\ adj. PROVISIONAL; EXPERIMENTAL. Your *tentative* plans sound plausible; let me know when the final details are worked out.

tenuous \'ten-yə-wəs, -yü-əs\ adj. THIN; RARE; SLIM. The allegiance of our allies is held by rather *tenuous* ties.

tenure \'ten-yər *also* -ˌyůr\ n. HOLDING OF AN OFFICE; TIME DURING WHICH SUCH AN OFFICE IS HELD. He has permanent *tenure* in this position and cannot be fired.

tepid \'te-pəd\ adj. LUKEWARM. During the summer, l like to take a *tepid* bath, not a hot one.

terminate \'tər-mə-ˌnāt\ v. TO BRING TO AN END. When his contract was *terminated* unexpectedly, he desperately needed a new job.

terminology \ˌtər-mə-'nä-lə-jē\ n. TERMS USED IN A SCIENCE OR ART. The special *terminology* developed by some authorities in the field has done more to confuse the layman than to enlighten him.

terrestrial \tə-'res-t(r)ē-əl; -'res-chəl, -resh-\ adj. ON THE EARTH. We have been able to explore the *terrestrial* regions much more thoroughly than the aquatic or celestial regions.

terse \'tərs\ adj. CONCISE; ABRUPT; PITHY. I admire his *terse* style of writing; he comes directly to the point.

testy \'tes-tē\ adj. IRRITABLE; SHORT-TEMPERED. My advice is to avoid discussing this problem with him today as he is rather *testy* and may shout at you.

therapeutic \ˌther-ə-'pyü-tik\ adj. CURATIVE. These springs are famous for their *therapeutic* and healing qualities.

thermal \'thər-məl\ adj. PERTAINING TO HEAT. The natives discovered that the hot springs gave excellent *thermal* baths and began to develop their community as a health resort. //also n.

thespian \'thes-pē-ən\ adj. PERTAINING TO DRAMA. Her success in the school play convinced her she was destined for a *thespian* career. //also n.

thrifty \'thrif-tē\ adj. CAREFUL ABOUT MONEY; ECONOMICAL. A *thrifty* shopper compares prices before making major purchases.

throes \'thrōz\ n. VIOLENT ANGUISH. The *throes* of despair can be as devastating as the spasms accompanying physical pain.

throng \'thrȯŋ\ n. CROWD. *Throngs* of shoppers jammed the aisles. //also v.

thwart \'thwȯrt\ v. BAFFLE; FRUSTRATE. He felt that everyone was trying to *thwart* his plans and prevent his success.

timidity \tə-'mi-də-tē\ n. LACK OF SELF-CONFIDENCE OR COURAGE. If you are to succeed as a salesman, you must first lose your *timidity* and fear of failure.

timorous \'ti-mə-rəs, 'tim-rəs\ adj. FEARFUL; DEMONSTRATING FEAR. His *timorous* manner betrayed the fear he felt at the moment.

tirade \'tī-,rād *also* ti-'\ n. EXTENDED SCOLDING; DENUNCIATION. Long before he had finished his *tirade*, we were sufficiently aware of the seriousness of our misconduct.

titanic \tī-'ta-nik *also* tə-\ adj. GIGANTIC. *Titanic* waves beat against the shore during the hurricane.

titular \'ti-chə-lər, 'tich-lər\ adj. NOMINAL HOLDING OF TITLE WITHOUT OBLIGATIONS. Although he was the *titular* head of the company, the real decisions were made by his general manager.

tome \'tōm\ n. LARGE VOLUME. He spent much time in the libraries poring over ancient *tomes*.

topography \tə-'pä-grə-fē\ n. PHYSICAL FEATURES OF A REGION. Before the generals gave the order to attack, they ordered a complete study of the *topography* of the region.

torpor \'tȯr-pər\ n. LETHARGY; SLUGGISHNESS; DORMANCY.
Nothing seemed to arouse him from his *torpor*;
he had wholly surrendered himself to lethargy.
//torpid, adj.

torso \'tȯr-(,)sō\ n. TRUNK OF STATUE WITH HEAD AND LIMBS
MISSING; HUMAN TRUNK. This *torso*, found in the ruins
of Pompeii, is now on exhibition in the museum in
Naples.

touchstone \'təch-,stōn\ n. CRITERION; STANDARD; MEASURE.
What *touchstone* can be used to measure the character
of a person?

Each of the questions below consists of a word in capital letters followed by five words or phrases. Choose the word or phrase that is most similar in meaning to the word in capital letters and write the letter of your choice on your answer paper.

676. **TANTRUM**   (A) confetti   (B) crudity
     (C) stubborn individual   (D) angry outburst
     (E) melodious sound

677. **TAUTOLOGY**   (A) memory   (B) repetition
     (C) tension   (D) simile   (E) lack of logic

678. **TEDIOUS**   (A) orderly   (B) boring   (C) reclaimed
     (D) filtered   (E) proper

679. **TEMERITY**   (A) timidity   (B) resourcefulness
     (C) boldness   (D) tremulousness   (E) caution

680. **TEMPORAL**   (A) priestly   (B) scholarly   (C) secular
     (D) sleepy   (E) sporadic

681. **TENACIOUS**   (A) fast running   (B) intentional
     (C) obnoxious   (D) holding fast   (E) collecting

682. **TENACITY**   (A) splendor   (B) perseverance
     (C) tendency   (D) ingratitude   (E) decimation

683. **TENSILE**   (A) elastic   (B) likely   (C) absurd
     (D) festive   (E) servile

684. **TENTATIVE**   (A) prevalent   (B) portable
     (C) mocking   (D) wry   (E) experimental

685. **TEPID**   (A) boiling   (B) lukewarm   (C) freezing
     (D) gaseous   (E) cold

686. **TERRESTRIAL**   (A) vital   (B) earthly   (C) careful
     (D) dangerous   (E) frightening

687. **TERSE**   (A) concise   (B) poetic   (C) muddy
     (D) bold   (E) adamant

688. **TESTY**   (A) striped   (B) irritable   (C) quizzical
     (D) uniform   (E) trim

689. **THESPIAN**   (A) producer   (B) dreamer
     (C) philosopher   (D) thief   (E) actress

690. **THWART**   (A) hasten   (B) fasten   (C) frustrate
     (D) incorporate   (E) enlarge

toxic \'täk-sik\ adj. POISONOUS. We must seek an antidote for whatever *toxic* substance he has eaten. //toxicity, n.

tractable \'trak-tə-bəl\ adj. DOCILE. You will find the children in this school very *tractable* and willing to learn.

traduce \trə-'düs, -'dyüs\ v. EXPOSE TO SLANDER. His opponents tried to *traduce* the candidate's reputation by spreading rumors about the past.

trajectory \trə-'jek-t(ə-)rē\ n. PATH TAKEN BY A PROJECTILE. The police tried to locate the spot from which the assassin had fired the fatal shot by tracing the *trajectory* of the bullet.

tranquillity \tran-'kwi-lə-tē, traŋ-\ n. CALMNESS; PEACE. After the commotion and excitement of the city, I appreciate the *tranquillity* of these fields and forests. //tranquil, adj.

transcend \tran(t)-'send\ v. EXCEED; SURPASS. This accomplishment *transcends* all our previous efforts. //transcendental, adj.

transcribe \tran(t)-'skrīb\ v. COPY. When you *transcribe* your notes, please send a copy to Mr. Smith and keep the original for our files. //transcription, n.

transgression \tran(t)s-'gre-shən, tranz-\ n. VIOLATION OF A LAW; SIN. Forgive us our *transgressions*; we know not what we do. //transgress, v.

transient \'tran(t)-sh(ē-)ənt, 'tran-zē-ənt, 'tran(t)-sē-; 'tran-zhənt, -jənt\ adj. FLEETING; QUICKLY PASSING AWAY; STAYING FOR A SHORT TIME. This hotel caters to a *transient* trade because it is near a busy highway.

transition \tran(t)-'si-shən, tran-'zi-\ n. GOING FROM ONE STATE OF ACTION TO ANOTHER. During the period of *transition* from oil heat to gas heat, the furnace will have to be shut off.

translucent \tran(t)s-'lü-sᵊnt, tranz-\ adj. PARTLY TRANSPARENT. We could not recognize the people in the next room because of the *translucent* curtains that separated us.

transparent \tran(t)s-'per-ənt\ adj. PERMITTING LIGHT TO PASS THROUGH FREELY; EASILY DETECTED. Your scheme is so *transparent* that it will fool no one.

traumatic \trə-'ma-tik, trȯ-, traủ-\ adj. PERTAINING TO A PHYSICAL OR PSYCHOLOGICAL WOUND. In his nightmares, he kept on recalling the *traumatic* experience of being wounded in battle.

traverse \'tra-vərs *also* -'vərs, *also* trə-' *or* tra-'\ v. GO THROUGH OR ACROSS. When you *traverse* this field, be careful of the bull.

travesty \'tra-və-stē\ n. COMICAL PARODY; TREATMENT AIMED AT MAKING SOMETHING APPEAR RIDICULOUS. The ridiculous decision the jury has arrived at is a *travesty* of justice.

treatise \'trē-təs *also* -təz\ n. ARTICLE TREATING A SUBJECT SYSTEMATICALLY AND THOROUGHLY. He is preparing a *treatise* on the Elizabethan playwrights for his graduate degree.

trek \'trek\ n. TRAVEL; JOURNEY. The tribe made their *trek* further north that summer in search of game. //also v.

tremor \'tre-mər\ n. TREMBLING; SLIGHT QUIVER. She had a nervous *tremor* in her right hand.

tremulous \'trem-yə-ləs\ adj. TREMBLING; WAVERING. She was *tremulous* more from excitement than from fear.

trenchant \'tren-chənt\ adj. CUTTING; KEEN. I am afraid of his *trenchant* wit for it is so often sarcastic.

trepidation \,tre-pə-'dā-shən\ n. FEAR; TREMBLING AGITATION. We must face the enemy without *trepidation* if we are to win this battle.

tribulation \,tri-byə-'lā-shən\ n. DISTRESS; SUFFERING. After all the trials and *tribulations* we have gone through, we need this rest.

tribute \'tri-(,)byüt, -byət\ n. TAX LEVIED BY A RULER; MARK OF RESPECT. The colonists refused to pay *tribute* to a foreign despot.

trilogy \'tri-lə-jē\ n. GROUP OF THREE WORKS. Romain Rolland's novel *Jean Christophe* was first published as a *trilogy*.

trite \'trīt\ adj. HACKNEYED; COMMONPLACE. The *trite* and predictable situations in many television programs alienate many viewers.

trivia \'tri-vē-ə\ n. TRIFLES; UNIMPORTANT MATTERS. Too many magazines ignore newsworthy subjects and feature *trivia*. //trivial, adj.

truculent \'trə-kyə-lənt *also* 'trü-\ adj. AGGRESSIVE; SAVAGE. Clearly ready for a fight, the *truculent* youth thrust his chin forward aggressively as if he dared someone to take a punch at him.

truism \'trü-,i-zəm\ n. SELF-EVIDENT TRUTH. Many a *truism* is well expressed in a proverb.

truncate \'trəŋ-,kāt, 'trən-\ v. CUT THE TOP OFF. The top of a cone that has been *truncated* in a plane parallel to its base is a circle.

tumult \'tü-,məlt, 'tyü- *also* 'tə-\ n. COMMOTION; RIOT; NOISE. She could not make herself heard over the *tumult* of the mob.

tundra \'tən-drə *also* 'tun-\ n. ROLLING, TREELESS PLAIN IN SIBERIA AND ARCTIC NORTH AMERICA. Despite the cold, many geologists are trying to discover valuable mineral deposits in the *tundra*.

turbid \'tər-bəd\ adj. MUDDY; HAVING THE SEDIMENT DISTURBED. The water was *turbid* after the children had waded through it.

turbulence \'tər-byə-lən(t)s\ n. STATE OF VIOLENT AGITATION. We were frightened by the *turbulence* of the ocean during the storm.

turgid \'tər-jəd\ adj. SWOLLEN; DISTENDED. The *turgid* river threatened to overflow the levees and flood the countryside.

turmoil \'tər-ˌmȯi(-ə)l\ n. CONFUSION; STRIFE. Conscious he had sinned, he was in a state of spiritual *turmoil*.

turpitude \'tər-pə-ˌtüd, -ˌtyüd\ n. DEPRAVITY. A visitor may be denied admittance to this country if she has been guilty of moral *turpitude*.

tycoon \tī-'kün\ n. WEALTHY LEADER. John D. Rockefeller was a prominent *tycoon*.

tyranny \'tir-ə-nē\ n. OPPRESSION; CRUEL GOVERNMENT. Frederick Douglass fought against the *tyranny* of slavery throughout his life.

tyro \'tī-(ˌ)rō\ n. BEGINNER; NOVICE. For a mere *tyro*, you have produced some marvelous results.

ubiquitous \yü-'bi-kwə-təs\ adj. BEING EVERYWHERE; OMNIPRESENT. You must be *ubiquitous* for I meet you wherever I go.

Synonym Test • Word List 47

Each of the questions below consists of a word in capital letters, followed by five words or phrases. Choose the word or phrase that is most similar in meaning to the word in capital letters and write the letter of your choice on your answer paper.

691. **TRACTABLE** (A) manageable (B) irreligious (C) mortal (D) incapable (E) unreal

692. **TRADUCE** (A) exhume (B) increase (C) purchase (D) disgrace (E) donate

693. **TRANQUILLITY** (A) lack of sleep (B) placidity (C) emptiness (D) renewal (E) closeness

694. **TRANSIENT** (A) carried (B) close (C) temporary (D) removed (E) certain

695. **TREMULOUS** (A) trembling (B) obese (C) young (D) healthy (E) unkempt

696. **TRENCHANT** (A) sharp (B) windy (C) suspicious (D) confused (E) prevalent

697. **TREPIDATION** (A) slowness (B) amputation (C) fear (D) adroitness (E) death

698. **TRITE** (A) correct (B) banal (C) distinguished (D) premature (E) certain

699. **TRUCULENT** (A) juicy (B) overflowing (C) fierce (D) determined (E) false

700. **TRUISM** (A) silence (B) defeat (C) percussion (D) murder (E) axiom

701. **TURBID** (A) muddy (B) improbable (C) invariable (D) honest (E) turgid

702. **TURBULENCE** (A) reaction (B) approach (C) impropriety (D) agitation (E) hostility

703. **TURGID** (A) rancid (B) bloated (C) cool (D) explosive (E) painful

704. **TURPITUDE** (A) amplitude (B) heat (C) wealth (D) immorality (E) quiet

705. **TYRO** (A) infant (B) miser (C) sluggard (D) idiot (E) novice

ulterior \əl-'tir-ē-ər\ adj. SITUATED BEYOND; UNSTATED. You must have an *ulterior* motive for your behavior, since there is no obvious reason for it.

ultimate \'əl-tə-mət\ adj. FINAL; NOT SUSCEPTIBLE TO FURTHER ANALYSIS. Scientists are searching for the *ultimate* truths.

ultimatum \,əl-tə-'mā-təm, -'mä-\ n. LAST DEMAND; WARNING. Since they have ignored our *ultimatum*, our only recourse is to declare war.

unanimity \,yü-nə-'ni-mə-tē\ n. COMPLETE AGREEMENT. We were surprised by the *unanimity* with which our proposals were accepted by the different groups.

unassuming \,ən-ə-'sü-miŋ\ adj. MODEST. He is so *unassuming* that some people fail to realize how great a man he really is.

uncanny \,ən-'ka-nē\ adj. STRANGE; MYSTERIOUS. You have the *uncanny* knack of reading my innermost thoughts.

unconscionable \,ən-'kän(t)-sh(ə-)nə-bəl\ adj. UNSCRUPULOUS; EXCESSIVE. She found the loan shark's demands *unconscionable* and impossible to meet.

unctuous \'əŋ(k)-chə-wəs, -chəs, -shwəs\ adj. OILY; BLAND; INSINCERELY SUAVE. Uriah Heep disguised his nefarious actions by *unctuous* protestations of his "umility."

undermine \,ən-dər-'mīn\ v. WEAKEN; SAP. The recent corruption scandals have *undermined* many people's faith in the city government.

undulate \'ən-jə-lət, 'ən-dyə-, 'ən-də-, -,lāt\ v. MOVE WITH A WAVELIKE MOTION. The flag *undulated* in the breeze.

unearth \,ən-'ərth\ v. DIG UP. When they *unearthed* the city, the archeologists found many relics of an ancient civilization.

unequivocal \ˌən-i-ˈkwi-və-kəl\ adj. PLAIN; OBVIOUS; UNMISTAKABLE. My answer to your proposal is an *unequivocal* and absolute "no."

ungainly \ˌən-ˈgān-lē\ adj. AWKWARD. He is an *ungainly* young man; he trips over everything.

uniformity \ˌyü-nə-ˈfor-mə-tē\ n. SAMENESS; MONOTONY. After a while, the *uniformity* of TV situation comedies becomes boring. //uniform, adj.

unimpeachable \ˌən-im-ˈpē-chə-bəl\ adj. BLAMELESS AND EXEMPLARY. Her conduct in office was *unimpeachable* and her record is spotless.

unique \yü-ˈnēk\ adj. WITHOUT AN EQUAL; SINGLE IN KIND. You have the *unique* distinction of being the first student whom I have had to fail in this course.

unison \ˈyü-nə-sən, -nə-zən\ n. UNITY OF PITCH; COMPLETE ACCORD. The choir sang in *unison*.

unkempt \ˌən-ˈkem(p)t\ adj. DISHEVELED; WITH UNCARED-FOR APPEARANCE. The beggar was dirty and *unkempt*.

unobtrusive \ˌən-əb-ˈtrü-siv, -ziv\ adj. INCONSPICUOUS; NOT BLATANT. The secret service agents in charge of protecting the president tried to be as *unobtrusive* as possible.

unprecedented \ˌən-ˈpre-sə-ˌden-təd\ adj. NOVEL; UNPARALLELED. Margaret Mitchell's book *Gone with the Wind* was an *unprecedented* success.

unruly \ˌən-ˈrü-lē\ adj. DISOBEDIENT; LAWLESS. The only way to curb this *unruly* mob is to use tear gas.

unscathed \ˌən-ˈskāthd\ adj. UNHARMED. They prayed he would come back from the war *unscathed*.

unseemly \ˌən-ˈsēm-lē\ adj. UNBECOMING; INDECENT. Your levity is *unseemly* at this time of mourning.

unsullied \ˌən-ˈsə-lēd\ adj. UNTARNISHED. I am happy that my reputation is *unsullied*.

untenable \ˌən-ˈte-nə-bəl\ adj. UNSUPPORTABLE. I find your theory *untenable* and must reject it.

unwitting \,ən-'wi-tiŋ\ adj. UNINTENTIONAL; NOT KNOWING. She was the *unwitting* tool of the swindlers.

upbraid \,əp-'brād\ v. SCOLD; REPROACH. I must *upbraid* him for his unruly behavior.

upshot \'əp-shät\ n. OUTCOME. The *upshot* of the rematch was that the former champion proved that he still possessed all the skills of his youth.

urbane \,ər-'bān\ adj. SUAVE; REFINED; ELEGANT. The courtier was *urbane* and sophisticated. //urbanity, n.

usurpation \,yü-sər-'pā-shən *also* ,yü-zər-\ n. ACT OF SEIZING POWER AND RANK OF ANOTHER. The revolution ended with the *usurpation* of the throne by the victorious rebel leader. //usurp, v.

utopia \yü-'tō-pē-ə\ n. IMAGINARY LAND WITH PERFECT SOCIAL AND POLITICAL SYSTEM. Shangri-la was the name of James Hilton's Tibetan *utopia*.

vacillation \,va-sə-'lā-shən\ n. FLUCTUATION; WAVERING. His *vacillation* when confronted with a problem annoyed all of us who had to wait until he made his decision. //vacillate, v.

vacuous \'va-kyə-wəs\ adj. EMPTY; INANE. The *vacuous* remarks of the politician annoyed the audience, who had hoped to hear more than empty platitudes.

vagabond \'va-gə-,bänd\ n. WANDERER; TRAMP. In summer, college students wander the roads of Europe like carefree *vagabonds*. //also adj.

vagrant \'vā-grənt\ adj. STRAY; RANDOM. He tried to study, but could not collect his *vagrant* thoughts. //vagrancy, n.

valedictory \,va-lə'dik-t(ə-)rē\ adj. PERTAINING TO FAREWELL. I found the *valedictory* address too long; leave-taking should be brief.

validate \'va-lə-,dāt\ v. CONFIRM; RATIFY. I will not publish my findings until I *validate* my results.

valor \'va-lər\ n. BRAVERY. He received the Medal of Honor for his *valor* in battle. //valiant, adj.

vanguard \'van-,gärd *also* 'vaŋ-\ n. FORERUNNERS; ADVANCE FORCES. We are the *vanguard* of a tremendous army that is following us.

vapid \'va-pəd, 'vā-\ adj. INSIPID; INANE. She delivered an uninspired and *vapid* address.

variegated \'ver-ē-ə-,gā-təd\ adj. MANY-COLORED. He will not like this solid blue necktie as he is addicted to *variegated* clothing.

veer \'vir\ v. CHANGE IN DIRECTION. After what seemed an eternity, the wind *veered* to the east and the storm abated.

vegetate \'ve-jə-,tāt\ v. LIVE IN A MONOTONOUS WAY. I do not understand how you can *vegetate* in this quiet village after the adventurous life you have led.

vehement \'vē-ə-mənt\ adj. IMPETUOUS; WITH MARKED VIGOR. He spoke with *vehement* eloquence in defense of his client. //vehemence, n.

Each of the questions below consists of a word in capital letters, followed by five words or phrases. Choose the word or phrase that is most similar in meaning to the word in capital letters and write the letter of your choice on your answer paper.

706. **UNEARTH** (A) uncover (B) gnaw (C) clean (D) fling (E) react

707. **UNEQUIVOCAL** (A) clear (B) fashionable (C) wary (D) switched (E) colonial

708. **UNGAINLY** (A) ignorant (B) clumsy (C) detailed (D) dancing (E) pedantic

709. **UNIMPEACHABLE** (A) fruitful (B) rampaging (C) exemplary (D) pensive (E) thorough

710. **UNKEMPT** (A) bombed (B) washed (C) sloppy (D) showy (E) tawdry

711. **UNRULY** (A) chatting (B) wild (C) definite (D) lined (E) curious

712. **UNSEEMLY** (A) effortless (B) indecent (C) conducive (D) pointed (E) informative

713. **UNSULLIED** (A) immaculate (B) countless (C) soggy (D) permanent (E) homicidal

714. **UNTENABLE** (A) unsupportable (B) tender (C) sheepish (D) tremulous (E) adequate

715. **UNWITTING** (A) clever (B) intense (C) sensitive (D) freezing (E) accidental

716. **VACILLATION** (A) remorse (B) relief (C) respect (D) wavering (E) inoculation

717. **VALEDICTORY** (A) sad (B) collegiate (C) derivative (D) parting (E) promising

718. **VALOR** (A) admonition (B) injustice (C) courage (D) generosity (E) repression

719. **VANGUARD** (A) regiment (B) forerunners (C) echelon (D) protection (E) loyalty

720. **VEHEMENT** (A) unvanquished (B) fell (C) vigorous (D) exacting (E) believed

velocity \və-'lä-sə-tē, -'läs-tē\ n. SPEED. The train went by at considerable *velocity*.

venal \'vē-nəl\ adj. CAPABLE OF BEING BRIBED. The *venal* policeman accepted the bribe offered him by the speeding motorist whom he had stopped.

vendetta \ven-'de-tə\ n. BLOOD FEUD. The rival mobs engaged in a bitter *vendetta*.

veneer \və-'nir\ n. THIN LAYER; COVER. Casual acquaintances were deceived by his *veneer* of sophistication and failed to recognize his fundamental shallowness.

venerate \'ve-nə-ˌrāt\ v. REVERE. In China, the people *venerate* their ancestors. //venerable, adj.

venial \'vē-nē-əl, -nyəl\ adj. FORGIVABLE; TRIVIAL. We may regard a hungry man's stealing as a *venial* crime.

vent \'vent\ n. A SMALL OPENING; OUTLET. The wine did not flow because the air *vent* in the barrel was clogged.

vent \'vent\ v. EXPRESS; UTTER. He *vented* his wrath on his class.

ventriloquist \ven-'tri-lə-kwist\ n. SOMEONE WHO CAN MAKE HIS OR HER VOICE SEEM TO COME FROM ANOTHER PERSON OR THING. This *ventriloquist* does an act in which she has a conversation with a wooden dummy.

venturesome \'ven(t)-shər-səm\ adj. BOLD. A group of *venturesome* women were the first to scale Mt. Annapurna.

veracious \və-'rā-shəs\ adj. TRUTHFUL. I can recommend him for this position because I have always found him *veracious* and reliable. veracity, n.

verbalize \'vər-bə-ˌlīz\ v. TO PUT INTO WORDS. I know you don't like to talk about these things, but please try to *verbalize* your feelings.

verbatim \(ˌ)vər-'bā-təm\ adj. WORD FOR WORD. He repeated the message *verbatim*. //also adj.

verbiage \\'vər-bē-ij *also* -bij\ n. POMPOUS ARRAY OF WORDS. After we had waded through all the *verbiage*, we discovered that the writer had said very little.

verbose \\(ˌ)vər-'bōs\ adj. WORDY. This article is *verbose*; we must edit it.

verge \\'vərj\ n. BORDER; EDGE. Madame Curie knew she was on the *verge* of discovering the secrets of radioactive elements. //also v.

verisimilitude \\ˌver-ə-sə-'mi-lə-ˌtüd, -ˌtyüd\ n. APPEARANCE OF TRUTH; LIKELIHOOD. Critics praised her for the *verisimilitude* of her performance as Lady Macbeth. She was completely believable.

vernacular \\və(r)-'na-kyə-lər\ n. LIVING LANGUAGE; NATURAL STYLE. Cut out those old-fashioned thee's and thou's and write in the *vernacular*. //also adj.

versatile \\'vər-sə-təl, -ˌtī(-ə)l\ adj. HAVING MANY TALENTS; CAPABLE OF WORKING IN MANY FIELDS. He was a *versatile* athlete; at college he had earned varsity letters in baseball, football, and track.

vertex \\'vər-ˌteks\ n. SUMMIT. Let us drop a perpendicular line from the *vertex* of the triangle to the base.

vertigo \\'vər-ti-ˌgō\ n. DIZZINESS. We test potential plane pilots for susceptibility to spells of *vertigo*.

vestige \\'ves-tij\ n. TRACE; REMAINS. We discovered *vestiges* of early Indian life in the cave. //vestigial, adj.

vex \\'veks\ n. ANNOY; DISTRESS. Please try not to *vex* your mother; she is doing the best she can.

viable \\'vī-ə-bəl\ adj. WORKABLE; CAPABLE OF MAINTAINING LIFE. The infant, though prematurely born, is *viable* and has a good chance to survive.

vicarious \\vī-'ker-ē-əs, və-\ adj. ACTING AS A SUBSTITUTE; DONE BY A DEPUTY. Many people get a *vicarious* thrill at the movies by imagining they are the characters on the screen.

vicissitude \\və-'si-sə-ˌtüd, vī-, -ˌtyüd\ n. CHANGE OF FORTUNE. I am accustomed to life's *vicissitudes*, having experienced poverty and wealth, sickness and health, and failure and success.

vie \'vī\ v. CONTEND; COMPETE. When we *vie* with each other for his approval, we are merely weakening ourselves and strengthening him.

vigilance \'vi-jə-lən(t)s\ n. WATCHFULNESS. Eternal *vigilance* is the price of liberty.

vignette \vin-'yet, vēn-\ n. PICTURE; SHORT LITERARY SKETCH. *The New Yorker* published her latest *vignette*.

vigor \'vi-gər\ n. ACTIVE STRENGTH. Although he was over seventy years old, Jack had the *vigor* of a man in his prime. //vigorous, adj.

vilify \'vi-lə-ˌfī\ v. SLANDER. She is a liar and is always trying to *vilify* my reputation. //vilification, n.

vindicate \'vin-də-ˌkāt\ v. CLEAR OF CHARGES. I hope to *vindicate* my client and return him to society as a free man.

vindictive \vin-'dik-tiv\ adj. REVENGEFUL. She was very *vindictive* and never forgave an injury.

viper \'vī-pər\ n. POISONOUS SNAKE. The habitat of the horned *viper*, a particularly venomous snake, is in sandy regions like the Sahara or the Sinai peninsula.

virile \'vir-əl, 'vir-ˌī(-ə)l\ adj. MANLY. I do not accept the premise that a man is *virile* only when he is belligerent.

virtuoso \'vər-(ˌ)chü-'ō-(ˌ)sō, -(ˌ)zō\ n. HIGHLY SKILLED ARTIST. Heifetz is a violin *virtuoso*.

virulent \'vir-ə-lənt, 'vir-yə-\ adj. EXTREMELY POISONOUS. The virus is highly *virulent* and has made many of us ill for days.

virus \'vī-rəs\ n. DISEASE COMMUNICATOR. The doctors are looking for a specific medicine to control this *virus*.

viscous \'vis-kəs\ adj. STICKY; GLUEY. Melted tar is a *viscous* substance. //viscosity, n.

visionary \'vi-zhə-ˌner-ē\ adj. PRODUCED BY IMAGINATION; FANCIFUL; MYSTICAL. She was given to *visionary* schemes that never materialized. //also n.

vitiate \'vi-shē-ˌāt\ v. SPOIL THE EFFECT OF; MAKE INOPERATIVE. Fraud will *vitiate* the contract.

vitriolic \ˌvi-trē-'ä-lik\ adj. CORROSIVE; SARCASTIC. Such *vitriolic* criticism is uncalled for.

vituperative \vī-'tü-p(ə-)rə-tiv, -pə-ˌrā-\ adj. ABUSIVE; SCOLDING. He became more *vituperative* as he realized that we were not going to grant him his wish.

vivacious \və-'vā-shəs *also* vī-\ adj. ANIMATED. She had always been *vivacious* and sparkling.

vociferous \vō-'si-f(ə-)rəs\ adj. CLAMOROUS; NOISY. The crowd grew *vociferous* in its anger and threatened to take the law into its own hands.

vogue \'vōg\ n. POPULAR FASHION. Jeans became the *vogue* on many college campuses.

Each of the questions below consists of a word in capital letters, followed by five words or phrases. Choose the word or phrase that is most similar in meaning to the word in capital letters and write the letter of your choice on your answer paper.

721. **VENAL** (A) springlike (B) corrupt (C) angry
(D) indifferent (E) going

722. **VENERATE** (A) revere (B) age (C) reject
(D) reverberate (E) degenerate

723. **VENIAL** (A) minor (B) unforgettable
(C) unmistaken (D) fearful (E) fragrant

724. **VERACIOUS** (A) worried (B) slight (C) alert
(D) truthful (E) instrumental

725. **VERBOSE** (A) poetic (B) wordy (C) sympathetic
(D) autumnal (E) frequent

726. **VERTEX** (A) sanctity (B) reverence (C) summit
(D) rarity (E) household

727. **VESTIGE** (A) trek (B) trail (C) trace
(D) trial (E) tract

728. **VIABLE** (A) effective (B) salable (C) useful
(D) foolish (E) inadequate

729. **VICARIOUS** (A) substitutional (B) aggressive
(C) sporadic (D) reverent (E) internal

730. **VICISSITUDE** (A) wand (B) counterargument
(C) change of fortune (D) orchestra
(E) return to power

731. **VIGILANCE** (A) bivouac (B) guide
(C) watchfulness (D) mob rule (E) posse

732. **VILIFY** (A) erect (B) degrade (C) better
(D) verify (E) horrify

733. **VINDICTIVE** (A) revengeful (B) fearful
(C) divided (D) literal (E) convincing

734. **VIRULENT** (A) sensuous (B) malignant
(C) masculine (D) conforming (E) approaching

735. **VOGUE** (A) doubt (B) personality (C) humility
(D) fashion (E) armor

volatile \\'vä-lə-təl, -ˌtī(-ə)l\ adj. EVAPORATING RAPIDLY; LIGHTHEARTED; MERCURIAL. Ethyl chloride is a very *volatile* liquid.

volition \vō-'li-shən, və-\ n. ACT OF MAKING A CONSCIOUS CHOICE. She selected this dress of her own *volition*.

voluble \\'väl-yə-bəl\ adj. FLUENT; GLIB. She was a *voluble* speaker, always ready to talk.

voluminous \və-'lü-mə-nəs\ adj. BULKY; LARGE. Despite her family burdens, she kept up a *voluminous* correspondence with her friends.

voluptuous \və-'ləp(t)-shə-wəs, -shəs\ adj. GRATIFYING THE SENSES. The nobility during the Renaissance led *voluptuous* lives.

voracious \vȯ-'rā-shəs, və-\ adj. RAVENOUS. The wolf is a *voracious* animal, its hunger never satisfied.

vulnerable \\'vəl-n(ə-)rə-bəl, 'vəl-nər-bəl\ adj. SUSCEPTIBLE TO WOUNDS. Achilles was *vulnerable* only in his heel.

vying \\'vī-yiŋ\ v. CONTENDING. Why are we *vying* with each other for her favors? //vie, v.

waive \\'wāv\ v. GIVE UP TEMPORARILY; YIELD. I will *waive* my rights in this matter in order to expedite our reaching a proper decision.

wallow \\'wä-(ˌ)lō\ v. ROLL IN; INDULGE IN; BECOME HELPLESS. The hippopotamus loves to *wallow* in the mud.

wan \\'wän\ adj. HAVING A PALE OR SICKLY COLOR; PALLID. Suckling asked, "Why so pale and *wan*, fond lover?"

wane \\'wān\ v. GROW GRADUALLY SMALLER. From now until December 21, the winter equinox, the hours of daylight will *wane*.

wanton \\'wȯn-tᵊn, 'wän-\ adj. UNRULY; UNCHASTE; EXCESSIVE. His *wanton*, drunken ways cost him many friends.

warrant \'wȯr-ənt, 'wär-\ v. JUSTIFY; AUTHORIZE. Before the judge issues the injunction, you must convince her this action is *warranted*.

warranty \'wȯr-ən-tē, 'wär-\ n. GUARANTEE; ASSURANCE BY SELLER. The purchaser of this automobile is protected by the manufacturer's *warranty* that he will replace any defective part for five years or 50,000 miles.

wary \'wer-ē\ adj. VERY CAUTIOUS. The spies grew *wary* as they approached the sentry.

wax \'waks\ v. INCREASE; GROW. With proper handling, his fortunes *waxed* and he became rich.

wean \'wēn\ v. ACCUSTOM A BABY NOT TO NURSE; GIVE UP A CHERISHED ACTIVITY. He decided he would *wean* himself away from eating junk food and stick to fruits and vegetables.

weather \'we-thər\ v. ENDURE THE EFFECTS OF WEATHER OR OTHER FORCES. He *weathered* the changes in his personal life with difficulty, as he had no one in whom to confide.

wheedle \'hwē-dəl, 'wē-\ v. CAJOLE; COAX; DECEIVE BY FLATTERY. She knows she can *wheedle* almost anything she wants from her father.

whet \'hwet, 'wet\ v. SHARPEN; STIMULATE. The odors from the kitchen are *whetting* my appetite; I will be ravenous by the time the meal is served.

whimsical \'hwim-zi-kəl, 'wim-\ adj. CAPRICIOUS; FANCIFUL; QUAINT. *Peter Pan* is a *whimsical* play.

wily \'wī-lē\ adj. CUNNING; ARTFUL. She is as *wily* as a fox in avoiding trouble.

wince \'win(t)s\ v. SHRINK BACK; FLINCH. The screech of the chalk on the blackboard made her *wince*.

windfall \'win(d)-ˌfȯl\ n. UNEXPECTED LUCKY EVENT. This huge tax refund is quite a *windfall*.

winnow \\'wi-(,)nō\\ v. SIFT; SEPARATE GOOD PARTS FROM BAD. This test will *winnow* out the students who study from those who don't bother.

wither \\'wi-thər\\ v. SHRIVEL; DECAY. Cut flowers are beautiful for a day, but all too soon they *wither*.

witless \\'wit-ləs\\ adj. FOOLISH; IDIOTIC. Such *witless* and fatuous statements will create the impression that you are an ignorant individual.

witticism \\'wi-tə-,si-zəm\\ n. WITTY SAYING; FACETIOUS REMARK. What you regard as *witticisms* are often offensive to sensitive people.

wizardry \\'wi-zə(r)-drē\\ n. SORCERY; MAGIC. Merlin amazed the knights with his *wizardry*.

wizened \\'wi-zᵊnd *also* 'wē-\\ adj. WITHERED; SHRIVELED. The *wizened* old man in the home for the aged was still active and energetic.

worldly \\'wər(-ə)ld-lē, 'wərl-lē\\ adj. ENGROSSED IN MATTERS OF THIS EARTH; NOT SPIRITUAL. You must leave your *worldly* goods behind you when you go to meet your Maker.

wrath \\'rath\\ n. ANGER; FURY. She turned to him, full of *wrath*, and said, "What makes you think I'll accept lower pay for this job than you get?"

wreak \\'rēk *also* 'rek\\ v. INFLICT. I am afraid he will *wreak* his vengeance on the innocent as well as the guilty.

wrench \\'rench\\ v. PULL; STRAIN; TWIST. She *wrenched* free of her attacker and landed a powerful kick to his kneecap.

writhe \\'rīth\\ v. SQUIRM, TWIST. He was *writhing* in pain, desperate for the drug his body required.

wry \\'rī\\ adj. TWISTED; WITH A HUMOROUS TWIST. We enjoy Dorothy Parker's verse for its *wry* wit.

xenophobia \\,ze-nə-'fō-bē-ə, ,zē-\\ n. FEAR OR HATRED OF FOREIGNERS. When the refugee arrived in America, he was unprepared for the *xenophobia* he found there.

yen \'yen\ n. LONGING; URGE. She had a *yen* to get away and live on her own for a while.

yoke \'yōk\ v. PIN TOGETHER, UNITE. I don't wish to be *yoked* to him in marriage, as if we were cattle pulling a plow. //also n.

zany \'zā-nē\ adj. CRAZY; COMIC. I can watch the Marx brothers' *zany* antics for hours.

zealot \'ze-lət\ n. FANATIC; PERSON WHO SHOWS EXCESSIVE ZEAL. It is good to have a few *zealots* in our group for their enthusiasm is contagious. //zealous, adj.

zenith \'zē-nəth\ n. POINT DIRECTLY OVERHEAD IN THE SKY; SUMMIT. When the sun was at its *zenith*, the glare was not as strong as at sunrise and sunset.

zephyr \'ze-fər\ n. GENTLE BREEZE; WEST WIND. When these *zephyrs* blow, it is good to be in an open boat under a full sail.

Each of the questions below consists of a word in capital letters, followed by five words or phrases. Choose the word or phrase that is most similar in meaning to the word in capital letters and write the letter of your choice on your answer paper.

736. **VOLUBLE**   (A) worthwhile   (B) serious   (C) terminal   (D) loquacious   (E) circular

737. **VORACIOUS**   (A) ravenous   (B) spacious   (C) truthful   (D) pacific   (E) tenacious

738. **WAIVE**   (A) borrow   (B) yield   (C) punish   (D) desire   (E) qualify

739. **WAN**   (A) clear   (B) pale   (C) dire   (D) jovial   (E) victorious

740. **WANTON**   (A) needy   (B) passive   (C) rumored   (D) oriental   (E) unchaste

741. **WARRANTY**   (A) threat   (B) guarantee   (C) order for arrest   (D) issue   (E) fund

742. **WARY**   (A) rough   (B) cautious   (C) mortal   (D) tolerant   (E) belligerent

743. **WAX**   (A) grow   (B) journey   (C) rest   (D) delay   (E) survive

744. **WHEEDLE**   (A) delay   (B) greet   (C) becloud   (D) press   (E) coax

745. **WHET**   (A) complain   (B) hurry   (C) request   (D) sharpen   (E) gallop

746. **WINDFALL**   (A) unexpected gain   (B) widespread destruction   (C) calm   (D) autumn   (E) wait

747. **WITLESS**   (A) negligent   (B) idiotic   (C) married   (D) permanent   (E) pained

748. **WIZENED**   (A) magical   (B) clever   (C) shriveled   (D) swift   (E) active

749. **YEN**   (A) regret   (B) urge   (C) lack   (D) wealth   (E) rank

750. **ZEALOT**   (A) beginner   (B) patron   (C) fanatic   (D) murderer   (E) leper

Each of the questions below consists of a sentence from which one word is missing. Choose the most appropriate replacement from among the five choices.

1. King Lear lamented vociferously when his daughters demanded that he travel with a smaller _____.
   (A) simile   (B) stratagem   (C) yoke
   (D) trek   (E) retinue

2. I could not imagine my _____ grandmother behaving raucously at a party.
   (A) staid   (B) strident   (C) ribald
   (D) resilient   (E) retroactive

3. The _____ teacher seemed to take great pleasure in assigning overwhelming amounts of homework to her suffering students.
   (A) sagacious   (B) torpid   (C) sadistic
   (D) voluble   (E) wary

4. The suspect chose to _____ his right to have an attorney present during his questioning.
   (A) winnow   (B) surpass   (C) sedate
   (D) waive   (E) scrutinize

5. Beneath his calm facade, the jilted groom was _____ with anger and humiliation.
   (A) seething   (B) skulking   (C) surmising
   (D) terminating   (E) venting

6. She committed herself to a mental hospital when she realized that she was on the _____ of a nervous breakdown.
   (A) vanguard   (B) temerity   (C) verge
   (D) tenet   (E) schism

7. The sumptuous smell of the holiday meal _____ my appetite.
   (A) wheedled   (B) withered   (C) wallowed
   (D) surfeited   (E) whetted

8. Some sort of corroborating evidence will be needed to _____ your alibi.
   (A) saturate   (B) substantiate   (C) scoff
   (D) revere   (E) wax

9. As television viewing has increased, book and periodical reading has _____.
   (A) weathered (B) waned (C) sundered
      (D) retorted (E) sedated

10. Recalling the president's previous, lengthy State of the Union speech, I hoped that his new presentation would be more _____.
    (A) tepid (B) therapeutic (C) vicarious
       (D) salient (E) sententious

11. Many critics of public education argue that the academic standards for new teachers should be more _____.
    (A) rigorous (B) shrewd (C) subtle
       (D) rudimentary (E) ribald

12. A _____ understanding cannot be enforced as a contract, the terms of a contract must be explicit.
    (A) trenchant (B) verbose (C) sacrosanct
       (D) retrenched (E) tacit

13. While it is debatable whether the death penalty deters crime, it certainly provides society with an opportunity for _____.
    (A) stoicism (B) stupor (C) retribution
       (D) temerity (E) xenophobia

14. The driver of the car became an _____ accomplice to murder when his passenger shot a rival gang member.
    (A) unruly (B) unwitting (C) unscathed
       (D) unctuous (E) unassuming

15. Despite his _____, the nervous debater stood up well under cross-examination.
    (A) travesty (B) veneer (C) yen
       (D) trepidation (E) semblance

ANSWER KEY

Test • Word List 1

1. E	6. E	11. A
2. A	7. B	12. A
3. C	8. A	13. A
4. D	9. E	14. D
5. B	10. E	15. C

Test • Word List 2

16. E	21. A	26. B
17. B	22. A	27. D
18. A	23. B	28. B
19. D	24. B	29. C
20. A	25. B	30. D

Test • Word List 3

31. C	36. E	41. B
32. C	37. C	42. E
33. D	38. B	43. E
34. D	39. E	44. C
35. A	40. D	45. A

Test • Word List 4

46. A	51. C	56. E
47. A	52. A	57. C
48. B	53. C	58. D
49. D	54. B	59. D
50. B	55. D	60. C

Test • Word List 5

61. E	66. A	71. D
62. D	67. C	72. C
63. B	68. C	73. C
64. C	69. B	74. B
65. C	70. C	75. D

Test • Word List 6

76. D	81. A	86. C
77. B	82. B	87. A
78. D	83. B	88. E
79. A	84. E	89. E
80. E	85. E	90. C

Test • Word List 7

91. B	96. B	101. D
92. B	97. A	102. B
93. B	98. D	103. A
94. D	99. B	104. A
95. B	100. C	105. B

Test • Word List 8

106. D	111. A	116. B
107. E	112. B	117. D
108. A	113. C	118. A
109. C	114. D	119. C
110. E	115. D	120. B

Test • Word List 9

121. D	126. E	131. A
122. E	127. A	132. D
123. E	128. D	133. C
124. C	129. B	134. B
125. C	130. E	135. A

Test • Word List 10

136. E	141. B	146. E
137. B	142. E	147. E
138. D	143. D	148. C
139. C	144. D	149. A
140. A	145. D	150. D

Comprehensive Test •
Word Lists 1–10

1. A	6. C	11. A
2. C	7. A	12. B
3. B	8. C	13. A
4. D	9. A	14. C
5. D	10. D	15. E

Test • Word List 11

151. B	156. C	161. B
152. B	157. C	162. D
153. A	158. E	163. D
154. A	159. E	164. A
155. A	160. B	165. B

Test • Word List 12

166. B	171. C	176. B
167. C	172. B	177. B
168. C	173. A	178. A
169. D	174. A	179. C
170. D	175. B	180. A

Test • Word List 13

181. A	186. A	191. C
182. E	187. B	192. B
183. D	188. C	193. E
184. D	189. B	194. A
185. A	190. C	195. A

Test • Word List 14

196. D	201. C	206. B
197. E	202. C	207. D
198. B	203. C	208. C
199. A	204. B	209. E
200. C	205. B	210. D

Test • Word List 15

211. C	216. C	221. B
212. A	217. A	222. E
213. D	218. A	223. A
214. D	219. C	224. A
215. D	220. D	225. B

Test • Word List 16

226. D	231. B	236. A
227. A	232. C	237. D
228. C	233. D	238. A
229. E	234. C	239. C
230. E	235. E	240. B

Test • Word List 17

241. A	246. C	251. D
242. A	247. A	252. A
243. B	248. A	253. E
244. E	249. C	254. B
245. E	250. D	255. B

Test Word • List 18

256. A	261. D	266. A
257. A	262. D	267. A
258. D	263. E	268. C
259. C	264. C	269. B
260. A	265. B	270. E

Test • Word List 19

271. A	276. A	281. A
272. D	277. A	282. D
273. E	278. D	283. C
274. C	279. C	284. B
275. E	280. B	285. C

Test • Word List 20

286. A	291. A	296. E
287. D	292. A	297. D
288. B	293. D	298. A
289. B	294. C	299. A
290. B	295. C	300. B

**Comprehensive Test •
Word Lists 11–20**

1. B	6. A	11. B
2. B	7. E	12. A
3. D	8. B	13. C
4. D	9. C	14. A
5. A	10. E	15. E

Test—Word List 21

301. B	306. E	311. E
302. B	307. C	312. A
303. C	308. B	313. B
304. C	309. D	314. D
305. C	310. D	315. C

Test • Word List 22

316. D	321. E	326. C
317. A	322. A	327. C
318. A	323. B	328. A
319. D	324. C	329. B
320. A	325. E	330. D

Test • Word List 23

331. B	336. A	341. A
332. A	337. C	342. E
333. B	338. D	343. A
334. E	339. C	344. B
335. C	340. D	345. A

Test • Word List 24

346. C	351. D	356. B
347. B	352. A	357. C
348. C	353. A	358. A
349. A	354. A	359. B
350. B	355. B	360. D

Test • Word List 25

361. A	366. B	371. E
362. E	367. B	372. B
363. B	368. C	373. D
364. D	369. D	374. C
365. E	370. A	375. A

Test • Word List 26

376. C	381. B	386. B
377. A	382. A	387. E
378. B	383. C	388. E
379. B	384. C	389. E
380. B	385. C	390. A

Test • Word List 27

391. A	396. E	401. B
392. D	397. E	402. B
393. B	398. C	403. A
394. D	399. A	404. C
395. B	400. D	405. B

Test • Word List 28

406. B	411. B	416. B
407. A	412. E	417. D
408. E	413. D	418. A
409. C	414. E	419. D
410. E	415. C	420. A

Test • Word List 29

421. B	426. D	431. A
422. A	427. E	432. C
423. B	428. B	433. B
424. B	429. A	434. C
425. C	430. E	435. A

Test • Word List 30

436. A	441. A	446. E
437. A	442. B	447. B
438. B	443. D	448. C
439. D	444. B	449. E
440. C	445. A	450. B

Comprehensive Test • Word Lists 21–30

1. E	6. A	11. C
2. A	7. C	12. C
3. B	8. E	13. A
4. C	9. C	14. B
5. D	10. A	15. D

Test • Word List 31

451. B	456. A	461. E
452. E	457. C	462. C
453. C	458. C	463. A
454. C	459. A	464. B
455. B	460. B	465. A

Test • Word List 32

466. B	471. D	476. D
467. C	472. C	477. B
468. C	473. B	478. A
479. A	474. A	479. C
470. C	475. B	480. A

Test • Word List 33

481. C	486. A	491. E
482. B	487. B	492. C
483. E	488. C	493. E
484. D	489. D	494. B
485. B	490. B	495. A

Test • Word List 34

496. D	501. B	506. D
497. A	502. B	507. D
498. D	503. A	508. C
499. A	504. E	509. C
500. E	505. C	510. A

Test • Word List 35

511. A	516. C	521. C
512. C	517. B	522. E
513. C	518. D	523. A
514. C	519. C	524. E
515. B	520. A	525. E

Test • Word List 36

526. A	531. E	536. A
527. D	532. B	537. D
528. A	533. C	538. D
529. B	534. C	539. D
530. E	535. B	540. D

Test • Word List 37

541. C	546. A	551. A
542. C	547. A	552. C
543. D	548. C	553. B
544. E	549. B	554. E
545. C	550. A	555. A

Test • Word List 38

556. E	561. E	566. D
557. D	562. E	567. E
558. C	563. B	568. C
559. B	564. A	569. D
560. B	565. A	570. C

Test • Word List 39

571. B	576. C	581. B
572. B	577. D	582. C
573. E	578. A	583. A
574. A	579. C	584. D
575. A	580. E	585. A

Test—Word List 40

586. E	591. C	596. D
587. B	592. A	597. D
588. D	593. B	598. B
589. C	594. A	599. D
590. A	595. D	600. E

Comprehensive Test • Word Lists 31–40

1. E	6. B	11. B
2. A	7. B	12. C
3. D	8. A	13. D
4. A	9. C	14. E
5. D	10. D	15. A

Test • Word List 41

601. E	606. B	611. C
602. B	607. B	612. D
603. A	608. A	613. A
604. D	609. D	614. B
605. A	610. B	615. A

Test • Word List 42

616. C	621. D	626. B
617. A	622. D	627. D
618. B	623. A	628. A
619. C	624. D	629. D
620. E	625. C	630. E

Test • Word List 43

631. C	636. C	641. D
632. C	637. E	642. A
633. E	638. C	643. E
634. A	639. E	644. A
635. C	640. D	645. B

Test • Word List 44

646. A	651. B	656. A
647. B	652. A	657. B
648. D	653. D	658. A
649. A	654. C	659. C
650. E	655. C	660. C

Test • Word List 45

661. C	666. C	671. C
662. C	667. B	672. D
663. A	668. A	673. A
664. C	669. A	674. D
665. B	670. A	675. A

Test • Word List 46

676. D	681. D	686. B
677. B	682. B	687. A
678. B	683. A	688. B
679. C	684. E	689. E
680. C	685. B	690. C

Test • Word List 47

691. A	696. A	701. A
692. D	697. C	702. D
693. B	698. B	703. B
694. C	699. C	704. D
695. A	700. E	705. E

Test • Word List 48

706. A	711. B	716. D
707. A	712. B	717. D
708. B	713. A	718. C
709. C	714. A	719. B
710. C	715. E	720. C

Test • Word List 49

721. B	726. C	731. C
722. A	727. C	732. B
723. A	728. A	733. A
724. D	729. A	734. B
725. B	730. C	735. D

Test • Word List 50

736. D	741. B	746. A
737. A	742. B	747. B
738. B	743. A	748. C
739. B	744. E	749. B
740. E	745. D	750. C

Comprehensive Test • Word Lists 41–50

1. E	6. C	11. A
2. A	7. E	12. E
3. C	8. B	13. C
4. D	9. B	14. B
5. A	10. E	15. D

WORD
PARTS
REVIEW

If you are familiar with these word parts, you can often decipher the meaning of unfamiliar words, even words you have never seen before. In the following lists, each element is followed by its meaning in parentheses and one or more words formed with it.

PREFIXES

These are the parts that are placed in front of words to change or modify the meaning. For example, pre- is a prefix meaning in front, before. Added to fix, it creates a word meaning "to place in front."

Positive or intensifying prefixes:

arch- (chief): *archbishop*, a bishop of the highest rank; *architect*, the designer of a building (originally the chief builder)

bene- (good, well): *benefactor*, one who does good; *benevolent*, wishing well

eu- (good, well, beautiful): *eulogize*, speak well of someone, praise; *euphemism*, pleasant way of saying something unpleasant

extra- (beyond, outside): *extraordinary* unusual, exceptional; *extracurricular*, outside the usual course of studies

hyper- (above, excessively): *hyperbole*, overstatement

pro- (for, before, in front of): *proponent*, supporter; *progress*, advancement, going forward or further

super- (over, above): *supernatural*, beyond the normal; *superintendent*, one who watches over or is in charge

ultra- (beyond, excessively): *ultraconservative*, overly conservative, reactionary

Negative prefixes:

an-, a- (without): *anarchy*, without government

anti- (against, opposite): *antidote*, remedy for poison; *antipathy*, dislike, aversion

contra- (against): *contradict*, disagree; *controversy*, dispute, argument

de- (down, away from): *debase*, lower in value; *decant*, pour off

dis-, di-, dif- (not, apart): *discord*, lack of harmony; *dismember*, separate into parts; *diverge*, go in different directions

ex-, e-, ef- (out, off, from): *exhale*, breathe out; *eject*, throw out

in-, ig-, il-, im-, ir- (not): *incorrect*, wrong; *illegal*, against the law; *immature*, not fully grown

mal-, male- (bad, badly): *malediction*, curse; *malefactor*, evil doer

mis- (wrong, ill, not): *misbehave*, act badly; *misfortune*, bad luck

non- (not): *nonsense*, something absurd

ob-, oc-, of-, op- (against): *object*, give reasons against; *oppose*, resist, stand in the way of

sub-, suc-, suf-, sug- (under): *subjugate*, bring under control

un- (not): *untrue*, false

Other prefixes:

ab-, abs- (from, away from): *abduct*, lead away, kidnap; *abnormal*, strange, not following the usual pattern

ad-, ac-, af-, ag-, an-, ap-, ar-, as-, at- (to, forward): *advance*, go forward; *aggravate*, make worse

ambi- (both): *ambivalent*, having conflicting emotions (leaning both ways)

ante- (before): *antebellum*, before the war (usually the Civil War)

auto- (self): *automobile*, a vehicle that moves by itself

bi- (two): *biennial*, every two years

cata- (down): *cataclysm*, upheaval; *catastrophe*, calamity

circum- (around): *circumspect*, cautious (looking around)

com-, co-, con- (with, together): *combine*, merge with

di- (two): *dichotomy*, division into two parts; *dilemma*, choice between two poor alternatives

en-, em- (in, into): *emphasize*, put stress on

in-, il-, im-, ir- (in, into): *invade*, go in like an enemy

inter- (between, among): *intervene*, come between

intra, intro- (within): *introvert*, person who turns within himself

meta- (involving change): *metamorphosis*, change of shape

mono- (one): *monolithic*, uniform; *monotony*, boring sameness

multi- (many): *multiplicity*, numerousness

neo- (new): *neophyte*, beginner

pan- (all, every): *panorama*, comprehensive view; *panacea*, cure-all

per- (through): *perforate*, make holes through

peri- (around, near): *perimeter*, outer boundary; *peripheral*, marginal, outer

pre- (before): *precede*, go before

re- (back, again): *respond*, answer

se- (apart): *segregate*, set apart

syl, sym, syn, sys- (with, together): *symmetry*, congruity; *synchronous*, occurring at the same time

trans- (across, beyond, through): *transparent*, letting light through

vice- (in place of): *vicarious*, acting as a substitute

ROOTS

You will be surprised by how many English words are derived from just these 29 roots.

ac, acr (sharp): *acerbity*, bitterness of temper; *acrimonious*, bitter, caustic

ag, act (to do): *act*, deed; *agent*, doer; *retroactive*, having a backward action

am (love): *amicable*, friendly

anthrop (man): *anthropoid*, manlike; *misanthrope*, man-hater

apt (fit): *aptitude*, skill or fitness; *adapt*, make fit

auto (self): *autocracy*, rule by one person (self)

cap, capt, cep, cip (to take): *participate*, take part; *capture*, seize; *precept*, a wise saying (originally a command)

ced, cess (to yield, to go): *recede*, go back; *antecedent*, that which goes before

celer (swift): *celerity*, swiftness; *decelerate*, reduce speed

chron (time): *anachronism*, a thing out of its proper time

cred, credit (to believe): *incredulous*, not believing, skeptical; *incredible*, unbelievable

curr, curs (to run): *excursion*, journey; *cursory*, brief; *precursor*, forerunner

dic, dict (to say): *abdicate*, renounce; *diction*, speech; *verdict*, decision or statement of a jury

duc, duct (to lead): *aqueduct*, artificial waterway; *education*, training (leading out); *conduct*, lead or guide

fac, fic, fec, fect (to make or do): *factory*, place where things are made; *fiction*, made-up story; *affect*, cause to change

fer, lat (from an irregular Latin verb meaning to bring, to carry): *transfer*, to bring from one place to another; *translate*, to bring from one language to another

graph, gram (writing): *epigram*, a pithy statement; *telegram*, a message sent over great distances; *graphite*, a soft carbon that is so named because you can write with it

leg, lect (to choose, read): *election*, choice; *legible*, able to be read; *eligible*, able to be selected

mitt, miss (to send): *missile*, projectile; *admit*, let in; *dismiss*, send away; *transmit*, send across

mori, mort (to die): *mortuary*, funeral parlor; *moribund*, dying; *immortal*, never dying

morph (shape, form): *amorphous*, shapeless

pon, posit (to place): *postpone*, place after or later; *positive*, definite, certain (definitely placed)

port, portat (to carry): *portable*, able to be carried; *transport*, carry across; *export*, carry out of the country

scrib, script (to write): *transcribe*, copy; *script*, writing; *circumscribe*, enclose, limit (write around)

sequi, secut (to follow): *consecutive*, following in order; *sequence*, arrangement; *sequel*, that which follows

spec, spect (to look at): *spectator*, observer; *aspect*, appearance; *inspect*, look at carefully

tang, tact (to touch): *tangent*, touching; *contact*, touching, meeting; *tactile*, having to do with the sense of touch

ten, tent (to hold): *tenable*, able to be held or maintained; *tenacious*, holding firm; *tenure*, term of office

veni, vent (to come): *intervene*, come between; *prevent*, stop; *convention*, meeting

ASPIRE HIGHER WITH THE POWER... OF WORDS!

504 ABSOLUTELY ESSENTIAL WORDS, 5th Edition
ISBN 978-0-7641-2815-8
Builds practical vocabulary skills through funny stories and cartoons plus practice exercises.

WORDFEST!
ISBN 978-0-7641-7932-7
Book and CD help improve students' word-power and verbal reasoning by offering word lists, a battery of short tests, vocabulary-building help, and recommended reading advice.

1100 WORDS YOU NEED TO KNOW, 5th Edition
ISBN 978-0-7641-3864-5
This book is the way to master more than 1100 useful words and idioms taken from the mass media.

WORDPLAY: 550+ WORDS YOU NEED TO KNOW, 2nd Edition
CD Package ISBN 978-0-7641-7750-7
Based on 1100 Words You Need to Know; included are five CDs presented in comedy-drama form to add in the dimension of dialogue and the spoken word.

A DICTIONARY OF AMERICAN IDIOMS, 4th Edition
ISBN 978-0-7641-1982-8
Over 8,000 idiomatic words, expressions, regionalisms, and informal English expressions are defined and cross-referenced for easy access.

HANDBOOK OF COMMONLY USED AMERICAN IDIOMS, 4th Edition
ISBN 978-0-7641-2776-2
With 1500 popular idioms, this book will benefit both English-speaking people and those learning English as a second language.

BARRON'S EDUCATIONAL SERIES, INC.
250 Wireless Boulevard
Hauppauge, New York 11788
Canada: Georgetown Book Warehouse
34 Armstrong Avenue
Georgetown, Ont. L7G 4R9

Please visit **www.barronseduc.com** to view current prices and to order books

(#14) R 12/08

No One Can Build
Your Writing Skills Better
Than We Can...

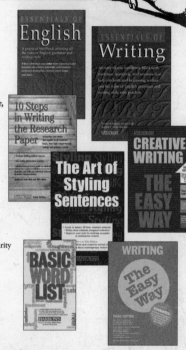

Essentials of English, 5th Edition
(978-0-7641-1367-3)
The comprehensive program for effective
writing skills.

Essentials of Writing, 5th Edition
(978-0-7641-1368-0)
A companion workbook for the material in
Essentials of English.

**10 Steps in Writing the Research Paper,
4th Edition**
(978-0-7641-1362-8)
The easy step-by-step guide for writing
research papers. It includes a section on
how to avoid plagiarism.

Creative Writing The Easy Way
(978-0-7641-2579-9)
This title discusses, analyzes, and offers
exercises in prose forms.

**The Art of Styling Sentences:
20 Patterns for Success, 4th Edition**
(978-0-7641-2181-4)
How to write with flair, imagination, and clarity
by imitating 20 sentence patterns and
variations.

Writing The Easy Way, 3rd Edition
(978-0-7641-1206-5)
The quick and convenient way to enhance
writing skills.

Basic Word List, 4th Edition
(978-0-7641-4119-8)
More than 2,000 words that are
found on the most recent major
standardized tests are thoroughly
reviewed.

BARRON'S EDUCATIONAL SERIES, INC.
250 Wireless Boulevard • Hauppauge, New York 11788
In Canada: Georgetown Book Warehouse
34 Armstrong Avenue • Georgetown, Ontario L7G 4R9

Please visit **www.barronseduc.com** to view current prices and to order books

(#15) R12/08